THE ORTHOL

THE APOCALYPSE
OF ST. JOHN

A Revelation of Love and Power

by Fr. Lawrence R. Farley

Ancient Faith Publishing
Chesterton, Indiana

THE APOCALYPSE OF ST. JOHN
A Revelation of Love and Power
© Copyright 2011 by Lawrence Farley

One volume of *The Orthodox Bible Study Companion Series*

All rights reserved. No part of this publication may be reproduced by any means, electronic, mechanical, photocopying, recording, scanning, or otherwise, without the prior written permission of the publisher.

Published by   Ancient Faith Publishing
A Division of Ancient Faith Ministries
P.O. Box 748
Chesterton, IN 46304

ISBN: 978-1-936270-40-8

Printed in the United States of America

Dedicated to
the Very Reverend Cyprian Hutcheon,
skillful physician, gentle shepherd,
best of companions.

Table of Contents and Outline

Introduction to the Series
A Word about Scholarship and Translation 9
Key to the Format of This Work..11

Introduction to the Apocalypse of St. John
The Apocalypse of St. John..13
Author and Date 14
The Purpose of the Apocalypse 15
The Apocalypse as Genre: True Vision or Literary Device?........17
The Apocalypse and the Fathers...19

I. **Opening** (1:1–20) 23
   1. Introduction (1:1–3) ॐ 23
   2. Episolary Greeting (1:4–6) ॐ 27
   3. The Things John Saw:
      The Vision of Christ's Glory (1:7–20) ॐ 30

II. **The Things Which Are:**
    Messages to the Seven Churches of Asia
    (2:1—3:22) 37
    The Structure of the Messages to the Seven Churches ॐ 37
   1. To the Church at Ephesus (2:1–7) ॐ 39
   2. To the Church at Smyrna (2:8–11) ॐ 43
   3. To the Church at Pergamum (2:12–17) ॐ 45
   4. To the Church at Thyatira (2:18–29) ॐ 49
   5. To the Church at Sardis (3:1–6) ॐ 53
   6. To the Church at Philadelphia (3:7–13) ॐ 56
   7. To the Church at Laodicea (3:14–22) ॐ 61

III. The Things Which Will Take Place Hereafter: Visions of Judgment, Persecution, and Triumph (4:1—11:14) 67
  1. The Worship of God, the Creator (4:1–11) ॐ 67
  2. The Worship of the Lamb, the Redeemer (5:1–14) ॐ 72
  3. The Opening of the Seven Seals (6:1–17) ॐ 78
  4. Interlude: The Church Sealed and Prepared for the Conflict (7:1–17) ॐ 90
  5. The Opening of the Seventh Seal: Final Wrath Begins—The Seven Trumpets (8:1—9:19) ॐ 101

  The Seven Trumpets and the Language of the Apocalyptic Genre ॐ 101

  6. Interlude: John Eats the Little Book and Measures the Temple; the Church Preaches the Gospel through Persecution (10:1—11:14) ॐ 114

IV. The End of All Things (11:15—18:24) 127
  1. The Blowing of the Seventh Trumpet: The Last Outpouring of Wrath Begins (11:15–19) ॐ 127
  2. Interlude: Signs in Heaven—The Church Is Persecuted by the World (12:1—15:4) ॐ 129
  3. The Seven Bowls: The Final Plagues of Judgment (15:5—16:21) ॐ 168
  4. The Judgment of Babylon the Great (17:1—18:24) ॐ 177

V. The New Beginning (19:1—22:21) 191
  1. The Second Coming of Christ: The Final Victory (19:1—20:15) ॐ 191
  2. The New Jerusalem: The Church's Inheritance and Reward (21:1—22:5) ॐ 210

3. Conclusion (22:6–20) ❧ 222
   4. Epistolary Blessing (22:21) ❧ 229
   A Practical Conclusion ❧ 229

Excurses:
❧ On the Beatitudes of the Apocalypse 26
❧ On the Wrath of the Lamb 88
❧ On the Church as Israel.. 93
❧ On the Transformation of Rome and the Rise of the Beast... 144
❧ On the Beast of the Apocalypse and the Final Antichrist..... 151
❧ On the Apocalyptic Church as Martyric 156

About the Author 233
Also in the Series 235

❦ Introduction to the Series ❧

A Word about Scholarship and Translation

This commentary was written for your grandmother. And for your plumber, your banker, your next-door neighbor, and the girl who serves you French fries at the nearby McDonald's. That is, it was written for the average layman, for the nonprofessional who feels a bit intimidated by the presence of copious footnotes, long bibliographies, and all those other things which so enrich the lives of academics. It is written for the pious Orthodox layman who is mystified by such things as Source Criticism, but who nonetheless wants to know what the Scriptures mean.

Therefore, it is unlike many other commentaries, which are written as contributions to the ongoing endeavor of scholarship and as parts of a continuous dialogue among scholars. That endeavor and dialogue is indeed worthwhile, but the present commentary forms no part of it. For it assumes, without argument, a certain point of view, and asserts it without defense, believing it to be consistent with the presuppositions of the Fathers and therefore consistent with Orthodox Tradition. It has but one aim: to be the sort of book a busy parish priest might put in the hands of an interested parishioner who says to him over coffee hour after Liturgy, "Father, I'm not sure I really get what St. Paul is saying in the Epistles. What does it all mean?" This commentary tries to tell the perplexed parishioner what the writers of the New Testament mean.

Regarding the translation used herein, an Italian proverb says, "All translators are traitors." (The proverb proves its own point, for it sounds better in Italian!) The point of the proverb, of course, is that no translation, however careful, can bring out all the nuances and meanings of the original, since no language can be the mathematical equivalent of another. The English translator is faced, it would seem,

9

with a choice: either he can make the translation something of a rough paraphrase of the original and render it into flowing sonorous English; or he can attempt to make a fairly literal, word-for-word translation from the original with the resultant English being stilted, wooden, and clumsy.

These two basic and different approaches to translation correspond to two basic and different activities in the Church. The Church needs a translation of the Scriptures for use in worship. This should be in good, grammatical, and flowing English, as elegant as possible and suited to its function in the majestic worship of the Liturgy. The Church also needs a translation of the Scriptures for private study and for group Bible study. Here the elegance of its English is of lesser concern. What is of greater concern here is the bringing out of all the nuances found in the original. Thus this approach will tend to sacrifice elegance for literality and, wherever possible, seek a word-for-word correspondence with the Greek. Also, because the student will want to see how the biblical authors use a particular word (especially St. Paul, who has many works included in the canon), a consistency of translation will be sought and the same Greek word will be translated, wherever possible, by the same English word or by its cognate.

The present work does not pretend to be anything other than a translation for private Bible study. It seeks to achieve, as much as possible, a literal, word-for-word correspondence with the Greek. The aim has been to present a translation from which one could jump back into the Greek original with the aid of an interlinear New Testament. Where a single Greek word has been used in the original, I have tried to find (or invent!) a single English word.

The result, of course, is a translation so literally rendered from the Greek that it represents an English spoken nowhere on the planet! That is, it represents a kind of "study Bible English" and not an actual vernacular. It was never intended for use outside the present commentaries, much less in the worship of the Church. The task of producing a flowing, elegant translation that nonetheless preserves the integrity and nuances of the original I cheerfully leave to hands more competent than mine.

Key to the Format of This Work:
- The translated text is first presented in boldface type. Italics within these biblical text sections represent words required by English syntax that are not actually present in the Greek. Each translated text section is set within a shaded grey box.

> ࿐ ࿐ ࿐ ࿐ ࿐
> 2 who witnessed to the Word of God and to the witness of Jesus Christ, *even* whatever *things* he saw.

- In the commentary sections, citations from the portion of text being commented upon are given in boldface type.

> John begins by giving his credentials. He **witnessed to the Word of God and to the witness of Jesus Christ**. That is, he witnessed to the Gospel (**the Word of God**) through his preaching and pastoral ministry in Asia.

- In the commentary sections, citations from other locations in Scripture are given in quotation marks with a reference; any reference not including a book name refers to the book under discussion.

> For St. John, our faith in Christ and His Cross also "overcomes the world" (1 John 5:5). Thus the Apocalypse speaks not only of us "making our robes white" in His Blood (7:14) but also of us overcoming Satan "by the Blood of the Lamb" (12:11).

- In the commentary sections, italics are used in the ordinary way—for emphasis, foreign words, etc.

> The word *signified* (Gr. *semaino*) is used in John 21:19 for Christ's enigmatic prophecy to Peter regarding his martyrdom.

☙ Introduction ❧

The Apocalypse of St. John

Sometimes, it seems to me, the Church is almost embarrassed that the Book of Revelation made it into the canon of Scripture. (Indeed, it almost didn't make it, and its status as a late arrival is reflected in its absence from the Lectionary, which took shape before the Apocalypse secured its place in the canon.) That is, we are sometimes tempted to regard the Apocalypse as we do an eccentric and loud second cousin—interesting, but best kept quiet at social gatherings. We're glad he's in the extended family, but it's best not to let him speak.

This ecclesiastical ambivalence to the Apocalypse was also discerned by such Orthodox writers as the Russian theologian Sergius Bulgakov. He contended that there was, in the Church, a continuing struggle against the Book of Revelation, whether secretly or openly, whether actively or passively. In his work *The Apocalypse of John* (published in 1948, four years after his death), Fr. Sergius suggested we have all become disillusioned and tired of waiting for the Second Coming, and "the fiery Christian hope" has given way "to a lukewarm certainty that through being in the church, we already possess all fullness and need no denouement." In fact, he says, "We fear the Apocalypse and hide ourselves from it because it calls us to that last and awesome prayer *Maranatha!* 'Even so, may the Lord come!'. . . By this prayer, nothing halfway can be meant. Life will not be left unchanged." In his understanding, we fear the Apocalypse because it challenges our complacency.

Though Fr. Sergius was perhaps being a bit hard on the Church, there is no doubt that the Apocalypse is indeed a challenge to our complacency. It puts the eternal issues of spiritual life and death right in our face (usually with extravagantly bizarre imagery) in a way that is hard to ignore.

But many people do manage to ignore it. Though certain people seem to specialize in the Apocalypse and use it as the prism through which to see everything in the Christian life (people in what Fr. Sergius characterized as "mystically minded and fanatical sects" who were "lacking in spiritual balance"), many Christians are a little reluctant to deal with the Apocalypse. The Gospels they like to read, and the Epistles of St. Paul they will read also. But they draw the line at the Book of Revelation. It is almost as if for them the New Testament canon ends just before it, with the Epistle of St. Jude.

Why is this? I do not think it is solely (or even mainly) because they fear the challenge to complacency. I think it is because they do not know how to read apocalyptic literature *per se*. They have lost both the ability to read it (or shall we say "decode it") and also the taste for it. (Perhaps the taste for it left along with the ability to read it.)

If this is true, it would be a good thing to recover this ability. For by effectively bypassing the Apocalypse we forfeit a blessing. St. John, in the opening verses of the book, offers and pronounces a blessing on the one "who reads" and on those "who hear" the prophetic words (1:3). This blessing is our inheritance as Orthodox Christians. The Church, in her Spirit-led wisdom, included the Apocalypse in the New Testament canon (and not without some considerable struggle and thought). She must have had a good reason for doing so. The commentary that follows is offered in the hope that, as we prayerfully read the Apocalypse, we will discover what that reason was.

Author and Date

Few things are more contested in modern scholarship than the assertion that St. John, the Beloved Disciple and author of the Fourth Gospel, also wrote the Apocalypse. Certainly the Greek of the Fourth Gospel is much more polished than the Greek of the Apocalypse. Nonetheless, Tradition ascribes the work to St. John the Beloved Disciple with impressive consistency and antiquity.

St. Justin the Philosopher and Martyr (d. AD 166) ascribed the work to St. John in his *Dialogue with Trypho* (81:15), as did

St. Irenaeus (d. AD 202) in his *Against Heresies* (5.26.1). Regarding the date of the work, St. Irenaeus, again in his *Against Heresies* (5.30.3), dates it "toward the end of Domitian's reign" (i.e. before AD 96), when John was an old man.

What are we to make, however, of the differing quality of the Greek used? The differences are adequately accounted for if we suppose that John used an amanuensis or secretary for his Gospel (and for his three Epistles), who, according to the custom of the day, would have polished up John's Greek. When John was sent into exile on Patmos, we may suppose that such secretarial help was not sent with him, so that the Apocalypse represents his own unretouched Greek. This would also account for the multitude of Hebraisms used throughout the work.

We therefore see no compelling reason to abandon the ancient patristic view regarding the authorship or the date of the Apocalypse.

The Purpose of the Apocalypse
The Apocalypse was given to the Church by our Lord as a part of His pastoral care for it. At the end of the first century, the Church was about to undergo its first major persecution—although the Christians in Rome in the mid-60s had already experienced a foretaste of it under the Emperor Nero. At the end of the first century, however, the persecution was about to begin in earnest and would continue, in differing measures and at different times and places, until the Coming of the Lord. Suffering was one of the characteristics of the Church, and the people of God had to be steeled and prepared for the trial.

The immediate trial came in the form of enforced emperor worship. As a way of unifying the empire, the emperor demanded that all citizens swear by his divinity. One had to simply burn a pinch of incense before an image of the emperor, assert "Caesar is Lord," and offer sacrifice to the gods. The little ceremony did not mean that one actually believed in the divinity of the reigning emperor; it only signified one's civic loyalty. By acknowledging Caesar as supreme, one could then get on with the business of life and continue to worship one's own favored deities as one wished. (The gods could be important, in the Roman scheme of things, just not as important as Caesar.)

It was precisely this admission that the Christians could not make. Caesar could be important, and the Christians were loyal subjects. But they could never worship anyone other than God, nor give supreme place to any other. Caesar demanded that civic loyalty be the supreme loyalty, and this is just what the Christians could not admit. Thus the Church's worship was forbidden, their faith branded a *religio illicita* ("illegal religion"), and the persecution begun.

The Emperor Domitian, in promoting this cult of emperor worship, made it a punishable offense to fail to offer the mandated worship. As with all persecutions of the Church, the clergy were the first to suffer, since they were the most prominent. St. John had already been exiled to Patmos. A few others had suffered martyrdom in recent memory (such as Antipas of Pergamum). Now the full brunt of state persecution was about to be felt by the poor Christian rank and file. They needed to be prepared for the onslaught, to be steeled to remain steadfast in the face of the imminent attack—an attack which would sweep away fathers, mothers, teens, and even young children. The Book of Revelation was addressed to a frightened people, to those who lived in fear of the policeman's knock on their doors (or the ancient equivalent).

There were other challenges to the Church as well. Heretical movements (such as the "Nicolaitans") preached an easy compromise and co-existence of Church and pagan state. This option was all the more tempting in the face of the coming persecution. Also, as always, there were the Jews, who were taking the opportunity of state hostility to express their own hatred of the "heretical" Christians. Everywhere on earth one looked, there were problems, obstacles, failures, disasters. Where was God in all this? The might of Rome looked all but invincible; its power, unchallengeable; its claims, unanswerable. The Christians, by contrast, were pathetic and powerless. Had God abandoned them?

The Apocalypse of St. John is God's answer. He had *not* abandoned them. St. John was given a vision of heaven and of the might of God. Christ was not just the defeated, pathetic crucified carpenter

Rome knew—He was the dazzling Lord of Glory, exalted, immortal, living in the midst of His churches. The vision of Christ in chapter 1 answers to the Church's need to see their Lord as He is in glory. The Church was not just a marginalized and powerless group of slaves and poor. They were a kingdom, priests to God (1:6), part of an immense heavenly throng standing before the throne of God with the palms of victory in their triumphant hands. The vision of the Church of chapter 7 reveals her true dignity, answering the slanders of Rome.

There was more. The Apocalypse assured the Church that the course of history and its outcome lay not with Caesar, but with Christ. He is the Lamb, standing before the throne of God, receiving the scroll of the world's glorification. He is the one who will open the scroll and guide the world to peace. As a prelude to this glory, though, judgments must come. War and tumult, famine and pestilence, martyrdom and the shaking of the powers of heaven, blood, fire, and vapor of smoke—all this must precede the End. The Church must indeed enter its time of trial, striving against the Enemy, the ancient Dragon, the beast from the abyss. Many will shed their blood for Him and win their crowns. But at the end, Rome will fall, the final persecution will end, and the Lord will return in glory to overthrow all His foes and reward His persevering people. Then will be glory for all His saints.

This is the purpose of the Apocalypse—the pastoral reassurance of the Church as it enters the eschatological struggle of this age. Tears must indeed come first. But at the end (to quote Julian of Norwich), "all shall be well and all manner of thing shall be well." The servants of God shall see His Face and they shall reign to ages of ages (22:4–5).

The Apocalypse as Genre: True Vision or Literary Device?
The Apocalypse is, of course, a specific kind of literature, called by modern scholars "apocalyptic literature." It is a peculiarly Jewish type of literature, written especially during times of conflict and stress. It flourished in the Jewish community from the second century BC to the first century AD. Extrabiblical examples of it include the

Book of Enoch (mentioned in the Epistle of Jude) and 2 Esdras. It is characterized by a predominance of fantastic symbols and by a sense of the imminence of the coming Kingdom. Numerology abounds, as does a preoccupation with the coming judgments of God. It is aimed, not so much at the head or the heart, but at the nerves. It is a much more visceral genre than, for example, the prophecies of Isaiah—more direct and powerful, less finely nuanced.

Most Jewish apocalypses are pseudonymous—their authorship is ascribed to ancient worthies (such as Enoch) who received a vision and transmitted it secretly to the (then) present age. The ascribed ancient authorship is a part of the genre. The visions were not, of course, actually historically received by these ancient worthies—but the ascription of the writing to them was a way of setting the stage and lending to the message an air of authority. It was, in fact, a literary device.

But what about the Apocalypse of St. John? Did he actually receive such a vision? Did he see exactly what is written down, without any literary artistry, didactic purpose, or artful structuring? Was he simply transmitting his vision, like a person reporting the images seen on a television?

Opinion seems to be divided. Some scholars, acknowledging the indisputable fact that this is a species of apocalyptic literature and part of an obvious genre, say simply that John had no vision. The reporting of a vision was a recognized and received literary device, no more. Others say that biblical authority being what it is, if St. John says he had a vision, then he had a vision. These scholars would play down the apocalyptic elements in St. John's work and accentuate the differences between this and other Jewish apocalyptic works.

I would offer the following.

The Apocalypse is unlike other apocalyptic literature in that it is not pseudonymous. Generally speaking, pseudonymous writing by Christians was opposed because of the importance of apostolic authority. To write a book under the name of Solomon was one thing, for that was just to claim that the work in question was wise. But to claim to be an apostle was something else, for that would be to claim an unquestioned authority bestowed by Christ only upon certain men. (Thus Tertullian reports that a well-meaning presbyter was deposed when he admitted to writing a work and pseudonymously claiming Pauline authorship for it.) That in itself sets the present Apocalypse somewhat apart from other works in the same genre.

Also, John was an apostle, which meant that his main task was to tell the truth about what he had seen about Christ. Historicity was paramount. That St. John's text begins with historic events is made clear when he relates his exile to Patmos (1:9–10). That testimony continues without a break to his relating a theophanic vision of the Lord.

Further, John himself claims that his work is a prophecy (1:3; 22:6, 7, 18) and seems to regard the prophets of the Church as especially valuable (10:7; 16:6; 18:24), presumably because he considered himself to be one. This would indicate that the book was to be considered as a genuine vision, such as prophets received (such as in Acts 10:10f).

I would suggest therefore that John did indeed have a vision of the Lord, of His glory and coming judgments and of the triumph of the Kingdom of God. Like many visions of this kind, the reality was too great to be fully articulated in human words—one hears things that cannot be told, "unsayable sayings" (2 Cor. 12:4). I suggest that the present work is the attempted articulation of that vision, according to the recognized form and accepted literary conventions of the genre. As such, it contains all the literary structuring, artistic craftsmanship, and deliberate didactic purpose of that literature. It is a human work. But it is also an apostolic work, and as an apostle, John tells the truth, striving to convey to us the substance and power of what the Lord revealed to him for our sake.

The Apocalypse and the Fathers
The Apocalypse was revered and quoted by a number of Fathers, especially in the West. St. Justin the Philosopher quoted it, as did St. Irenaeus (as we have seen). St. Papias, Bishop of Hierapolis in the early second century, accepted it as canonical, as did Melito, Bishop of Sardis in about AD 175. The Roman Hippolytus (in the third century) quotes it repeatedly, as does Tertullian (in North Africa) about

the same time. Clement of Alexandria quoted from it as apostolic. Victorinus (d. AD 304) wrote a commentary on it. St. Augustine of Hippo comments on it at length in his work, *The City of God*. In the East, however, the Apocalypse was not universally regarded as apostolic or canonical. Eusebius of Caesarea questioned its apostolic authorship. It was also questioned in the fourth century by St. John Chrysostom, St. Cyril of Jerusalem, and Theodoret of Cyr.

Thus, one must exercise care in speaking about "the Fathers' view of the Apocalypse," since there was no unanimity about it, either about its interpretation or even about its canonicity. Some early writers (like Justin, Hippolytus, and Victorinus) interpreted its details literally, while later writers (like Augustine) did not. The temptation, yielded to by some, is to take the extant commentaries of a couple of Fathers (such as Victorinus in his *Commentary on the Apocalypse*, or Hippolytus in his *Christ and Antichrist*) and accept those as *the* authoritative patristic voice. It must be stressed that, strictly speaking, there *is* no single consistent patristic voice in interpreting details of the Book of Revelation, and modern Orthodox attempts to find such a voice are simply exercises in arbitrary selection of one patristic voice over others. The field of interpretation is more open than some would think (or like), and the insights of modern scholarship are not to be dismissed out of hand as "unpatristic."

And speaking of modern scholarly insights, we must acknowledge that some of the Fathers seem to show little awareness of the kind of distinct literary genre with which they were dealing. To be sure, the Fathers are reliable guides for the basics of understanding this work: they all apply it to the Church and her struggle with anti-Christian powers of this age, and see the Second Coming as the final consummation. But the nuances of the text, and in particular the way one reads the genre of apocalyptic literature, seem to escape them. What are we to make of this?

The Fathers were mostly Gentiles. As such, they would have had little occasion to steep themselves in as Jewish a literary genre as the apocalyptic. Perhaps the only example of this genre they had studied was, in fact, the Book of Revelation.

The closest thing to it in their own Gentile culture was the

Sibyl—an oracle who foretold the future in ambiguous, aphoristic speech. Lacking from the Sibylline literature were many basic apocalyptic features: the fantastic, symbolic animals; the concern for numerology; the visceral appeal to the nerves. The Sibylline oracles were not a truly adequate preparation for appreciating Jewish apocalyptic literature. But it was natural to view the Book of Revelation as if it were a Christian version of the Sibyl and to understand the text in a more literal, predictive way.

Although the Fathers may be of limited use in understanding all of the book's Jewish apocalyptic nuances, they do give us a basic grasp of the book as having to do with the struggle between Christ and Satan, between His Holy Church and the persecuting powers of this age.

I

OPENING
(1:1–20)

§I.1 Introduction

> **1** 1 The revelation of Jesus Christ, which God gave Him to show to His slaves the things which must happen soon; and He sent and signified *it* through His angel to His slave John,

The book begins by asserting that it is not just a literary work coming from the mind of man; it is a **revelation of Jesus Christ**, coming from God. In referring to **the revelation of Jesus Christ**, John does not mean that Jesus Christ is what is revealed, but rather that **God gave** this message to **Jesus Christ** as a gift to pass on to His Church. Jesus is not the substance of the revelation, but the bestower of it **to His slaves** and servants.

Furthermore, there is an urgency to this revelation. The events and realities of this book are not just for the "end times," the last few years before the Second Coming. Rather, they **must happen soon**. The time is imminent. Admittedly, there is in the Christian Faith (and especially in apocalyptic literature such as this) a sense of special imminence, of urgency, a viewing of events as a kind of psychological emergency that telescopes time and sees the end of all things as "at hand" (compare 1 Peter 4:7). Thus the Lord says in Revelation 22:7, "Behold, I am coming soon!"

Nonetheless, since **the things** referred to here are not just the

Second Coming but also the persecution of the Church, and since the book opens with the contemporary situation of the seven churches of Asia as they then existed, we are justified in reading this **soon** of verse 1 as having a chronological as well as an eschatological meaning. The prophesied events are **soon** to take place in the sense that there will not be a long delay; they will begin in a few years.

This message Christ **sent and signified**. That is, He gave the message in signs, oracles, symbols. The word *signified* (Gr. *semaino*) is used in John 21:19 for Christ's enigmatic prophecy to Peter regarding his martyrdom. There Christ did not simply say to Peter, "You will be martyred," but rather, "You will stretch out your hands, and another will gird you and bring you where you do not want to go." Thus we may expect Christ's message to be communicated in symbolic terms, with images that defy the commonplace.

To carry this message, Christ sent it **through His angel**, a special angelic envoy to bear this message **to His slave John**, perhaps carrying His own Presence. That the message was sent by Christ's **angel** shows the importance and immensity of the proffered revelation. It could have come by dream or vision (as St. Peter experienced in Acts 10). It could have come as a simple prophetic utterance (as with the prophet Agabus in Acts 21:11). But instead, Christ sent a special envoy, as one was sent to Daniel in Babylon (Dan. 10)—or as one was sent to the most-holy Theotokos at the Annunciation (Luke 1). And not just any angel was sent—not even one as important as Gabriel the Archangel. Rather, Christ's own angel, His special servant and ambassador and messenger, was sent. This special dignity of communication shows not just the importance of the message, but also Christ's loving care for His own Church. So much does He love us and take thought for our strengthening that He sends His own angel to bring us this revelation.

༄ ༄ ༄ ༄ ༄

2 who witnessed to the Word of God and to the witness of Jesus Christ, *even* whatever *things* he saw.

John begins by giving his credentials. He **witnessed to the Word of God and to the witness of Jesus Christ**. That is, he witnessed to the Gospel (**the Word of God**) through his preaching and pastoral ministry in Asia Minor, and also to all the things Jesus Christ showed him in the apocalyptic visions to follow, and he will faithfully recount **whatever *things* he saw**. John's past ministry reveals him as the faithful slave of Jesus (v. 1), and so his present testimony can be trusted. As a faithful slave, he does not offer his own message; rather, he simply passes on the message with which the Lord entrusted him.

We note in passing that John's insistence here on his status as witness well accords with the same insistence in the Gospel of John (19:35; 21:24). Similarly, the Apocalypse and the Gospel of John together are unique in referring to Christ as the Word and the Lamb (Rev. 5:8; 19:13; John 1:1, 29). Further, both the Apocalypse and the other clearly Johannine books stress the call of Christians to overcome and conquer like their Master (Rev. 2:7, 11, 17, 26f; John 16:33; 1 John 5:4–5). This is further confirmation that the beloved disciple is the author of the Apocalypse.

> ३ॐ ३ॐ ३ॐ ३ॐ ३ॐ
>
> 3   Blessed *is* the one who reads and the ones who hear the words of the prophecy and keep the things which are written in it; for the time *is* near.

A blessing is here pronounced on **the one who reads**. Because this message is the true word of Jesus Christ, given by Him to those of His Church, a great blessing is given if this message is faithfully received. Both **the one who reads** it (that is, aloud in the liturgical assembly) and **the ones who hear** the reading are blessed.

But the words of the prophecy must go into the heart and not simply bounce off the ears. All those who receive these words must also **keep** and observe **the things which are written** if they are to be truly blessed. This blessing is given to the Church if they will humbly receive the prophecy because **the time** for its fulfillment *is* **near**. Now is the time to heed the message. The challenges of the world and the persecution by the beast are at hand—and so is the blessing of God, if they will endure to the end. We note that the Apocalypse does not come to us simply as a series of predictions of future events; it comes as a challenge to the human heart. It does not simply inform us; it calls us to faithfulness and perseverance—even in the face of suffering and death.

❧ EXCURSUS
On the Beatitudes of the Apocalypse

The Apocalypse is intricately structured. Imbedded within it lie seven beatitudes. (This reminds us of other "sevens" in John's Gospel, such as the seven signs or miracles of Christ, as well as the Lord's seven "I Am" declarations.) The Apocalypse contains many pronouncements of judgment and wrath upon the unbelieving world, but it is a book of blessing as well. It indeed declares God's wrath against the persecuting world, but also pronounces His blessings upon the faithful martyric Church which withstands that persecution.

These blessings are pronounced upon:

1:3	"the one who reads and the ones who hear the words of the prophecy, and keep the things which are written in it"
14:13	the martyrs "who die in the Lord from now on"
16:15	"the one who keeps alert," faithfully awaiting the Lord's Coming
19:9	"those who are called to the wedding supper of the Lamb"
20:6	the martyrs who have "a part in the first resurrection"
22:7	all who "keep the words of the prophecy of this book"
22:14	all those in the martyric Church, "those who wash their robes, so that they may have their right to the tree of life, and may enter by the gates into the city."

Seven is the number of perfection, and by the giving of seven blessings, a perfect and full blessing is pronounced upon those faithful who conquer the world through their faith (compare 1 John 5:4).

The Lord, during His earthly ministry, had pronounced His beatitudes upon His disciples, speaking to those who were poor in spirit, who were persecuted for righteousness' sake and for His sake (Matt. 5:3–11). The Apocalypse offers a new set of beatitudes for the Church under persecution, restating the blessedness of Christian discipleship under these new conditions.

By studding the Apocalypse with blessings, St. John reveals that its message is not aimed merely at the head, but also at the heart. He does not present a series of predictions so that we can satisfy our curiosity. He presents a way of life, a challenge to live with fearless faithfulness to Christ, which alone can secure the blessings of God. In the "traditional" Beatitudes of Matthew 5:1 and Luke 6:20f we see how our Lord promises a heavenly reward to those who persevere as His disciples, living lives of meekness and faithfulness in the face of worldly opposition. These apocalyptic beatitudes reconfirm these promises, holding out the reward of eternal blessedness to those who would persevere.

§I.2 Epistolary Greeting

4 John to the seven churches that are in Asia: Grace to you and peace, from Him *who* is and was and *who is* coming, and from the seven spirits before His throne,

5 and from Jesus Christ, the faithful witness, the firstborn of the dead, and the ruler of the kings of the earth. To Him who loves us and loosed us from our sins by His blood

> 6 and made us *to be* a kingdom, priests to His God and Father—to Him *be* the glory and the might to the ages of ages. Amen.

John sends this message to the **seven churches in Asia** who were under his pastoral care. By choosing but **seven** of these churches, John widens the intended audience, for seven is also the number symbolic of perfection. Thus the Revelation is intended not only to the seven churches of Asia, but also for the perfect totality of all God's churches.

In calling God **Him *who* is and was and *who is* coming**, John describes God the Father as the One who is sovereign over time and history and therefore over all the historical events that touch us. God sits enthroned as Lord of the present, the past, and the future, and therefore there is nothing in the past, present, or future that can ever hurt us. God is the Lord of time and of all our days.

The message not only comes from the hand of God, it also comes from the entire heavenly court. All in heaven offer the Church on earth this word of encouragement and triumph. The **seven spirits before His throne** are the seven archangels (see 5:6, "the seven spirits of God sent forth into all the earth," and 8:2, the "seven angels who stand before God"). (In chapter 20 of the Book of Enoch, these angels are listed as Uriel, Raphael, Raguel, Michael, Saraqael, Gabriel, and Remiel.) Once again, the number **seven** is symbolic, an image for all the archangels who stand closest to God's throne and hear His counsel. In saying that this message comes from the **seven spirits before His throne**, John means that this message comes directly from the Throne itself, with secrets not given to the world at large.

Later liturgical usage, in which reference to the Father and the Son was always followed by reference to the Holy Spirit, has misled some interpreters into seeing this reference to the **seven spirits** as a reference to the Holy Spirit. But when the Holy Spirit is mentioned in the Book of Revelation, He is referred to simply as "the Spirit" (e.g. 2:7; 14:13; 22:17), always in the singular and never as "seven spirits" or as a "sevenfold" Spirit. These seven spirits stand **before**

God's **throne**; that is, they are portrayed as waiting upon God as a part of His heavenly court. It is inconceivable that the Divine Spirit, co-eternal and consubstantial with the Father and the Son, could be portrayed as such a servant. Indeed, the other references to the Spirit in the Apocalypse carry the suggestion of His sovereignty and authority.

The message also comes **from Jesus Christ, the faithful witness** (Gr. *martus*; compare our English "martyr"). Christ bore faithful witness before Pilate to the Truth, even at the cost of His Life (1 Tim. 6:13); John stresses this so that we may imitate His faithfulness. The Lord does not call us to walk in any place where He has not gone before.

Jesus is further described as **the firstborn of the dead**. In using this Jewish concept of the firstborn (in which the firstborn son is the main heir), John shows that Jesus Christ is the heir of the whole age to come; the entire coming Kingdom belongs to Him. His faithfulness unto death resulted in His victory and His inheriting all the world. Our faithfulness unto death will result in our sharing that victory. Death has no terrors for Jesus Christ, and so it need have none for us.

Thus Christ is also **the ruler of the kings of the earth**. Caesar may think he has no superior or master, but Jesus, the humble carpenter crucified under the governor Pontius Pilate, is the true Master of the Roman Empire and indeed of the whole cosmos. The Christians of St. John's day, haunted by a sense of their own powerlessness and humility, were thus made to see their true dignity and power.

The Church is described as those whom the Lord **loves** and therefore continues to protect and care for (the present tense is used to denote Christ's ongoing care), and as those who were **loosed from** their **sins by His Blood.** This is an important theme in the Apocalypse. The Cross of Christ was seen by secular Rome as His defeat and proof of how pathetic and deluded the Christians were—that they would worship a crucified man. But for John, the Cross is proof of the power of God that defeats all other powers. The Lord Himself said of the Cross, "I have overcome the world" (John 16:33). For St. John, our faith in Christ and His Cross also "overcomes the world"

(1 John 5:5). Thus the Apocalypse speaks not only of us "making our robes white" in His Blood (7:14) but also of us overcoming Satan "by the Blood of the Lamb" (12:11). The Christians are not to be ashamed of Christ's Cross, for through His Blood they overcome death, Satan, and the whole world.

In describing the Christians as **a kingdom, priests to His God and Father**, John asserts the privileges of the Christians in the face of the pride of Rome. The Roman powers may think the Christians are but poor, uneducated, and powerless, to be utterly disdained. John knows them to be God's own Kingdom, one destined to outlast all the kingdoms of the earth, and to be priests to God Himself, with access to His awe-inspiring Presence. Priests had status and honor in the Roman secular world, and St. John says this is the true status of the Christians before God.

§I.3. The Things John Saw: The Vision of Christ's Glory

> ༄ ༄ ༄ ༄ ༄
>
> 7 Behold, He is coming with the clouds, and every eye will see Him, even those who pierced Him; and all the tribes of the earth will lament over Him. Yes! Amen!
> 8 "I *Myself* am the Alpha and the Omega," says the Lord God, "who is and who was and who is coming, the Almighty."

At the very beginning of the work, John holds aloft the hope of the Second and glorious Coming as the blessed hope for the Church under persecution. Drawing together language from Daniel 7:13 about Messiah's universal authority and from Zechariah 12:10 about Messiah's vindication before those who had rejected Him, John declares that at the Second Coming, when He **comes with the clouds, all the tribes of the earth will lament over Him**. That is, all the nations will lament that they rejected Him and persecuted His Church. John's faithful heart strains toward this day, and he cries out as if standing on tiptoe, **Yes! Amen!**

To this assertion by St. John is added the voice of God the Father. **The Lord God** declares (in an echo of His declaration in Is. 44:6), "**I *Myself* am the Alpha and the Omega.**" In the Isaiah 44 passage, Yahweh declares, "I am the First and the Last; besides Me there is no God." That is, Yahweh has no rivals to his authority over all the nations, no other gods to contest His will. This same God rules world history still and is sovereign over all the ages. He is the One **who is and who was and who is coming, the Almighty** (Gr. *Pantokrator*), exalted above all the earth. What is the might of Rome compared to His might? With such a God in control, the Christians have nothing to fear.

> ꙮ ꙮ ꙮ ꙮ ꙮ
>
> 9 I, John, your brother and co-sharer in the tribulation and Kingdom and perseverance *which are* in Jesus, was on the island called Patmos because of the Word of God and the witness of Jesus.
> 10 I became in the Spirit on the Lord's day, and I heard behind me a great voice like a trumpet,
> 11 saying, "Write what you see in a book, and send *it* to the seven churches: to Ephesus and to Smyrna and to Pergamum and to Thyatira and to Sardis and to Philadelphia and to Laodicea."

St. John, like a good shepherd, does not place himself above his flock, but is in solidarity with them. Though their chief pastor, he is also their **brother** and suffers with them. Thus He is a **co-sharer** with them in all their lot. He shares **in the tribulation** they are undergoing, as well as **the Kingdom** for which that suffering is making them worthy, and that **perseverance** which is demanded of those who are **in Jesus**. Though separated from them in body, John is with his flock in spirit, and his sufferings mirror theirs.

St. John has been exiled to **the island called Patmos**, a small rocky island off the coast of Miletus in the Aegean Sea, for preaching the Gospel, **the Word of God,** and for his proclamation of

the witness of Jesus. John relates how he received his message. He suddenly **became in the Spirit**. That is, he received an ecstatic vision, which fell on him all at once from the hand of God. Like St. Paul, who was caught up to the third heaven, John also found the island of Patmos receding from his sight, to be replaced by higher realities.

This took place **on the Lord's day**, on Sunday, though whether it took place during the worship of the Church or not is not stated. Certainly by stressing that this vision was received on the Lord's day, St. John intends it to be set in a liturgical context. As we will see in examining chapter 4 (where the image of God seated on a throne surrounded by His elders mirrors the eucharistic image of the bishop-celebrant sitting on his *cathedra*, surrounded by his presbyters), our earthly worship mirrors and manifests the worship of heaven. Indeed, spiritually speaking, our worship finds its true locus in heaven, where Christ has made us sit with Him, sharing His throne and His glory in the heavenly places (see Eph. 2:6). In this sense, the Apocalypse is all about our liturgical experience of the heavenly and glorified Christ.

This theophany of the glorified Lord begins with a ringing voice, a sovereign command. With **a great voice like a trumpet**, the Lord orders His beloved disciple to write what he sees and send it to the churches under his care, the **seven churches** of Asia. The Lord is here portrayed not in tenderness, but in power—the worthy Master of the world, to whom the great Caesar and all the powers of the Roman Empire must bow and obey.

ॐ ॐ ॐ ॐ ॐ

12 Then I turned back to see the voice that was speaking with me. And having turned back I saw seven golden lampstands;
13 and in the middle of the lampstands I saw one like a son of man, clothed *in a garment reaching* to *His* feet, and girded around His breast with a golden belt.
14 His head and hair *were* white as white wool,

> as snow; and His eyes were as a flame of fire.
> 15 His feet were like burnished bronze, as if fired in a furnace, and His voice was like the voice of many waters.
> 16 In His right hand He had seven stars, and out of His mouth proceeded a sharp two-edged sword; and His appearance was as the sun shining in its power.

A description of the Lord who spoke to him now follows, replete with all the usual symbolism of apocalyptic imagery. John **turned back to see the voice that was speaking** to him. By mentioning this detail (that Christ first appeared *behind* John), John shows that the vision came to him unexpectedly, from without. It was not the product of his own desire or his own subconscious longing. It was a true vision, given by the Lord.

Christ is seen standing **in the middle** of His local church communities, imaged by **seven golden lampstands**. He is pictured as **one like a son of man**—a reference to Daniel 7:13, where Daniel sees the Kingdom embodied as a human being, in contrast to the Gentile kingdoms, which were embodied as brutal animals. By hearkening back to the passage in Daniel, St. John reveals Jesus in all His messianic power, exalted above all the pagan kingdoms of the earth.

Image is piled upon image to convey the majesty of the Lord Messiah, exalted in His holy churches. He is vested as a high priest, **clothed** *in a* priestly *garment reaching to His* **feet, girded around** with the priestly **golden belt**. The **hair** on his **head** and beard was **white as white wool, as snow,** an allusion again to the vision of Daniel 7, where the eternal God, the Ancient of Days, is described as having raiment "white as snow and the hair of his head like pure wool" (Dan. 7:9). Christ is thus described as possessing divine eternity, as befits One who is co-eternal with the Ancient of Days.

His eyes are **as a flame of fire**, seeing all the works of men, piercing through all excuses, into the deepest recesses of our hearts and motives. **His feet were like burnished bronze**, portraying Him as stable, immovable, steady, and dependable in His saving strength. He **had seven stars**, which, as He says in verse 20 below, are the angels of the seven churches (that is, Christ carries and cares for all His people). **Out of His mouth** comes the **sharp sword** of judgment, the power with which He will smite and conquer all the world (compare 19:15). He is full of transfigured glory, resplendent with the blinding brilliance of God, **His appearance as the sun shining in its power**.

In all this imagery, we see our Lord, mighty to save us, exalted in a power greater than that of any of our adversaries—eternal, venerable, invincible, sovereign, and serene. This is our source of hope and joy in the midst of our tribulations—that Christ the Unconquerable is in our midst.

> ॐ ॐ ॐ ॐ ॐ
>
> 17 When I saw Him, I fell at His feet as *if* dead. And He put His right *hand* on me, saying, "Do not be afraid; I Myself am the first and the last,
>
> 18 "and the Living One; and I became dead, and behold, I am alive to ages of ages, and I have the keys of death and of Hades.
>
> 19 "Therefore write the things which you have seen, and the things which are, and the things which are about to happen after these things.
>
> 20 "*As for* the mystery of the seven stars which you saw in My right *hand*, and the seven golden lampstands: the seven stars are the angels of the seven churches, and the seven lampstands are the seven churches."

Like those receiving such theophanic appearances in Old Testament days (e.g. Ezek. 1:28; Dan. 8:17), John **fell at His feet as *if* dead**. Even though he had leaned in familiarity upon His breast at the Last Supper (John 13:23), yet such is the power of the Lord in His heavenly exaltation that even the beloved disciple is overwhelmed. The Lord restores him in preparation to **write the things** he has seen and will see.

I. Opening   Revelation 1:17–20

He tells John, **"Do not be afraid,"** and in this He tells all of John's churches not to fear. They need not fear death, martyrdom, or anything in all the world. Why? Because Christ has overcome the world, trampling down death by death. He **became dead**, but now He is **alive to ages of ages**. As such, He is **the first and the last**, sovereign over all (compare God as the Alpha and Omega in 1:8) **and the Living One**, the source of all life. He had authority over **death and Hades** by His Resurrection. Death cannot now separate us from Him, for He is Lord of both the living and the dead.

Then Christ gives John a command: he is to **write the things which** he has **seen, and the things which are, and the things which are about to happen after these things** and send them to the main churches under his care in Asia. (From these seven main locations, they could be sent out to other smaller church communities as well.) This gives a basic outline of the Book of Revelation as a whole: it relates what John has seen (the vision of Christ in ch. 1), the things which are (the present state of the churches, described in chs. 2–3), and the things which are about to happen in the future (the prophecies of chs. 4–22).

The introduction concludes with an explanation of the meaning of **the seven stars** in His hand and **the seven lampstands** among which He stands. The **seven lampstands are the seven churches** of Asia, and the **seven stars are the angels of the seven churches**. This is a reference to what may be termed the individual corporate personality of each church community. Each local church is thus portrayed as having an angel, even as each person has his guardian angel. Just as a person's guardian angel resembles that person (see those who reacted to the announcement that Peter was standing unexpectedly at the door by suggesting that it was not Peter but his angel; Acts 12:15), so the church's angel sums up and embodies the local church. The angel of the church is an image of the strengths and weaknesses of each church. In writing to the angel of the church of Ephesus, the Lord actually speaks to the church of Ephesus in its corporate aspect. We see this today as well, in that church communities have corporate characteristics—some are loving, some judgmental, some zealous, some lax. The reference to each church's "angel" is a way of addressing each community *as a community*, using the language of the apocalyptic.

❧ II ☙

THE THINGS WHICH ARE:
MESSAGES TO THE SEVEN CHURCHES OF ASIA
(2:1—3:22)

The Structure of the Messages to the Seven Churches
Each one begins by addressing the recipient of the message, such as "To the angel of the church in___." That is, each message is addressed to one of seven churches of Asia in its corporate aspect, as imaged by the guardian angel of each church.

These messages are not so much letters in themselves, for they lack the usual epistolary form (such as "Christ to the church of Ephesus, greetings"). Rather, each is in the form of a prophecy, an oracle. Each begins with the words "Thus says" (Gr. *tade legei*), followed by a description of the glorified Lord who speaks to them. This stylized beginning is consciously modeled after the oracles given through the prophets. Thus (for example) God spoke through the prophet Isaiah in Isaiah 1:24 LXX, beginning His oracle with the formula "Thus says the Lord" (Gr. *tade legei kurios*). By beginning with this same formula, the seven messages establish themselves as authoritative prophecies, like the prophecies of old.

The opening formula is followed by a description of the Lord, drawn mostly from the images of the previous theophany recorded in 1:13–16. There is thus a continuity between John's vision and our experience of Christ in liturgical worship. That is why the details of the theophany in chapter 1 find their way into each of the messages to the seven churches: Christ has spoken prophetically to St. John as he experienced His glory, and we experience this same glory in each of our communities when we worship the Lord in our Sunday Liturgies.

After this description of Christ, the Lord speaks (where possible) a word of commendation and only then a word of rebuke and correction. We can see here His love for us, which delights to bless and not to chide. His favored words are words of encouragement and commendation; only reluctantly does He rebuke, and that only for our salvation.

Each message concludes with a call to heed the words of commendation and rebuke as well as a promise to "the one who conquers"—that is, to the one who will remain steadfast in faith through the coming persecution. This reveals the pastoral context of the seven messages—and indeed, of the Book of Revelation as a whole. It was meant to strengthen and steel the Church in the face of lethal onslaught, so that the time of trial might not separate us from the Lord.

Each call to heed the words of commendation and rebuke is phrased as a call "to hear what the Spirit says to the churches." That is, Christ calls us to recognize these words, given through John, as authoritative prophecy. Just as the Spirit speaks to the Church through the prophets (compare the prophet Agabus prefacing his message with the authoritative "Thus says the Holy Spirit" in Acts 21:11), so John by the Spirit conveys Christ's true word to the churches. In calling these messages of Christ the word that the Spirit is speaking to the churches, Christ confirms these messages as true prophecy. For all prophecy, including such visions as the Apocalypse, comes from the Spirit acting on the hearts of men (see Acts 2:17).

In all these seven messages, there is no suggestion of a chronological, historical aspect. Some have suggested that each of the seven churches represents not only that church community at the time of the first century, but also successive periods of church history. According to this theory, the first church mentioned (Ephesus) is symbolic of the first period of church history (the early Church), and the final church mentioned (Laodicea) represents the final end-times Church, with the churches in between symbolic of intervening successive epochs in history. This theory is flawed, for there is no suggestion in the messages themselves that they are to be taken in this way. And the theory is impossible to apply, since we do not know the time of the Second Coming, and therefore have no way of determining which epoch we are in.

§II.1. To the Church at Ephesus

> **2** 1 To the angel of the church in Ephesus write: "Thus says the One who holds the seven stars in His right *hand*, who walks in the middle of the seven golden lampstands:

It is not accidental that the first church to be addressed was the one in **Ephesus**, for Ephesus was not only the most important city in the Roman province of Asia, it was also the place where St. John lived prior to his exile.

The Lord reveals Himself as the same One who **holds** all **the seven stars in His** mighty **right** *hand*, protecting them from all assaults of the devil and the world. The church in Ephesus (and Asia Minor generally), as it endures persecution and harassment, might be tempted to feel abandoned by God and left to the mercy of the world. It is not so. Christ holds them in His hand, caring for them and watching over them (compare John 10:28). All are safe with Him. Christ also **walks in the middle of the seven golden lampstands**, manifesting Himself to them in their worship and in their daily lives. That is, He lives and moves among them and is familiar with all their works. He knows all they do and experience, all their deeds and labor and perseverance (v. 2).

> 2 "I know your works and your toil and perseverance, and that you cannot bear wicked *men*, but tested those who call themselves apostles, and they are not, and you found them *to be* liars;
> 3 "and you have perseverance and have borne *trials* for My Name, and have not wearied.

The Church in Ephesus is commended for its **works** and its **toil** (such as its care of the poor) and for its **perseverance** under trial. They have a great concern for correctness and orthodoxy—both in life and doctrine. They **cannot bear wicked *men*** —in particular, those wicked men who are false prophets, false **apostles**. These they have **tested** and **found them *to be* liars**.

The reference to "apostles" here is not to men who claim to be of the Twelve. Rather, the term "apostle" has a wider meaning. In the *Didache*, a church manual written around this time, the local church is warned about "apostles," or traveling evangelists and prophets, who would stay with the church for a few days before they moved on. They are styled "apostles" since they had the same right to be supported and welcomed and fed as did the Twelve (compare 1 Cor. 9:4–14). Some were true apostles, true prophets who desired only to serve the Lord and His Church. They lodged with the local community for a day or two, teaching and prophesying, and then moved on.

But others were false and charlatans. "If he stay with you three days or more," the *Didache* warns, "he is a false prophet. Let the apostle, when leaving, receive food. But if he asks for money, he is a false prophet" (*Didache* ch. 11). The Ephesian church had experienced these false prophets, tested them, and rejected them. Here is a lesson for the church today. We are not to believe any and all claims to piety; naiveté is not one of the fruits of the Spirit. Christ calls us to examine all claims on our generosity and reject the spurious and unworthy.

More than this, the Ephesians **have perseverance and have borne *trials*** and persecution for the sake of the Lord, because they confess His **Name** (compare Matt. 24:9). They have soldiered on through all this and **have not wearied**. Trials and persecution always tempt us to lose heart, to give up on God and renounce our faith. The enemy is ever at hand to discourage us. The church at Ephesus has suffered for their Lord and still come back for more. For all this they are commended by the Lord of Glory.

> 🙵 🙵 🙵 🙵 🙵
> 4 "But I have *this* against you, that you have left your first love.
> 5 "Remember therefore from where you have fallen, and repent and do the first works; if not, I am coming to you and will move your lampstand from its place—unless you repent.
> 6 "Yet this you do have, that you hate the works of the Nicolaitans, which I also hate.

The Lord now offers a word of rebuke. Their very strength is also their weakness. They have a concern for orthodox doctrine, for correctness, for righteousness, but this very zeal leaves them open to a spiritual coldness of heart. In closing their hearts to sin, they have closed them to the sinner also. In concentrating so much on doctrine, they have forgotten the Lord and have **left** their **first love**, allowing their love for Jesus to cool in their hearts. Thus they are called to **repent and do the first works**, returning to the way of life they had when first converted. If they do not, the Lord will come invisibly in judgment and **move** their **lampstand from its place**. That is, He will reject them from being a part of His people and will not recognize them as His Church on the last day. If the Church in Ephesus is to survive (as the Anaphora of St. Basil prays that this holy house of the local church may be preserved "until the end of the world"), it must turn from its way and strive to please the Lord.

This rebuke the Lord cushions by placing it between two words of commendation, showing that He is eager to bless and approve. And what He approves is this: that they **hate the works of the Nicolaitans, which** He **also hates**.

These Nicolaitans were a short-lived sect that seems to have made a comfortable compromise with the world. They seem to have been a movement that professed to reject the false rigorism (as they thought it) of the mainline Church. They were characterized by laxity: they allowed eating food that had been offered to idols and winked at the immorality rampant in society in that day (2:14, 20–21).

The Lord states that He also hates such works as idolatry and immorality. Christ is not simply the kind, benevolent Galilean, tolerant of everything. He is also the Lord of Hosts, who hates evil and commands that we hate it as well. In denouncing the Nicolaitans, the Lord thereby warns His Church in all ages not to compromise her standards or to tolerate sin, as if we could somehow make a treaty with the world, the flesh, and the devil and bless evil in the name of being "relevant" or "modern." Sin always destroys the sinner, and in His love for the sinner, Christ is unrelenting in His hatred of sin. He calls us to share that saving and holy hatred too, calling all men to repentance, life, and joy.

> 7 "He who has an ear, let him hear what the Spirit says to the churches. To the one who conquers, I will give to eat of the tree of life, which is in the Paradise of God."

The appeal ends with a promise for the one who **hears what the Spirit says to the churches**. At the end, for **the one who conquers** all temptations to apostatize in the coming persecution, our primordial joy and bliss will be restored. Such a one will be **given to eat of the tree of life, which is in the Paradise of God**. The eternal life originally meant for us in Eden will be his to enjoy and possess again. This eternal reward awaits us, like fruit hanging on the tree of life in Paradise, waiting for us to come and taste it. Christ, the Lord of Paradise, will open the way to that eternal garden of delight and give us the fruit of life with His own hand. Here we find a call to conquer, an incentive to overcome whatever obstacles we may face.

§II.2. To the Church at Smyrna

> 8 And to the angel of the church in Smyrna write: "Thus says the first and the last, who became dead and who *came to* life:
> 9 "I know your tribulation and your poverty (but you are rich), and the blasphemy from those who say they themselves are Jews and are not, but *are* a synagogue of Satan.
> 10 "Do not be afraid of what you are about to suffer. Behold, the devil is about to cast some of you into prison, that you may be tested, and you will have tribulation for ten days. Be faithful until death, and I will give you the crown of life.
> 11 "He who has an ear, let him hear what the Spirit says to the churches. The one who conquers will never be hurt by the second death."

Next Christ speaks to the church in **Smyrna**, located about 35 miles north of Ephesus, on the west shore of the Aegean Sea.

The Lord is described as **the first and the last**, the One **who became dead and who *came to* life**. That is, He is present to the church in Smyrna as the sovereign ruler over all, the One with the power over death. This is of particular comfort to the church in Smyrna, since it undergoes such fierce persecution. As a small, powerless, marginalized group, the church there needs to know the Lord remains in control over all things, both in life and in death.

Christ acknowledges that His people in Smyrna are poor, as the world counts poverty, saying, **I know your poverty**. But the world does not see things as they truly are, but through the distorted lens of external appearances. The Lord, however, does not look and judge as the world does. Inwardly, the church at Smyrna is **rich** in good works, in being a healing and loving community, in helping the poor and storing up for themselves treasures in heaven (Matt. 6:20). The church there can take comfort in recognizing their true wealth in God's eyes and the inadequacy of the world's judgment.

Part of the Church's **tribulation** there comes from persecution, and the persecution here (as in many places in the early Church) is aided and abetted by the Jewish communities, who in **blasphemy** deride the Christians as heretics and their Lord as a deceiver. (Thus the Jews at Smyrna will later delight in the martyrdom of Bishop Polycarp—compare *Martyrdom of Polycarp* ch. 13). Such Jews are not true Jews at all. They may **say they** are **Jews**, but they **are not, but are** a **synagogue of Satan**, not of God. The title "Jew" is a title of honor, and a true Jew is one who is circumcised in his heart (Rom. 2:28–29). The Jews of Smyrna, through their opposition to Christ, are thus not true Jews at all.

The church of Smyrna is about to experience another such onslaught, but they must **not be afraid of what** they are **about to suffer. The devil is about to cast some** of them **into prison**, and for **ten days** (until the release of those imprisoned?), they will **have tribulation**.

The experience of imprisonment is a **test**, for it will reveal the sincerity of their faith and the genuineness of their devotion to Christ. **The devil** may work this out of malice, but the Lord uses it to try them, that they may receive a final reward. Let them continue in their steadfastness and not be shaken by this latest trial. Christ has foreseen it and is forewarning them that it will not last forever. Let them ride out the storm. Let them **be faithful** through all such tests, *even* **until death**, and then Christ will trample down that death by **giving** them **the crown of life**, the reward of eternal joy.

The Lord concludes His message with a promise—**the one who conquers will never be hurt by the second death**, the lake of fire, the suffering of final separation from God (20:14). The world may have the power to inflict death on some of them, but the second and final death will have no power over them at all. If they will but persevere in their faith, they will pass through the final judgment unscathed.

§II.3. To the Church at Pergamum

> ৩৹ ৩৹ ৩৹ ৩৹ ৩৹
>
> 12 And to the angel of the church in Pergamum write: "Thus says the One who has the sharp two-edged sword:

North from Smyrna was **Pergamum**, the official center of emperor worship in Asia Minor. The description of Jesus having **the sharp two-edged sword** is drawn from the initial theophany of 1:16. The **sword** of His mouth is the word of judgment He utters against all ungodliness, both in the world and in the Church. The church at Pergamum can take comfort in knowing that Christ's sword will be turned against their persecutors. The Christians may seem to be helpless, but the Lord rules from heaven as their strong defender.

> ৩৹ ৩৹ ৩৹ ৩৹ ৩৹
>
> 13 "I know where you dwell, where Satan's throne *is*; you hold onto My Name and did not deny My faith even in the days of Antipas, My witness, My faithful one, who was killed among you, where Satan dwells.

Christ knows their situation and their suffering. He **knows where** they **dwell, where Satan's throne** is. That is, they live in the very mouth of the lion, in the center for the emperor's cult in all the East.

And He knows their great perseverance, how they **hold onto** His **Name and did not deny** His **faith, even in the days** of especially fierce persecution when **Antipas**, His **witness**, His beloved **faithful one, was killed among** them, **where Satan** himself **dwells**. The reference to Pergamum as Satan's dwelling place is repeated in this verse to show that Christ knows the intensity of their struggle. The greatness of their struggle will contribute ultimately to the greatness of their reward.

Who was this Antipas, described in glowing terms of praise by

Christ as **My witness** (*Gr. martus*, compare the English "martyr"), **My faithful one**? One tradition relates that Antipas, the bishop of Pergamum, was killed by being slowly roasted to death inside a brazen bull during the reign of Domitian in about AD 92 (Antipas' feast day is April 11). This happened just a few years before the Apocalypse was written, and so it would be vivid in the memory of the church in Pergamum. It must have been traumatic indeed, causing all the faithful to fear they were next. But they kept the faith, even though they lived at the epicenter of Satan's persecution. Even the death of their leader could not break their spirit nor make them cower in fear.

> 14 "But I have a few things against you, because you have there some who hold onto the teaching of Balaam, who taught Balak to throw a stumbling block before the sons of Israel, that they might eat things sacrificed to idols and fornicate.
> 15 "Thus you also have some who likewise hold onto the teaching of the Nicolaitans.

Despite such courage, the Lord still **has a few things against** them. (We may note in passing that our good works do not blind the eyes of God to our sins.) For they tolerate **some** in their midst who **hold onto the teaching of Balaam**. The reference is once again to the teaching of the Nicolaitans. The church in Ephesus resisted the infiltration of such teaching, excommunicating those who embraced it (2:6), but those in Pergamum are more reluctant to expel such people.

The teaching of Balaam, who taught Balak to throw a stumbling block before the sons of Israel, refers to the notorious false prophet who opposed Israel in his worldliness (Numbers 22ff). Balak, a pagan king, hired Balaam to curse Israel so that he might overcome them in battle. When that failed, Balaam, allied with the Midianite enemy, induced Israel to accept, in a kind of tolerant syncretism, the idol Baal-Peor, sacrificing to him and immorally marrying pagan women. God punished Israel for the idolatrous betrayal by sending a plague upon them (Num. 25:1–9; 31:16). By identifying the Nicolaitan teaching with that of Balaam, the Lord denounces it as an example of false prophecy and as a poison to be vigorously ejected from the Church. The Nicolaitan laxity in permitting the eating of food that had been offered to idols and in tolerating fornication is nothing less than the disastrous work of Balaam within the people of God.

> ❧ ❧ ❧ ❧ ❧
> 16 "Repent, therefore; or else I am coming to you quickly, and I will war against them with the sword of My mouth.

The church at Pergamum is exhorted to **repent** of this toleration and to be more zealous in excommunicating those who are committed to the Nicolaitan teaching and laxity. If they do not, the Lord will **come quickly** in judgment, visiting a plague upon the church there, **warring against them with the sword of** His **mouth**.

Of what would this war consist? We can only guess. But in 1 Corinthians 11:29–30, St. Paul tells the Corinthian church that their laxity at the Lord's Supper has brought judgment on them. The Corinthians were "not discerning the Lord's Body," not discerning that they were the true Body of Christ and behaving accordingly. The rich despised the poor; the poor went away hungry from the eucharistic agape meal, while the rich were drunk. For this reason, St. Paul says, "many are weak and sick among you and many sleep" in death (1 Cor. 11:21–30).

It would seem that this is the judgment with which the Lord threatens His church in Pergamum. If they persist in heretical and worldly Nicolaitan laxity, the Eucharist will then be to their judgment as well. This will be the utterance of judgment against them—a special outbreak of sickness such as is occasioned by offenses against the holiness of the Lord's sacramental Presence among them. Christ has the sharp **sword of His mouth** (2:12), and with it He will judge all ungodliness, **warring** against the ungodly in the world and against the Church also, if they side with the world and behave like them.

> 17 "He who has an ear, let him hear what the Spirit says to the churches. To the one who conquers, to him I will give *some* of the hidden manna, and I will give him a white pebble, and a new name written on the pebble which no one knows except him who receives *it*."

The Lord holds out a promise to the one who **conquers** and perseveres under trial. Even as Israel was feasted with a miraculous provision of manna in the wilderness, as a proof and token that God cared for them as His own, so will the faithful and persevering Christians be feasted at the heavenly banquet with **hidden manna**, the food which is hidden from the world and which it cannot receive. After the trial and battle of the wilderness of this age, they will be nourished, cared for, and rewarded by God in the age to come.

Also, they will be **given a white pebble**. In those days, such tokens were used for many purposes. They were, for example, given to victorious gladiators who were publicly admired and allowed to retire from combat. The **white pebble** thus serves as a wonderful image of our admission to the messianic banquet, after we victoriously retire from the combat of this age.

The inner struggle of each individual person in this combat no one else can tell. We are all alone, in one sense, with our struggles, and no one else fully knows our secret griefs and tears, only the Lord. That is the sense in which **a new name** will be **written on the pebble which no one knows except him who receives it**. The Lord knows our true self, our private and secret warfare, and rewards us with healing in the age to come, drying our secret tears and giving us our **new name**, our new life and corresponding reward. In one sense, there is no such thing as Christian individualism, for we are all saved as part of a body, the Church. But in another sense, each of us enjoys a secret communion with the Lord that is utterly unique.

This is the authentic individualism, as Christ speaks to our soul truths which are for no one other than ourselves.

§II.4. To the Church at Thyatira

The church at **Thyatira**, located inland and southeast from Pergamum, is in fact the smallest, outwardly most insignificant of the seven churches of Asia. Nonetheless, it is the recipient of the longest message of the seven. This shows once again that the Lord does not judge as man does; the outwardly small and unimportant may have a greater importance to Him than others the world deems more important and impressive. The tiniest mission station in the Church may be more central to heaven's purpose than the oldest and biggest cathedral.

> ꙮ ꙮ ꙮ ꙮ ꙮ
>
> 18 And to the angel of the church in Thyatira write: "Thus says the Son of God, who has eyes as a flame of fire, and His feet like burnished bronze:
> 19 "I know your works, and your love and faith and service and perseverance, and that your last works are more *than* the first.
> 20 "But I have *this* against you, that you leave *in peace* the woman Jezebel, who calls herself a prophetess, and she teaches and deceives My slaves so that they fornicate and eat things sacrificed to idols.
> 21 "I gave her time that she might repent, and she does not want to repent of her fornication.
> 22 "Behold, I am casting her on a bed, and those who commit adultery with her into great tribulation, unless they repent of her works.
> 23 "And I will kill her children with death, and all the churches will know that I *Myself* am He who examines the minds and hearts; and I

> will give to each one of you according to your works.

The description of the Lord as the exalted **Son of God who has eyes as a flame of fire** reveals Him as the One who sees all, who knows all that we do. He sees all that goes on in Thyatira and thus **knows** their **works**—their **love, faith, service and perseverance** (v. 19). Nothing is hidden from His gaze, which burns through all the lying façades we might erect to shield ourselves from His scrutiny. More than that, He stands firm, immovable, with **feet like burnished bronze**, strong, set as Judge over all.

Despite the word of threat and rebuke that He has to offer the Church in Thyatira, Christ begins with a word of commendation, praising them that their **last** and latest **works are more *than*** their **first**. Whatever their defects, their **works** of mercy have increased. Christ knows this too, and commends them.

But He has this against them: like others in Asia Minor, they tolerate the Nicolaitan movement. It would seem that in Thyatira, the teaching is being spread by a **woman**, given the label **Jezebel** after the worldly queen in Israel, who warred against Elijah and the true prophets (1 Kings 16:31; 19:1–2). She **calls herself a prophetess** and claims authority for her teaching under this title, and the church there is content to **leave** her *in peace* and not excommunicate her. Like others spreading the teaching of the Nicolaitans, she **teaches and deceives** Christ's own **slaves** and servants, usurping an authority which is not hers and thus interfering with the slaves of Another, so that they **fornicate and eat things sacrificed to idols**.

She has evidently been warned by some in the community against spreading this teaching, for Christ says that He **gave her time** to **repent**. But it is all for naught. **She does not want to repent of her fornication**—that is, she refuses to cease pretending to be a true prophet and to cease spreading the morally lax teaching of the Nicolaitans.

The time for divine judgment has come. If she persists in eucharistic communion with the Church, she will be **cast upon a**

bed (that is, a bed of sickness). Joining her in this judgment will be **those who commit adultery with her** (described in v. 23 as **her** spiritual **children**). By **adultery** is meant those who share her spiritual adultery and her partners in her unfaithfulness to God (not physical adultery with her). Like Israel of old, who was rejected by Yahweh for the spiritual adultery of worshipping idols (compare Jer. 3:1, 9; Hos. 2:2), so the Nicolaitan acceptance of food offered to idols is adultery against God.

As suggested above, this judgment would seem to be like that experienced by some of the Corinthians. It is described here as being **cast into great tribulation** and as being **killed with death** (that is, with pestilence). By this, a special outbreak of sickness seems intended. This judgment will be so severe that the impenitent heretics of Thyatira will become a byword to the Christians round about them, as **all the churches will know** that Christ Himself is the One **who examines the minds and hearts; and** He **will give to each one** of His people **according to** their **works**. With such a mighty judgment impending, let the impenitent repent of the false prophetess's works before it is too late. Christ's word has already gone forth from Him (present tense, **"I am casting her"**): let them quickly turn back.

༄ ༄ ༄ ༄ ༄

24 "But I say to you, the rest who are in Thyatira, as many as do not have this teaching, who have not known the deep *things* of Satan, as they say—I cast no other burden on you.
25 "But what you have, hold onto until I come.

There seem to have been more things wrong with the embattled little community in Thyatira, but Christ in mercy does not ask them to correct them now. **The rest in Thyatira, as many as do not have this** Nicolaitan **teaching**, are given no other **burden**. It is enough for them to deal with the false prophetess and her followers. They have **not known the deep *things* of Satan**. But let them not let the true Faith slip away, which they have so far retained unsoiled by heresy and moral laxity. Let them simply **hold onto** what they **have until** the Lord **comes**.

The Nicolaitan teaching is here called **the deep *things* of Satan**, a term that seems to have come from the main body of the Thyatiran church, which did **not have this teaching**. This term is how **they say** and describe it. What is meant by this term?

It would seem some of the Nicolaitans boasted that their teaching contained a more mature, deeper Christianity than that held by the others—that the everyday apostolic Christianity was good enough for lightweights and beginners, but the "real" and serious Christians would want to embrace their movement. They were the ones who could really plumb the depths and know the secret teachings of God. It would seem they referred to their teachings as "the deep things of God"—and the others, those in Thyatira who resisted their teaching, responded that they were teaching rather **the deep *things* of Satan**. In His commendation of those who resist, Christ agrees with their polemical assessment.

> ꕀ ꕀ ꕀ ꕀ ꕀ
> 26 "The one who conquers, and the one who keeps My works until the end, I will give him authority over the nations;
> 27 "and he will shepherd them with a rod of iron, as the vessels of pottery are broken, as I also have received from My Father;
> 28 "and I will give him the morning star.
> 29 "He who has an ear, let him hear what the Spirit says to the churches."

Christ concludes with His promise that the one who conquers, that is, who keeps His works until the end, remaining unsullied by heresy or apostasy, will have **authority over the nations** and **will shepherd them with a rod of iron**. They will receive authority in the age to come, just **as** He **also had** now **received** authority **from** His **Father**. The allusion is to Psalm 2:8–9, where the Messiah is given authority over the nations to rule them with a rod of iron, shattering all resistance **as vessels of pottery are broken**. Christ promises to share His messianic authority with the humble and powerless believers of Thyatira in the age to come. Here is an amazing promise of power given to a tiny powerless community. Christ received all the authority of the Father as He sat down at His right hand, and Christ now promises to share this authority with His disciples. That is, believers are to exercise all the authority of God Himself in the age to come. Doubtless this is what St. Paul meant when he said we were to judge the world and even the angels (1 Cor. 6:2–3). This bestowal of full messianic authority upon the followers of Messiah is held out as incentive to the believers of Thyatira, ignored by the world as of no account, to persevere in their holy faith.

Moreover, Christ **will give** the one who overcomes **the morning star**. The morning star (the first "star" seen in the morning, actually the planet Venus) is an image of celestial beauty. Thus the inner beauty for which we yearn and strive (found for us in the Lord—He is the true Morning Star; 22:16) will be finally bestowed and manifested in us. Here and now our attempts at glorious holiness are paltry and failing. At the End we will enjoy the holiness for which we now strive. In this age, most if not all of our attempts at transformed and holy living are disappointing. We long to reflect the Lord's glory more adequately and to live a life of radiant holiness, but too often find this hope frustrated by our weakness and sinfulness. Finally, however, these deepest longings will be fulfilled, and we will shine as the divine masterpieces we yearn to be. We will never disappoint our loving Lord again.

§II.5. To the Church at Sardis

> **3** 1 To the angel of the church in Sardis write: Thus says He who has the seven spirits of God and the seven stars: "I know your works, that you have a name that you live, but you are dead.

> 2 "Be alert, and establish the things that remain, which are about to die; for I have not found your works fulfilled before My God.
> 3 "Remember therefore what you have received and heard; and keep *it*, and repent. Therefore if you do not keep alert, I will come as a thief, and you will never know at what hour I will come upon you.

Christ speaks here as the One who is sovereign over **the seven spirits of God**, that is, over the great archangels who stand before God's Throne, over all the court of heaven. He also is sovereign over **the seven stars**, that is, over the angels of the seven churches, the churches of Asia Minor on earth. He therefore speaks as ruler over things above and things below, having received all authority in heaven and on earth (Matt. 28:18). The coupling of the **seven spirits** above with the **seven stars** below is not coincidental, for the Church on earth mirrors the Church of the firstborn above (compare Heb. 12:23), even as our earthly worship blends with the worship of heaven. Christ, ruling both above and below, is empowered to **know** the **works** of the Christians in Sardis, even their secret doings, and to pronounce judgment.

As the all-seeing One, He knows they **have a name** (that is, a reputation) **that** they **live,** even though they **are dead**. Sardis enjoyed a great reputation for being a spiritual powerhouse, an impressive and important part of the Christian community in Asia, perhaps because so many worldly rich people of substance and importance had joined their church. Nonetheless, the Lord's verdict is succinct and damning: **you are dead**. In the Greek this is expressed by two brief words, *nekros ei*, which would enter their heart like a two-edged sword and a sentence of doom. Whatever impresses man does not impress the secret Seer of hearts. He tells them to **be alert and establish the things that remain, which are about to die**. Things are not hopeless. The Lord still loves them and calls them to Life.

But they are hovering on the brink of spiritual death as a community and need to wake up to their true condition.

Their problem is not, it would seem, that they are tainted by the Nicolaitan movement which is ravaging Asia Minor. But their **works** are **not fulfilled**; they are incomplete, only half-done. They are being done without fervor. Those who do these works of mercy take their faith for granted, being Christians in name only.

Thus they are counseled by Christ to **remember** the precious gift of the Gospel which they **have received and heard and keep it.** They are sleepwalking through their faith—now is the time to **repent**, appreciating the Lord's grace and living in zealous gratitude for it. Otherwise, if they do **not keep alert**, the Lord **will come** as suddenly **as a thief** at the Second Coming and find them spiritually asleep and unprepared.

> 4 "But you have a few names in Sardis who have not defiled their garments; and they will walk with Me in white, for they are worthy.
> 5 "The one who conquers will thus be clothed in white garments; and I will not wipe his name from the book of life, and I will confess his name before My Father and before His angels.
> 6 "He who has an ear, let him hear what the Spirit says to the churches."

The Lord, who sees all, does not overlook the few faithful souls in the mass of the merely nominal. We are never lost in a crowd with Him. He sees in Sardis that there are **a few names** or persons who have **not defiled their garments** with the stain of worldliness and who have preserved their sincerity and zeal. In the culture of that day, one could not come to a sacrifice or worship one's god in soiled clothes, for this disqualified the worshipper and dishonored the deity. The majority of the church in Sardis have done this, soiling their garments spiritually through their moral compromises with the pagan world around them. But **a few** have not done so, and Christ commends them for their dedication. Such will **walk with** Him **in white** in the age to come, that is, in purity and joy, for through endurance they will be made **worthy** of this final beatitude.

Christ holds out a promise for **the one who conquers** and endures faithfully to the end. In the age to come, this one too will **be clothed in white garments**, in festal joy. And he will not be denied before the Throne at the Last Judgment, as the apostates will (compare Matt. 10:32–33). Christ will **not wipe his name from the book of life**, the register of God's favorites, of His true and faithful people, but will **confess his name before** His **Father and before His angels**, acknowledging him as His own before the whole court of heaven.

§II.6. To the Church at Philadelphia

The Church at **Philadelphia** is the only church of the seven addressed here that is given no word of rebuke. The church of brotherly love (Gr. *philadelphia*) therefore stands as an example for all, for it witnesses to the possibility of attaining a standard that is genuinely pleasing to the Lord. It is not the case that the Lord will always find something to criticize. Pleasing Him is a possibility open to all.

> 7 And to the angel of the church in Philadelphia write: "Thus says the Holy One, the True One, the One who has the key of David, who opens and no one will shut, and who shuts and no one opens:

The Lord is described in Old Testament terms as **the Holy One** (compare Is. 40:25 LXX), **the True One** (compare Ex. 34:6 LXX). That is, Christ is the Holy God who revealed Himself to Israel (for the Father always reveals Himself through His Word and Son); Christ is the One who is dependable and faithful to His word. He has promised life to those who persevere, and this promise can be trusted.

He is also described as **the One who has the key of David, who opens and no one will shut, and who shuts and no one opens**. This image is drawn from Isaiah 22:22. In this passage, Shebna, the chief steward over the royal House of David, was declared deposed from office, and Eliakim was put in his place. To Eliakim was given the "key of the House of David," or authority to govern the royal affairs as he saw fit. He was the King's plenipotentiary. This image of authority is applied to the glorified Christ. He is given **the key of David**, the authority as Messiah over the Kingdom of God. Christ **opens and no one shuts,** and what He **shuts no one opens**. His decision is sovereign and cannot be overruled by any. Access to the heavenly Kingdom is determined by His word alone.

---

8 "I know your works. Behold, I have granted an opened door before you which no one is able to shut, because you have a little power, and have kept My word, and did not deny My Name.

9 "Behold, I will grant *that* some from the synagogue of Satan, who say they are Jews and are not, but lie—I will make them come and worship before your feet, and make them know that I *Myself* have loved you.

This controversy with the Jews of Philadelphia is reflected in the words that follow. It would seem that some of the Philadelphian church are Jews who were put out from the synagogue for their faith in Christ. Those in the synagogue presume to speak for God, saying the Christians are heretics and will never enter the Kingdom. In so doing, they declare the door of the Kingdom firmly shut to the Christian "heretics."

In contradiction of such claims, Christ assures His followers in Philadelphia that *He alone* is the One with divine authority to admit or bar the way into the Kingdom, to declare heaven's door open or shut. He Himself has opened the way for them, and no one can shut it. The Christians of Philadelphia need not fear any Jewish excommunication. In fact, the Jews who excommunicated them are denounced as not true Jews at all; they **say they are Jews and are not, but lie**. As noted in the comments on 2:9, the title "Jew" is one of honor, and a true Jew, one who truly loves God, may wear it proudly. The Jews of Philadelphia are not such but are Jews only racially, in name only and not in their hearts (compare Rom. 2:29). By their opposition to Christ and His Church, they have lost the right to be considered true Jews.

The Lord **knows** the **works** of His own little ones, the Christians of Philadelphia—their faith and their love for Him. Though they have only **a little power**—are few in numbers and have no social influence—they nonetheless have **kept** His **word**, obeying the Gospel, and **did not deny** His **Name**, even under Jewish pressure to do so. Because of this, Christ has **granted an opened door before** them into the Kingdom, **which no one**—not even the Jews of the local synagogue—**is able to shut**. Though the Jews would close the door of heaven to them, Jesus is the One with all authority, and He overrules their worthless excommunication.

Christ will give something else as well. Besides granting an opened door, He also **will grant *that* some from the synagogue of Satan** will come and **worship before** their **feet**. (Such Jews are denounced as a **synagogue of Satan** and not a synagogue of God, since Satan works through them as they persecute the Christians. Thus they **say they are Jews and are not, but lie**, for a true Jew would confess Jesus as Messiah; compare 2:9.)

The image of having one's foes come in defeat and bow themselves down before one's feet is a common one in the Old Testament. The word used here and translated *worship* is the Greek *proskuneo*, which means "to bow oneself down." Whether this indicates the worship and adoration due to God alone (compare such a use in Ex. 20:5 LXX) or merely the respect given to social superiors in an Oriental context (compare such a use of the word in Gen. 33:3 LXX) depends on the context. Obviously the latter use is intended here.

It was the expectation of the Jews that, in the messianic age, their Gentile foes would come and worship or bow down before their feet (see Is. 45:14; 60:14). Ironically, this messianic salvation will be fulfilled *in the Christians*, not in them. In the age to come, they (the Jews) will be the ones to come and **worship before** the Christians' **feet**, confessing that the Christians are **loved** by Jesus, the true Messiah, that the Christians are the true people of God, and that the Jews erred in their rejection of Jesus as Messiah. The unbelieving Jews of Philadelphia must tyrannize the helpless Christians now, but Jesus will vindicate His followers in the age to come.

> ꙳ ꙳ ꙳ ꙳ ꙳
> 10 "Because you have kept the word of My perseverance, I also will keep you from the hour of trial, that hour which is about to come upon the whole world, to try those who dwell upon the earth.
> 11 "I am coming soon; hold onto what you have, that no one takes your crown.

Christ has yet a further reward for His people. Because they **have kept the word of** His **perseverance** (that is, have kept His Word and remained true to Him, persevering through trial and persecution), He in turn **also** will **keep** them **from the** coming **hour of trial**.

This **hour** is the time of persecution that is imminent. The faithful believers He promises to **keep from** it. The preposition *from* is the Greek *ek,* which is capable of several meanings. Here it means that when the universal time of trial **comes upon the whole world**, these faithful in Philadelphia will be sustained so as to emerge from it unscathed. They must enter that fire of testing, for **the whole world** must enter it. It will come to **try** all **those who dwell upon the earth**. But Christ will be with them in that fire (compare Dan. 3:25, in which one "like a son of God" was with the three young men in the furnace) and will sustain them by His supernatural strength.

The thought is the same as that in Luke 21:34–36. There the Lord says we must take heed to ourselves, lest our hearts be weighed down with carousing, drunkenness, and the cares of life so that the Day of Judgment comes upon us unexpectedly. If we will take heed, living in watchful righteousness, we will not be snared by it; rather, we will escape all these things and stand before the Son of Man.

This is the Lord's promise to His beloved Philadelphians. He will strengthen them so that their faith will not fail in the trial (compare Luke 22:32). But the promise is also a call to action; they are not to rest complacently. The Second Coming will happen **soon** (compare 1:1). It is imminent in that there is no place for lack of vigilance. Christ's servants must not rest and slide into moral laxity, saying to themselves, "My master is not coming for a long time" (see Matt. 24:48). Rather, they must retain a sense of eschatological urgency and **hold onto what** they **have**, **so that no one takes** their **crown** of victory by causing them to apostatize. The image of the crown would have particular resonance for those in Philadelphia, for it was there that festivals and athletic games were held, with the victor in the games receiving a crown.

> ༄ ༄ ༄ ༄ ༄
>
> 12 "The one who conquers, I will make him a pillar in the sanctuary of My God, and he will never go out from it any longer; and I will write upon him the Name of My God, and the name of the city of My God, the new Jerusalem, which comes down from heaven from My God, and My new Name.
> 13 "He who has an ear, let him hear what the Spirit says to the churches."

Christ's promise to **the one who conquers** is that He will **make him a pillar in the sanctuary of** His **God**. That is, they will be an immovable and permanent part of God's dwelling place. The image of being a **pillar** has a nonarchitectural nuance as well, for distinguished and honored men are called pillars (see Gal. 2:9). As pillars, the Philadelphians will thus know security with honor in the age to come. Indeed, they will **never go out from it** (i.e. from the **sanctuary**) **any longer**, but God will dwell among them, even as He dwelt in the earthly Sanctuary of Solomon. They will never be deprived of His Presence and protection to ages of ages. In an area that experienced many earthquakes, which made its populace go out from the city in panic to find safety in the countryside, this promise would be especially welcome. Christ will provide them with a security in the Kingdom which they never knew on earth.

Also, Christ promises to **write upon him the Name of** His **God, and the name of the city of** His **God, and** His **new Name.** To write on someone is to claim that person as one's own. Thus in Isaiah 44:5, the faithful write on their hand, "Belonging to Yahweh," which marks them as His own servants and possessions. The promise here does not refer to any physical writing or mark upon us, but rather a spiritual mark (compare 14:1). For the Lord to write on us is to claim us as belonging exclusively to Him and thus being under His protection.

Our reward is to be claimed as belonging to the Father, to His City, the new Jerusalem, and to Jesus Christ, glorified in the new Kingdom of the age to come. The world and its powers, Caesar and his successors, may claim authority over us (see 13:16f), but we belong to a higher One than Caesar. We do not belong to this age at all, in fact, but to the new City that will descend from heaven, adorned as a bride for her husband (21:2). Here in this age the Philadelphians may have felt small and powerless. But they do not belong to this age or to its king, but to the age to come and its King.

§II.7. To the Church at Laodicea

The last church addressed is that in Laodicea. This is the only church of the seven addressed here that is given no word of commendation, but only of rebuke.

> ৩৯ ৩৯ ৩৯ ৩৯ ৩৯
> 14 To the angel of the church in Laodicea write:
> "Thus says the Amen, the faithful and true
> witness, the Beginning of the creation of God:

Christ is described as **the Amen** because He is the fulfillment of all the Father's promises for redemption. As St. Paul said, all the promises God has made to His people Israel are fulfilled in Christ (2 Cor. 1:20), and all creation finds its fulfillment and "yes" to God in Him. Christ is also **the faithful and true witness** (Gr. *martus*, compare our English word "martyr") because He faithfully witnessed to the truth of God before Pontius Pilate, even to the death. By this He set the example for His people, for the Church also is called to witness to His truth when brought to stand before the powers of this age. Finally, Christ is described as **the Beginning** or Source (Gr. *arche*) **of the creation of God**, for God the Father created all through the Son. Through Jesus all things exist (1 Cor. 8:6); all things were made through Him, and without Jesus, nothing was made that was made (John 1:3). Thus all creation looks to Him as its Beginning and Source. In this message to the last of the seven churches, Christ stands revealed as the End and the Beginning, the One who fulfills all the saving promises of God and witnesses to them as well.

> 15 "I know your works, that you are neither cold nor hot; I would that you were cold or hot!
> 16 "Thus because you are lukewarm, and neither hot nor cold, I am about to vomit you from My mouth.
> 17 "For you say, 'I am rich, and have become rich, and have need of nothing!' and do not know that you *yourself* are miserable and pitiable and poor and blind and naked.
> 18 "I counsel you to buy from Me gold purified by fire that you may be rich, and white garments that you may be clothed, and that the shame of your nakedness will not be manifested; and salve to anoint your eyes that you may see.
> 19 "As many as I *Myself* love, I reprove and discipline; therefore be zealous and repent.

Once again the Lord declares that He **knows** their **works** (compare 2:2, 18; 3:1, 8). In particular, He knows they are **lukewarm, neither cold nor hot**. That is, they are neither **hot** and fervent in their love for Christ nor **cold** and hostile to Him. Rather, they have the form of godliness, but by their deeds deny its power to change lives (compare 2 Tim. 3:5). This is the worst state of all, and the Lord **would** that they **were** either **cold or hot.** For if they were coldly hostile to Him (as Saul the persecutor was; Acts 8:1, 3), they might be brought to know their peril and repent. But as lukewarm, they are blind to their true state. They think they are spiritually healthy, but are mortally ill. So ill, in fact, that if they do not repent, the Lord is **about to vomit** them **from** His **mouth** as a noxious, sickening substance. (The word rendered *vomit* is the Greek *emeo*; compare our English word "emetic.")

Their blindness is profound. As a prosperous and worldly church, they judge things according to the world's standards. They look at their worldly wealth and boast, **"I am rich, and have become rich, and have need of nothing!"** That is, not only are they rich, but they have achieved their wealth by their own power and now need rely on no one. One can almost see the chests of the rich church members swell with pride as they breathe out their boast.

In their blindness, they think their spiritual prosperity is commensurate with their physical prosperity. Here we see the danger of riches and their tendency to deaden the hearts and blind the eyes. They have wealth and so have been lulled into a sense of complacency and self-satisfaction—sure signs of spiritual death. The Lord, in love, reveals their true state: they are not rich, but on the contrary, *they* are the ones (the pronoun **you** is emphatic in the Greek) who are **miserable and pitiable and poor and blind and naked**. Like desperate infants abandoned to die in the street, they are not (as they think) in **need of nothing** but in need of everything.

From the Lord, though, can come all they need. He will provide the **gold purified by fire** they need to truly **be rich**, and **white garments** to cover **the shame of** their **nakedness**, and eye **salve** to **anoint** and heal their blinded **eyes**. (We detect a local flavor to these references, since Laodicea was famous for its wealth, its textile industry, and its medical school, which produced a famous eye salve.)

What would the Laodiceans use to **buy** from the Savior this gold, these white garments, and this eye salve? The money in their purses, now used to pamper themselves. In speaking of buying these things, Christ urges them to almsgiving and to works of mercy. Their money can be used to help the poor and thus provide themselves true riches in heaven (Matt. 6:20; Luke 12:33). This will constitute their repentance. Then they will have true **gold**, a lasting wealth in heaven. Then they will have a **white** festal **garment**, in which to feast with the King, purchased through their righteous deeds (see 19:8). Then they will have healing eye **salve** and perceive spiritual realities now opaque to them. In this extended parabolic metaphor, we see the condescension of the Savior. The rich worldlings of the Laodicean church understand the world of commerce very well, and so Christ uses terms they can comprehend to lead them to a higher world.

This is a devastating rebuke. But Christ again tempers it with love. He is not rebuking them because He does not love them, but rather because He *does*. For **as many as** He **loves** (the pronoun **I** is emphatic in the Greek, stressing that this is how the Lord deals with His beloved, contrary to the ways of the world), He **reproves** and **disciplines** or punishes. Let them **be zealous and repent**. Let them accept this word of rebuke as the word of love it is.

ॐ ॐ ॐ ॐ ॐ

20 "Behold, I stand at the door and knock; if anyone hears My voice and opens the door, I will come in to him and will sup with him, and he with Me.

Christ makes a further offer. The wealthy of Laodicea are accustomed to sup and dine well. They delight to dine with important people and to have them at their table. Christ affirms that, through their self-sufficiency and pride, they have excluded Him from their eucharistic agape meals. Salvation consists of dining with Him in His Kingdom (Luke 22:30), of which the eucharistic Supper is a foretaste. Yet these men have exiled the Lord and are unknowingly dining without Him. He is on the outside of their church door and they do not know it. Yet in His amazing humility and condescension, He **stands** outside that **door and knocks**, awaiting entrance.

Each man of the community is called to repent, hearkening to the sound of His knocking, and to **open the door**. If this is done, the Lord will **come in** to him and sup with **him** (Gr. *deipneo*; compare *deipnon*, "supper," as used of the eucharistic meal in 1 Cor. 11:20). If the church of Laodicea will open their hearts to Christ, He will fill their eucharistic meals with the fullness of His Presence, bestowing salvation.

> ৡ ৡ ৡ ৡ ৡ
> 21 "The one who conquers, I will grant to him to sit with Me on My throne, as I also conquered and sat with My Father on His throne.
> 22 "He who has an ear, let him hear what the Spirit says to the churches."

The Lord offers a final promise to **the one who conquers** and endures suffering to the end. The Lord will **grant** to such a one **to sit with** Him **on** His **throne** in the age to come, **as** He **also conquered** through enduring the Cross **and sat with** His **Father on His throne**. The Christian who endures to the end will share all the royal authority of Christ in the Kingdom of God, being the heir of God and the co-heir of Christ (Rom. 8:17). Christ shares all the authority of God and, staggering as it may seem, offers to share that immensity of divine authority with us as well. But one must conquer in order to rule, and must die before one can truly live. There is no possibility of experiencing the joy of Pascha without first enduring the darkness of Holy Friday, and no possibility of ruling in the age to come without overcoming the temptations to apostasy. The path to glory is always through the Cross.

❧ III ☙

THE THINGS WHICH WILL TAKE PLACE HEREAFTER: VISIONS OF JUDGMENT, PERSECUTION, AND TRIUMPH
(4:1—11:14)

Here begins the futuristic portion of St. John's prophecy. Chapter 1 described his theophanic vision of Christ, and chapters 2 and 3 detail the messages he received for the seven churches of Asia. The remainder of the Apocalypse concerns "the things which will happen after these things" (1:19)—that is, events and realities commencing in the immediate future reaching until the time of the Second Coming and the eternal consummation.

§III.1. The Worship of God, the Creator

4 1 After these things I looked, and behold! a door opened in heaven, and the first voice which I had heard speaking with me as a trumpet said, "Come up here, and I will show you the things which must happen after these things."
2 Immediately I became in the Spirit; and behold! a throne was set in heaven, and One sitting upon the throne.
3 And He who was sitting *was* in appearance like a jasper stone and a sardius; and there was a rainbow around the throne, in appearance like an emerald.

> 4 And around the throne *were* twenty-four thrones; and upon the thrones *were* twenty-four elders sitting, clothed in white garments, and upon their heads *were* golden crowns.

The visions begin with a dramatic cry, **behold!** introducing a sudden shift of perception. John has been looking at the glorified Christ, who was giving him messages for His churches in Asia. Then he suddenly sees something else—**a door opened in heaven**, standing as if bidding him to enter and to see mysteries hidden from the children of men. The Lord who first revealed Himself (in the vision of chapter 1) has yet more to reveal, and John hears that **voice speaking as a trumpet** (compare 1:10), summoning him to **come up here**, through the door, that Christ may **show** him **the things which must happen after these things**.

After this, **immediately** John **became in the Spirit**. That is, once again he saw things in a visionary ecstasy as in 1:10. The things he saw, therefore, were no fantasies or projections of his own ideas. They were true visions, such as God gives to His prophets (compare Acts 2:17; 10:10f), and as such came with the full authority of God.

Once again, John introduces his vision with the dramatic cry of **behold!** And what John sees is **a throne set in heaven and One sitting upon the throne**. The **throne** is an image of the invincible and eternal sovereignty of God. This is the governing image of the Apocalypse (the word *throne* being used more than forty times). It reveals that in the face of the eternal might of God's Kingdom, the authority and power of Caesar and the world are as nothing. He is the true *Pantocrator*, and all earthly events must ultimately bow to Him and fulfill His purposes.

John goes on to relate the vision in greater detail, even as Ezekiel related in detail the vision of God's glory he saw. **He who was sitting** on the throne was **in appearance like a jasper stone**, which was clear as a crystal (see 21:11), and **a sardius,** which was blood red and named after the city of Sardis, near which it was found. **Around the throne** shone **a rainbow**, which was **in appearance like an emerald**. With this wealth of imagery, we are given a picture

III. The Things Which Will Take Place   Revelation 4:5–8

of God's throne as shining with unapproachable light. The images echo those of Ezekiel 1:26–28, which also speaks of God's throne, radiant with sapphire and the light of the rainbow. In John's vision, God's throne blazes with the **jasper** brilliance of crystal purity; it is resplendent with the **sardius** red fire of God's Presence; it shines like **an emerald**, reflecting like a prism all the many-colored mercies of the **rainbow**, that ancient symbol of God's mercy to man (Gen. 9:13f).

Around the throne *were* **twenty-four thrones**, and upon these were **twenty-four elders sitting, clothed in white garments** (symbolic of festal joy; compare 3:4–5), wearing **golden crowns upon their heads** (symbolic of the authority they share with God).

These are the thrones of God's heavenly court. Even as earthly kings were surrounded by their attendants, so God also has His heavenly court. The scene would be a familiar one for the Christians, for they saw the bishop thus surrounded by his presbyters every Sunday at the Eucharist. The bishop would be seated on his "throne" or *cathedra* (chair) as he presided at the service, while his presbyters were seated around him on either side, on a bench later called the *synthronos*. Thus the Sunday eucharistic Liturgy is an image and participation in the heavenly worship above.

Why **twenty-four** thrones? Just as twenty-four courses of Aaronic priests were appointed for the worship of the Temple (1 Chr. 24:5), so there were a corresponding number in the heavenly temple, since the earthly was but a copy of the heavenly (compare Heb. 8:5).

🙖 🙖 🙖 🙖 🙖

5 Out from the throne come forth *flashes of* lightning and sounds and *peals of* thunder. And *there were* seven lamps of fire burning before the throne, which are the seven spirits of God;

6 and before the throne *there was* as *it were* a sea of glass, like crystal; and in the middle of the throne and around the throne *were* four living *things* full of eyes in front and behind.

7 The first living *thing was* like a lion, and the

> second living *thing* like a calf, and the third living *thing* had a face as of a man, and the fourth living *thing was* like a flying eagle.
> 8 And the four living *things*, each one of them having six wings, are full of eyes around and within; and day and night they do not have rest, saying, "Holy, holy, holy, the Lord God Almighty, who was and who is and who is coming!"

The throne is described in all its terrifying majesty. There **come forth** from the Presence of God *flashes of* **lightning and sounds** (rumbling sounds?) **and** *peals of* **thunder**. Such sounds of the storm often accompanied the divine Presence throughout the Old Testament: the appearance at Sinai was full of such fearful phenomena (Ex. 19:16), and the theophanies hymned by David saw such a storm (Ps. 18:12f; 77:17f). Indeed, thunderstorms mirrored the terrifying might of the Most High.

The seven archangelic spirits wait upon Him, like **seven lamps of fire burning before the throne**, even as the seven-branched lampstand burned before the Face of God in the earthly sanctuary (Ex. 25:37). **Before the throne** *there was* **as** *it were* **a sea of glass, like crystal**. Glass in the ancient world was dim and somewhat opaque, but this **glass** was clear as **crystal**, shining with a pure radiance. The **sea** in those days was a dangerous barrier to men, separating one from another, and it was not so easily navigable as now. Thus it is a suitable image for the crystal purity of God, which separates all profane creation from His Presence.

In the middle of the throne and around the throne (that is, standing near the throne and surrounding it as an inner circle) were **four living** *things*, living creatures or animals (Gr. *zoa*), **full of eyes in front and behind**, that is, standing fully intent upon their task of worship, alert, illumined, watchful, completely focused on their Lord God. Here is an image of all animate creation waiting on God their Creator.

The image draws its inspiration from a similar image in Ezekiel

III. The Things Which Will Take Place   Revelation 4:9–11

1:5–10. The **first living *thing*** or creature was **like a lion**, the **second like a calf** (that is, a bull-calf), **the third** had **a face as of a man**, and the **fourth** was **like a flying eagle**. Thus creation is portrayed in four basic aspects of strength, fertility, reason, and soaring freedom. Creation, in all its manifold splendor, unites in giving praise to its Creator. In this work of ceaseless praise the living creatures are even as the seraphim, for each has **six wings**, like the seraphim of Isaiah 6:2. And like the seraphim of Isaiah's vision, they find ceaseless joy and fulfillment in the unending adoration of God, so that **day and night they do not have rest**. Nor have they any need of it, for the sight of God is their refreshment and strength. In perpetual bliss, they cry **Holy, holy, holy, the Lord God Almighty, who was and who is and who is coming!** Their eternal delight is in beholding God in His power and sovereignty. (Later allegories would view these animals as symbols of the four Gospels.)

> ॐ ॐ ॐ ॐ ॐ
>
> 9 And whenever the living *things* give glory and honor and thanksgiving to Him who sits upon the throne, to Him who lives to ages of ages,
> 10 the twenty-four elders will fall down before Him who sits upon the throne, and will fall *down* before Him who lives to ages of ages, and will cast their crowns before the throne, saying,
> 11 "Worthy are You, our Lord and our God, to receive glory and honor and power; for You created all things, and through Your will they were, and were created."

The worship of heaven joins with the worship of all animate creation. **Whenever the living *things* give glory and honor and thanksgiving** to God, the eternal one who **lives to ages of ages**, the heavenly court joins them in that glad doxology. The **twenty-four elders**, symbolic of the court of heavenly worshippers, also **fall down before** God and **cast their crowns before the throne**, acknowledging that all authority comes from God. They cry out, **"Worthy are You, our Lord and our God."** This cry of "Worthy are you!" was the cry with which crowds greeted the entrance of the emperor in triumphal procession. Moreover, Domitian (the emperor under whom St. John was exiled) introduced the imperial title of "Lord and God" as part of the emperor cult. Here these honors are given to the true King, the Lord and God of the Christians.

And the Christian God is praised for His sovereign act of creating the world, **for He created all things, and through His will they were, and were created**—God both designed all creation and created it according to His design. That God is the Creator, of course, we now take for granted. But then it was one of the central points of controversy. The Jews and Christians asserted that matter was not eternal (as pagans said) but was made from nothing through the free and gracious act of God. Thus creation was a gift that showed God's love and power.

This vision of the heavenly adoration of God on His throne was a sight to thrill and encourage the hearts of the faithful. They had seen the power and pomp of Caesar—the parades, the pageantry, the music of the earthly glory. Their own small chanting in their eucharistic assemblies seemed perhaps a pale and unworthy thing in comparison. But St. John saw the true pomp of the universe—the glory and splendor of their God in heaven. Here was something with which the powers of the world could not compete. Here was the true and lasting glory.

§III.2. The Worship of the Lamb, the Redeemer

This chapter forms the counterpoint to the previous chapter. Chapter 4 centers on the worship of God the Creator and climaxes with the cry, "Worthy are You, our Lord and our God . . . for You created all things!" (4:11). Chapter 5 centers on Christ the Lamb, the Redeemer of the world, and climaxes with the cry, "Worthy is the Lamb that was slaughtered!" (5:12).

It may be added that this does not, of course, deny that Jesus the Lamb is also, with the Father, the Creator of the world. It is indeed through the Son that the Father made all things (John 1:3). These chapters simply focus on Christ's redeeming work to the literary exclusion of anything else. St. John is writing an apocalypse, not a comprehensive theological treatise.

> ꙮ ꙮ ꙮ ꙮ ꙮ
>
> **5** 1 I saw in the right *hand* of Him who sat upon the throne a book written inside and behind, sealed up with seven seals.
> 2 And I saw a strong angel heralding with a great voice, "Who *is* worthy to open the book and to loose its seals?"
> 3 And no one in heaven or on the earth or under the earth was able to open the book or to look *into* it.
> 4 And I was weeping greatly because no one was found worthy to open the book or to look *into* it;

As John looked, he **saw in the right *hand* of Him who sat upon the throne a book written inside and behind** (that is, on front and back), **sealed up with seven seals**. It was somewhat unusual to write on both sides; writing on the reverse side of a papyrus scroll (where the fibers ran vertically) was difficult. But this scroll had so much on it that both sides were necessary. This was because the scroll contained God's plan for the eternal ages, the consummation of His love for the world and our final salvation. A full scroll indeed! It was **sealed up with seven seals** (a sign of its importance; Roman wills often were sealed with seven seals.)

John looked and **saw a strong angel** (present in the Apocalypse at key moments; compare 10:1; 18:21) **heralding with a great voice, "Who *is* worthy to open the book and to loose its seals?"** The angel called aloud, with a voice reaching out to all in the universe, to find someone **worthy to open the book** and to put into effect God's saving dispensation in the age to come. But **no one** in the wide world, neither angels **in heaven**, nor men **on the earth,** nor the dead in Sheol **under the earth** (John uses the convention of speaking of a three-tiered universe to indicate totality) was **able to open the book**. None was worthy to transform and heal the earth. St. John found himself **weeping greatly** because of this, for it meant that God's plan for the age to come would never be carried out. Such wonderful things were written in the scroll, and they would never see the light.

> ꙮ ꙮ ꙮ ꙮ ꙮ
>
> 5 and one from the elders says to me, "Do not weep; behold, the Lion of the tribe of Judah, the Root of David, has conquered *so as* to open the book and its seven seals."
> 6 And I saw in the middle of the throne and the four living *things* and the elders a Lamb standing, as *if* slaughtered, having seven horns and seven eyes, which are the seven spirits of God, sent out into all the earth.
> 7 And He came and took *it* from the right *hand* of Him who sat upon the throne.

Then comes the dramatic resolution. **One from the** twenty-four **elders**, the heavenly court, interrupts John's grief and **says** to him, **"Do not weep; behold, the Lion of the tribe of Judah, the Root of David, has conquered *so as* to open the book."** The image of the Messiah as a **Lion of the tribe of Judah** is from Genesis 49:9–10, which was considered a prophecy of Messiah; it is used here to show the great strength of Christ. This title is paired with **the Root of** Jesse, source of **David,** drawn from Isaiah 11:1. This title reveals Christ as the messianic King, who will vindicate the poor and strike the earth with the rod of His mouth (Is. 11:4). In the messages to the seven churches of Asia, Christ repeatedly spoke of the necessity of conquering (2:7, 11, etc.). Here we see that He has blazed the victory trail for us by **conquering** death Himself. The presence of the conquering Messiah is announced to all.

Then John looked and **saw in the middle of the throne and**

III. The Things Which Will Take Place   Revelation 5:8–10

the four living *things* and the elders (that is, in the center of all the assembled multitude) **a Lamb standing, as *if* slaughtered** and slain, with its mortal wounds visible to all. The contrast between the power of the lion and the meekness of a slaughtered lamb is stunning. A lion is announced, yet one sees a lamb come forward—and a slaughtered one at that. Here is the mystery of the Church—that Christ's power is made perfect in weakness (compare 2 Cor. 12:9). It is by weakness and death that death is overcome.

This Lamb stands forth, **having seven horns** (symbolic of the totality of power; Ps. 92:10) and **seven eyes, which are the seven spirits of God, sent out into all the earth** (showing that all the archangels of God are sent out on their tasks by Jesus; He is the One who has care of all the earth). Christ, led as a lamb to the slaughter of the Cross (Is. 53:7), boldly **came** to God and **took** the book **from the right *hand* of Him who sat upon the throne**. We should note this boldness. Christ did not wait until He was given the scroll. As the crucified, risen, and glorified Lord, He was worthy to be the Savior and Judge of the world, and He is portrayed as boldly approaching the throne and taking the scroll.

༄ ༄ ༄ ༄ ༄

8   And when He had taken the book, the four living *things* and the twenty-four elders fell *down* before the Lamb, each having a harp and golden bowls full of incense, which are the prayers of the saints.

9   And they sang a new song, saying, "Worthy are You to take the book and to open its seals; for You were slaughtered, and bought for God with Your blood *men* from every tribe and tongue and people and nation,

10 "and made them to be a kingdom and priests to our God; and they will reign on the earth!"

When Christ **had taken the book** (symbolic of His beginning His heavenly reign), **the four living *things* and the twenty-four**

elders fell down before Him. Just as the heavenly court had fallen down in worship before God the Creator in 4:10, so now they fall down before Christ the Lamb, for Christ is co-equal with the Father and shares His throne and His glory. It is as Jesus said on earth: One must honor the Son even as one honors the Father (John 5:23), for the Son is of one essence with Him.

The heavenly court of elders each had **a harp** and **golden bowls full of incense, which are the prayers of the saints**. That is, all those in heaven sang melodiously in adoration to Christ, and also offered the prayers of the Christians still on earth (see Tobit 12:12–15 for the Old Testament background and the notion that angels in heaven intercede for those on earth). The prayers of the Church on earth are compared to **incense**, which rises acceptably before God (Ps. 141:2). These prayers are offered by the saints in heaven, the twenty-four elders, as in **golden bowls**. Here we see the unity of the Church, in which the prayers and praises of all the Church, both those militant in earth and those glorified in heaven, rise as a single harmony before God.

As those in heaven fell down in worship, they **sang a new song** to Christ, saying, **"Worthy are You."** Once again, we see the same acclamation, before given to God the Creator (4:11), now given also to Christ. This hymn is called a new song because it is the song of the new messianic age, and its joy and glory were never before seen on earth. In Christ, all creation is made new (2 Cor. 5:17), and the song that rises from the hearts of His redeemed people is new also.

Why is the Lamb praised like this and given such divine honors? Because He was **slaughtered, and bought for God with** His **blood men from every tribe and tongue and people and nation, and made them to be a kingdom and priests to God**. That is, Christ is praised because of His work of redeeming the whole world and preparing a holy people for the Father. In the words of St. Paul, it was because Christ humbled Himself to death, even the death of the Cross, that God highly exalted Him (Phil. 2:8–9).

Before Christ, all the tribes and peoples of the earth were lost in darkness and subjugated under the authority of the Evil One. Now Christ has purchased men from throughout the world for

III. The Things Which Will Take Place   Revelation 5:11–14

God, making them His Church, transforming them so that they are God's **kingdom** and **priests**, as Israel was called to be of old (Ex. 19:6). God's people are now no longer confined to one nation, but are drawn from all the nations on earth to form one international nation, the Church of the living God. The Roman authorities who persecute them think them powerless and pathetic, but they are God's people, and as such, in the age to come **they will reign on the earth**. The power that now belongs to the godless will one day belong to the Christians.

> ⁂ ⁂ ⁂ ⁂ ⁂
> 11 And I looked, and I heard the voice of many angels around the throne and the living *things* and the elders; and the number of them was myriads of myriads, and thousands of thousands,
> 12 saying with a great voice, "Worthy is the Lamb that was slaughtered to receive power and riches and wisdom and strength and honor and glory and blessing!"
> 13 And every creature which *is* in heaven and on the earth and under the earth and on the sea, and all things in them, I heard saying, "To Him who sits upon the throne, and to the Lamb, *be* blessing and honor and glory and might to ages of ages!"
> 14 And the four living *things* were saying, "Amen," and the elders fell *down* and worshipped.

John continues to **look** and sees an overwhelming outpouring of praise. As he continued to gaze at His Lord, he **heard the voice of many angels around the throne and the living *things* and the elders**. To the court he first observed were joined many others, a vast throng of angels, and **the number of them was myriads of myriads, and thousands of thousands** (that is, a host beyond counting). All were **saying with a great voice** and shouting aloud, **"Worthy is** the Lamb that was slaughtered to receive power and riches and wisdom and strength and honor and glory and blessing!" Praise is piled upon praise, **power and riches** are heaped upon **wisdom,** which is piled upon **strength**, which is loaded atop **honor**, which is heaped upon **glory**, which is loaded upon **blessing**. Acclaim after acclaim is offered up in an attempt to praise Christ worthily for what He has done. The crowds on earth that acclaimed Caesar as worthy were nothing compared to this.

There is yet more. After this countless throng in heaven has praised the Lamb, all in creation join in as well. **Every creature which *is* in heaven and on the earth and under the earth and on the sea, and all things in them**, the vast totality of all living things throughout the cosmos, cries out in ecstatic praise. John **heard** their thunderous shout, **"To Him who sits upon the throne, and to the Lamb,** *be* **blessing and honor and glory and might to ages of ages!"** Once again we see the piling up of acclaim, as all the living strain to empty out the treasury of language to praise the Father and the Son. The **four living *things***, symbolic of all created nature, echo this praise, ecstatically **saying** over and over again, **"Amen"**; and **the elders** of heaven's court also **fall *down* and worship**, offering adoration to God and His co-eternal Son.

(We note too that the Father who **sits upon the throne** and Christ **the Lamb** receive the same praise, the same co-equal worship. Arians who deny Christ's divinity, both ancient and modern, are wrong in their refusal to give Him the same worship as is given to God the Father.)

Here is the decisive answer and antidote the struggling Christians need as they watch the all-but-invincible Caesar cheered by the multitudes. They, though powerless and few in the eyes of the world, are part of a large and more eternal throng.

§III.3. The Opening of the Seven Seals

The Opening of the Seals and the Structure of the Apocalypse

When all the seals are removed, then the book will be opened and the salvation of the world consummated. For before a sealed book can be opened, its seals must be removed. In the same way, before the new messianic age can begin, all these things must take place—wars, tumults, famines, pestilence and death, martyrdom and great signs from heaven. The image of the seven seals tells us that all these disasters are but signs of the coming End. They are not to be feared or taken for evidence that the world is out of control. Rather, the opposite: they are evidence that Christ is preparing to judge the world, opening the seals of the heavenly book. The more these disasters afflict the world, the more the Christians may rejoice, for they are heralds of the coming Kingdom.

As in classic apocalyptic form, the coming judgments are heavily stylized and arranged into a group of seven different judgments. In this literary arrangement, first comes war, then come tumults, then comes famine, then pestilence and death. Next comes martyrdom and finally, at the sixth seal, signs from heaven. One plague must pass before the next comes. This is the stylization characteristic of the apocalyptic genre.

In the actual historical outworking of these judgments, things are not of course neatly and chronologically arranged. War, famine, pestilence, and death are usually found together, along with martyrdom of the faithful. We see a less obscure presentation of the same teaching in Christ's Olivet Discourse in Luke 21 and its parallels (Matthew 24 and Mark 13). What is said symbolically in the Apocalypse was said in plainer language on the Mount of Olives. There the Lord says, "You will hear of wars and disturbances. . . . Nation will rise against nation . . . and there will be great earthquakes and in various places pestilences and famines; and there will be terrors and great signs from heaven" (Luke 21:9–11). Here the chronological order of these disasters is already different from the stylized order found in the Apocalypse.

Then the Lord goes on to say, "Before all these things, they will lay their hands on you and will persecute you" (Luke 21:12). In this account, the persecution *precedes* the wars, famines, and pestilences. All of this underscores the stylized nature and structure of the apocalyptic genre. The Lord goes on to describe "signs in the sun and moon and stars" (Luke 21:25) as a prelude to the Second Coming.

The point is this: It is a mistake to assume a strict one-to-one correspondence between the seals and other events of the Apocalypse and actual historical events. One may not say, "This or that historical event is the precise fulfillment of this or that seal or judgment in the Book of Revelation." No such correspondence is intended or possible. What is intended by the first seal of war is not this or that war, but *all* wars occurring throughout this age, as they occur with increasing frequency. The third seal of famine is not any particular famine, but *all* famines as signs and heralds of the End.

It may be said, however, that the seals reveal an *approximate* chronological timetable insofar as concerns the fifth to the seventh seals. For the fifth seal is the sign of martyrdom, which is expected to increase with the rise of the final Antichrist. Similarly, the sixth seal consists of supernatural signs from heaven, which are also expected to multiply at the time of the End, so that when there are "signs in the sun and moon and stars" and "the powers of the heavens are shaken" (Luke 21:25–26), it is a sign that "redemption is drawing near" (Luke 21:28).

Thus there is a rough sense of chronological advance in the arrangement of the seals, but this arrangement still partakes of the imprecision of the apocalyptic genre. (The martyrdom of the Church under the final Antichrist, for example, may still be occurring when the signs in the heaven occur.)

Further, we observe how the judgments of God increase in severity and number as the End approaches. This is expressed by the relationship of the seals (ch. 6) with the trumpets (ch. 8) and the bowls (ch. 16). Specifically, the seventh seal (8:1) consists of seven trumpets (8:2), and the seventh trumpet (11:15) consists of seven bowls (15:7). The seventh seal therefore *contains within itself all the other trumpets and the bowls.* The interrelationships of these three kinds of judgments (the seals, the trumpets, and the bowls) show that the time when the seventh seal is opened, toward the end of the age, is a time when God pours out His wrath in ever-escalating severity.

Finally, interspersed between these trumpets and bowls are several distinct visions of the Church under persecution: the Church is sealed and prepared for the struggle (7:1–17); the angel gives the

III. The Things Which Will Take Place   Revelation 6:1–8

little book to the Church, telling her to prophesy to the nations (10:1–11); the temple is measured, though the outer court is given over to the nations (11:1–2); two witnesses prophesy in sackcloth to the nations and are martyred (11:3–13); the woman clothed with the sun is attacked by the dragon (12:1–17); the beast from the abyss wars against the saints (13:1–18); the Lamb stands on the heavenly Zion with the martyred Church (14:1–20); and the martyrs sing the new song before God (15:1–4). With great artistry and deliberate purpose, it is thereby shown how the persecution of the Church occurs against the background of God's judgment on the world, revealing that the world suffers these disasters *because* it dares to persecute the Church. God's judgments on the earth are not random, arbitrary, or causeless—they occur as God's response to the Church's suffering and come as the Church's vindication.

❧ ❧ ❧ ❧ ❧

6 1 Then I saw when the Lamb opened one of the seven seals, and I heard one of the four living *things* saying as with a voice of thunder, "Come!"
2 I looked, and behold, a white horse! and he who sat on it had a bow; and a crown was given to him, and he went out conquering and that he might conquer.
3 When He opened the second seal, I heard the second living *thing* saying, "Come!"
4 And another horse went out, a red one; and to him who sat on it, it was given to take peace from the earth, and that men would slaughter one another; and a great sword was given to him.
5 When He opened the third seal, I heard the third living *thing* saying, "Come!" I looked, and behold! a black horse; and he who sat on it had *a pair of* scales in his hand.
6 And I heard as *it were* a voice in the middle of

> the four living *things* saying, "A quart of wheat *for* a denarius, and three quarts of barley *for* a denarius; and do not hurt the oil and the wine."
>
> 7 When the Lamb opened the fourth seal, I heard the voice of the fourth living *thing* saying, "Come!"
>
> 8 I looked, and behold! a pale horse; and he who sat upon it *had* the name "Death"; and Hades was following with him. Authority was given to them over a fourth of the earth, to kill with sword and with famine and with death and by the beasts of the earth.

As the prelude to opening the scroll and putting into effect God's plan for the transformation of the world, the Lamb begins to open the seven seals. When He **opened one of the seven seals**, John **heard one of the four living *things* saying as with a voice of thunder, "Come!"** It is significant that **one of the four living *things*** bids the judgment **come**. The four living creatures are images of animate creation—the same animate creation that suffers so much, groaning under the rule of sinful mankind. The thunderous cry of each of the living creatures in turn (6:1, 3, 5, 7) expresses the earth's desire for liberation from human tyranny. It is as if the earth itself invites God's judgment on our rebellious race, that all may sooner enjoy the glorious freedom of the children of God (Rom. 8:21).

The opening of the first four seals results in the loosing of four judgments upon the earth, imaged by four horsemen (the so-called "Four Horsemen of the Apocalypse"). The image of variously colored horses is drawn from Zechariah 1:8–11 and 6:1–8. There they are images of God's knowledge of all the nations: just as the Persian king then used swift horses as messengers to learn the state of his empire, so God is portrayed as using angelic horsemen to report to Him regarding the state of His world. The horses there were of different colors because they were sent to different nations. Here the horsemen are images of four different judgments sent out swiftly into all the earth.

III. The Things Which Will Take Place   Revelation 6:1–8

After **one of the seven seals** was opened, John **looked** and saw **a white horse**. (Its sudden dramatic appearance is stressed by the introductory **behold**). The horse was **white** to express the triumph it would enjoy. The rider **who sat on it had a bow**, the image of military power, and he **went out conquering and that he might conquer** ever further afield. That all efforts to avert war were doomed to fail is expressed by **the crown** of sovereignty **given to him** by God. War came on the earth as the judgment of God.

The Lamb **opened the second seal**, and **the second living *thing*** invited judgment, **saying "Come!" And another horse went out.** This horse was **a red one**, the color of bloodshed. The rider of this horse **was given** by God **to take peace from the earth, and that men would slaughter one another**. That is, this horseman symbolized tumults and disturbances, civil unrest and riots. The chaos and destruction were to be great, for **a great sword was given to him**. The first horseman was an image of one nation conquering another; this horseman is an image of the internal disintegration of nations.

Christ **opened the third seal**, and once again one of the living creatures invited the judgment of God. John **looked, and behold!** there appeared suddenly **a black horse**, the color of death, with its rider holding *a pair of* **scales in his hand**. Such scales were used then to weigh out money and the goods purchased with it. Its rider carries them because it brings great famine. The scales will be needed to dole out food by measure because of its scarcity (compare Lev. 26:26; Ezek. 4:16). **A denarius**, a day's wage for the working man, would then buy only **a quart of wheat** or **three quarts of barley** (a poorer grain)—scant supplies indeed. This represents ten to twelve times the usual price for these basic supplies. But the famine was limited, for **the oil and wine** would not be **hurt**, but would continue to be available. The roots of olive trees and grapevines go deep and would not be as easily affected by a drought that might cause a famine of grain. The **voice**, giving the limitation on the suffering, came from **the middle of the four living *things*** and was the voice of Christ Himself (see 5:6). Even in judgment, the Lord remembers mercy.

The Lamb **opened the fourth seal**, and John **heard the voice of the fourth living *thing* saying, "Come!"** And he **looked, and**

behold!—he suddenly saw **a pale horse,** the color of a corpse. This was fitting, for **he who sat upon it *had* the name "Death," and Hades,** the land of the dead, **was following with him**. Here was the culmination of all the previous judgments, for death is the result of wars, tumults, and famine. **Authority was given** to these two **over a fourth of the earth, to kill with sword and with famine and with death** (that is, with pestilence; compare 2:23) **and by the beasts of the earth,** which prowl among men in the aftermath of war. The depiction of the portion suffering judgment as **a fourth of the earth** is not meant to be an exact geographic or numerical description. It is aimed not at the head, but at the nerves, and signifies a large portion.

We note that in all the above judgments, God remains sovereign, and these things occur only by His permission. The disasters that strike the earth are all under God's control—they only come when the Lamb opens the seals. Thus, the authority these apocalyptic horsemen have is **given** to them by God: a crown was given to the first one; a sword and the ability to take peace from the earth were given to the second; and authority over a fourth of the earth was given to the fourth. The horsemen are not portrayed as independent agents, as being out of control, but as doing only what is given to them by God.

༄ ༄ ༄ ༄ ༄

9 And when He opened the fifth seal, I saw under the altar the souls of those who had been slaughtered because of the Word of God, and because of the witness which they had *kept*;

10 and they cried out with a great voice, saying, "How long, O Master, holy and true, before You will judge and avenge our blood on those who dwell upon the earth?"

11 And there was given to each of them a white robe; and it was told to them that they should rest for yet a little time, until the *number* of their fellow-slaves and their brothers should be

> fulfilled, who were about to be killed, as they themselves also had been.

The fifth seal represents martyrdom. Even as sacrificial blood falls and collects **under the altar**, so **the souls of those who had been slaughtered** for the sake of Christ are found beneath the heavenly altar, since they have made themselves a sacrifice to God. These are the martyrs of the Church who died up until that time, such as Antipas (2:13) and those who died under Nero's persecution. They died because they held to **the Word of God**, the Gospel, and **because of the witness** to it **which they had kept**. These **cried out** for vengeance **with a great voice**, echoing the cry of the Psalmist, **"How long, O Master?"** (Ps. 13:1; 79:5). The heavenly **Master** (Gr. *despotes*, used for the owner of slaves) was **holy and true**, and so could be expected to **judge and avenge** their **blood on those who dwell upon the earth**, their murderers and persecutors. (The phrase *those who dwell upon the earth* is used in the Apocalypse as a kind of technical term for the world in its hostility to God; compare 3:10; 8:13; 11:10; 13:8, 14; 17:8. The thought is of those whose sphere is confined to the earth—unlike the saints, whose dwelling-place is in heaven; 13:6.)

In response to the martyrs' cry, **there was given to each of them a white robe**, the image of festal joy (compare 3:5; 4:4). The joy of heaven and the festal worship of their Lord was the compensation and reward for their sacrifice. God would yet avenge their deaths, but meanwhile they were told that they **should rest for yet a little time, until the *number* of their fellow-slaves and brothers should be fulfilled**. That is, more martyrdoms would yet follow, and God would not judge their blood until the time was ripe.

It was the same in the time of Abraham. Abraham was told that God would not yet judge and dispossess the inhabitants of Canaan, for their iniquity was not yet complete (Gen. 15:16). Only when their sins were full would they be judged. Similarly, the justice of God waits until the earth is fully ripe for judgment. Only then will the divine vengeance fall.

The response is an encouragement to the suffering Church. It may seem that God's justice will never come and their blood never be avenged. But the Judge of all the earth will do justly (Gen. 18:25), and the judgment, though long delayed, will come at last.

> ॐ ॐ ॐ ॐ ॐ
> 12 And when He opened the sixth seal, I looked, and behold! a great earthquake happened; and the sun became black as sackcloth of hair, and the whole moon became as blood;
> 13 and the stars of heaven fell to the earth, as a fig tree casts its unripe figs when shaken by a great wind.
> 14 The heaven was separated like a scroll that is rolled up, and every mountain and island were moved from their places.
> 15 And the kings of the earth and the great *men* and the generals and the rich and the strong and every slave and free *man* hid themselves in the caves and in the rocks of the mountains;
> 16 and they say to the mountains and to the rocks, "Fall on us and hide us from the Face of Him who sits upon the throne, and from the wrath of the Lamb;
> 17 "for the great day of their wrath has come, and who is able to stand?"

The sixth seal represents the signs in the heavens that herald the End. As Christ said in His Olivet Discourse, "There will be signs in the sun and moon and stars" (Luke 21:25). St. Matthew's version of the same gives the more original Jewish rendering: "The sun will be darkened and the moon will not give its light and the stars will fall from heaven" (Matt. 24:29).

In St. John's apocalyptic vision, he **looked, and behold!**—suddenly **a great earthquake happened**. This earthquake signaled the overturning of order in the heavens. **The sun became black as sackcloth of hair** (that is, jet black, so that the earth was darkened),

III. The Things Which Will Take Place   Revelation 6:12–17

and the whole moon became as blood (shining with a red color, in unnatural defiance of the created order), **and the stars of heaven fell to the earth, as a fig tree casts its unripe figs when shaken by a great wind** (that is, all the visible stars seem to fall away, for unripe figs are easily blown off the fig tree by the wind). **The heaven was separated like a scroll that is rolled up, and every mountain and island were moved from their places.**

The word translated here *separated* is the Greek *apochorizo*. It is used in Acts 15:39 for the separation of Paul and Barnabas after a quarrel. The thought is of an unrolled papyrus scroll separating and splitting apart in the middle, so that each of the two ends of the scroll rolls up and the scroll itself vanishes from sight. In the same way the heaven itself will vanish, and **every mountain and island** will be **moved from their places** in the end-time series of cataclysms.

The thought in all these upheavals is that of the natural order being dislodged; of even the very fabric of the universe—which before was unchanging and secure—going to pieces. No wonder "men will faint from fear and from the expectation of what was coming upon the earth" (Luke 21:26).

In John's vision, these signs are recognized by all as signs of the End. Even the confident and secure, **the kings of the earth and the great *men* and the generals and the rich and the strong**, are struck with panic. So overwhelming are these omens that fear grips the trembling hearts of all—**every slave** and every **free *man***—everyone flees from **the Face** and Presence **of Him who sits upon the throne, and from the wrath of the Lamb**. They hide themselves in the caves and in the rocks of the mountains, as men do during an invasion, "going into the caves of the rocks and the clefts of the cliffs before the terror of the Lord" (see Is. 2:21). So great is their terror of the coming judgment that they even cry out **to the mountains and to the rocks, "Fall on us and hide us!"** (compare Hos. 10:8). Better the mountains should fall on them than that the wrath of God should overtake them! **The great day** of divine **wrath has come—who is able to stand** against it? The God of the Christians is striking back in judgment—how can any escape?

This picture, with its image of the powerful persecutors cowering before the God of the Christians, is meant to comfort the martyric Church. In this age, the persecutors seem all but invincible. But a day will come when the Church will be vindicated, and the towering pride of the godless will be humbled in the dust. The proud look of man will be abased, and the Lord alone will be exalted in that day (Is. 2:11).

> ### ✺ EXCURSUS
> #### On the Wrath of the Lamb
>
> The concept of divine wrath—and of the martyrs' prayer to God to pour out that wrath to avenge their deaths—has been thought problematic by some. When Christ died, He prayed that the Father would forgive those who were killing Him (Luke 23:34), and St. Stephen the protomartyr did much the same when he died (Acts 7:60). Was it not somehow sub-Christian for the martyrs of the Apocalypse, the souls underneath the heavenly altar, to pray, "How long, O Master, before You will judge and avenge our blood?" Certainly that prayer finds abundant answer in the chapters that follow, as Christ does indeed pour out His wrath upon the world (see, for example, 16:6, and all that chapter). Is this consistent with the rest of the New Testament, which portrays God as a God of love?
>
> It must be understood that the Book of Revelation is not a comprehensive treatise on the nature of God, but rather a pastoral letter to a suffering Church. It is addressed to humble rank-and-file Christians—those who had been marginalized by society, and who had no power or recourse—to Christians who were about to experience brutal persecution and death, and who had no power to protest it. It was addressed to simple men who would soon see their wives and young children slaughtered before their very eyes, and who would endure the same fate themselves.
>
> Men can endure such things only if they know the sufferings they will unjustly undergo will not be forgotten by

God. The words of the Psalmist give voice to the powerless and the oppressed of every generation: "Why should the nations say, 'Where is their God?' Let the vengeance for the outpoured blood of Your servants be known among the nations before our eyes!" (Ps. 79:10). When the rich and powerful oppress the helpless, it seems that God has abandoned the poor, that injustice will rule unchallenged forever, that the righteous are fools to side with Truth. Why should the righteous man persevere in his righteousness and his integrity? What is his reward? Should he not rather sell out and join the godless? Why be an oppressed victim when one can be a victorious oppressor?

The Apocalypse is the response to such questions. It affirms that God has not abandoned His poor and that injustice will not rule unchallenged forever. When the godless derisively demand, "Where is their God?" the Apocalypse answers, "Our God is in heaven; He does whatever He pleases" (Ps. 115:2–3). It may seem that the godless have slaughtered the Christians with impunity, tortured innocent men, women, and children to death and gotten away with it. But it is not so. Those helpless victims have a Champion—the Lamb of God, Himself slaughtered under Pontius Pilate, the One who now reigns from the Throne of God. He has not forgotten their cries and their pain. He will avenge their blood and demand an account from their oppressors.

The Book of Revelation therefore is to be read as God's assurance to those who are about to suffer horribly that justice will indeed be done. The martyrs can approach their trial confident that their tears will not fall to the ground unnoticed. The prayer of the souls underneath the altar in 6:10 is not given so much as a liturgical paradigm to be used by those who suffer (many of the martyrs did indeed pray for their persecutors) as it is God's assurance to those who suffer that their suffering will be avenged. The prayer is the expression, in the context of the apocalyptic genre in which it is found, of the human need for divine justice. Whether or not this need is liturgically expressed by the martyric Church, like all true needs, it will be met by God.

§III.4. Interlude: The Church Sealed and Prepared for the Conflict

7 1 After this I saw four angels standing at the four corners of the earth, holding onto the four winds of the earth, that no wind might blow on the earth or on the sea or on any tree.
2 And I saw another angel coming up from the rising of the sun, having the seal of the living God; and he cried out with a great voice to the four angels to whom it was given to hurt the earth and the sea,
3 saying, "Do not hurt the earth or the sea or the trees until we have sealed the slaves of our God upon their foreheads."

The opening of the seventh seal represents the final outpouring of divine wrath upon the world, with all the trials that will mean for the Church. As long ago as St. Paul's Second Epistle to the Thessalonians, the Church had been taught to expect a final persecution before the End (see 2 Thess. 2:3–8). The Church learned from the *Didache* (written about AD 100) to expect the same thing. There it was said that "in the last days, they shall hate one another and persecute and betray, and the world-deceiver shall appear as a Son of God and the earth shall be delivered into his hands. Then all mankind shall come into the fire of testing" (ch. 16). Before this final fire of testing comes upon the world, therefore, God in His mercy prepares His Church.

III. The Things Which Will Take Place   Revelation 7:1–3

This final conflict is compared to a mighty blast from **the four winds of the earth**. By the command of God, these hurricane forces are delayed until the Church has been protected. Thus John sees **four angels standing** like sentries **at the four corners of the earth, holding onto** those **four winds, that no wind might blow** anywhere **on the earth** until the Church is ready.

And as he looked he **saw another angel coming up from the rising of the sun**, from the east. This is the direction the Church faces in prayer, indicating that this angel comes bringing help from God, in answer to their prayers.

This angel **had the seal of the living God**, with which he was to **seal the slaves of God upon their foreheads**, marking them for protection, giving them immunity from the coming storm of divine wrath.

What is this **seal**? The image is drawn from Ezekiel 9. In this passage, angels were to slay all in Jerusalem that rebelled idolatrously against Yahweh. But before they began their dreadful task, one angel went through the city and, at the divine command, put "a mark" (in Hebrew a *tau*) on all who were faithful (Ezek. 9:4). To be thus marked on the forehead is to enjoy the protection of God and an immunity from coming judgment.

The letter *tau* in Hebrew is shaped like a cross. The destroying angels were not to touch anyone on whom was the *tau* or mark. For the Christians, there could hardly have been a clearer prophecy of their baptism and chrismation. In the Orthodox baptismal ritual of that time, one was immersed thrice in water and then marked with a cross, in holy oil, on the forehead. The Ezekiel passage speaks to them of their baptismal rite and reveals its significance: as faithful regenerated believers, they are forgiven their sins and protected from the coming wrath of God. This mark was called "the seal" (Gr. *sphragis*) and the rite itself, the "Sealing."

In this prophecy, the sealing administered by the angel echoes their own baptismal rite and reveals its meaning, for it asserts that God has claimed them as His own and will protect them in the coming conflict. The angel from the east comes to **seal the slaves of God**, marking them as God's own possession. Thus, in the coming storm, they will be identifiable as God's own servants and will be spared His wrath.

> 4 And I heard the number of those who were sealed, one hundred and forty-four thousand sealed from every tribe of the sons of Israel:
> 5 From the tribe of Judah, twelve thousand were sealed, from the tribe of Reuben twelve thousand, from the tribe of Gad twelve thousand,
> 6 from the tribe of Asher twelve thousand, from the tribe of Naphtali twelve thousand, from the tribe of Manasseh twelve thousand,
> 7 from the tribe of Simeon twelve thousand, from the tribe of Levi twelve thousand, from the tribe of Issachar twelve thousand,
> 8 from the tribe of Zebulun twelve thousand, from the tribe of Joseph twelve thousand, from the tribe of Benjamin, twelve thousand were sealed.

John then **heard the number of those who were sealed**, and it was **one hundred and forty-four thousand from every tribe of the sons of Israel**, twelve thousand from each tribe. The concept of numbering a people or of taking a census originally had a military feel to it. Israel of old was thus numbered before entering into battle (see Num. 1:2; 1 Sam. 14:15). Kings would count their soldiers so they could have some notion of whether victory was assured or impossible. A king had to decide "whether he was strong enough with ten thousand to meet the one coming against him with twenty thousand" (Luke 14:31). These ancient census numbers therefore were not theoretical, but had practical military significance.

In numbering the servants of God who were sealed, the angels present the Church as the army of God mustered for battle, as **the sons of Israel** ready to follow the Lord, the heavenly Commander.

For the Church is the true Israel and the inheritor of all God promised in the Law and the Prophets.

As is usual in apocalyptic literature, the numbers here have symbolic significance. One **thousand** is the number of vast plurality. To say that God owns "the cattle on a thousand hills" (Ps. 50:10) is to say that He owns the cattle on *all* the hills. Further, **twelve** is the number that denotes completeness—such as in the twelve tribes of Israel, the twelve apostles. To say that **twelve thousand were sealed** from each of the twelve tribes is therefore to speak of vastness and completion, to say that all the People of God were included in this sealing; not the least one was left out. All were counted and cared for.

Some may ask why the tribe of Dan was omitted from this list of the twelve tribes and the half-tribe of Manasseh (which with the half-tribe of Ephraim made up the tribe of Joseph) put in its place. It is impossible to say with certainty. It may be noted, however, that in apocalyptic literature, the tribe of Dan had a reputation for idolatry and evil. First Kings 12:29 mentions an idolatrous shrine as being located in Dan. Whether for this reason or some other, the apocalyptic *Testament of Dan* describes Satan as the prince of that tribe. If the Apocalypse is heir to this tradition, the omission of the tribe of Dan expresses the truth that the Church, mustered by God and preserved by Him, is devoid of any evil and treason. "Those who are with Him are called and chosen and faithful" (Rev. 17:14).

❧ EXCURSUS
On the Church as Israel

It is significant that the Church on earth is portrayed as the totality of tribal Israel. This is not new: St. Paul referred to the Church as "the commonwealth of Israel" (Eph. 2:12) and as "the Israel of God" (Gal. 6:16). The Church was the true remnant of Israel, inheriting all its Old Testament promises (Rom. 11:5). But here this old truth receives fresh emphasis. The Church is presented consistently in Jewish terms: It is the numbered muster "from every tribe of the sons of Israel" (7:4), and it will be gathered with the Lamb on Mount Zion (14:1); it is the Sanctuary of God, the true Temple and dwelling-place of the God of Israel (11:1); its call is to inherit the new Jerusalem (21:2).

This relentless identification of the Church with Israel has as its background the struggle of the Church with Judaism. As mentioned above (see comments on 2:9), the Jews of Asia Minor strenuously opposed the Christians and delighted to help the Romans in their persecution of the Church. They arrogantly insisted they were the heirs to all God's promises for salvation found in the Law and the Prophets, and the Christians would suffer from God the punishment due to apostates and heretics.

It is against this controversy that the Apocalypse was written. It insists that the Jews of Asia Minor who persecuted the Christians were not true Jews at all, and that their gatherings were not *sunagogai* (or assemblies) of God, but rather synagogues of Satan. The Christian assemblies were the true synagogues or assemblies of God; the Christians were truly God's Chosen People. The Jews had forfeited those blessings and that status through their rejection of Jesus as Messiah.

It is important to note in passing that careful exegesis does not apply these terrible condemnations of the Jews of Asia Minor in the first century to all Jews living today. Such an application is not warranted. For anyone to deserve such condemnation, he must be fierce and unrelenting in his persecution of Christ's Church. Such denunciations as the Jews of Philadelphia being "a synagogue of Satan" (3:9) must not be ripped from their immediate context and made the justification for anti-Semitism, which is always demonic in all its forms.

One need only look at any iconostasis in any church to see our debt to Israel according to the flesh: Christ, His most-pure Mother, His Forerunner, and His Apostles are all there, and are all Jewish. (One may even suggest that the

III. The Things Which Will Take Place   Revelation 7:9–12

archangels Michael and Gabriel are spiritually Jewish, for they have Jewish names and were sent to guard the Jewish people.) The New Testament is a Jewish document, and its quarrel with "the Jews" is an "in-house" quarrel. In declaring the Church to be the true Israel, we are not indulging in anti-Semitism. Rather, this declaration not only reveals the Church's true Jewish nature and foundation, but also reveals the final destiny of the Jewish people, who will one day find their true identity in the Christ of God (see Rom. 11:25f).

ॐ ॐ ॐ ॐ ॐ

9 After these things I looked, and behold! a great crowd which no one was able to number, from every nation and all tribes and peoples and tongues, standing before the throne and before the Lamb, clothed in white robes, and palm branches *were* in their hands.
10 And they cry out with a great voice, saying, "Salvation to our God who sits upon the throne, and to the Lamb!"
11 And all the angels stood around the throne and around the elders and the four living *things*; and they fell on their faces before the throne and worshipped God,
12 saying, "Amen! The blessing and glory and wisdom and thanksgiving and honor and power and strength to our God to ages of ages! Amen!"

The scene then switches from earth to heaven (with another sudden **behold!**), and John looks upon **a great crowd which no one was able to number, from every nation and all tribes and peoples and tongues**. The contrast between the two multitudes is a stark one. The first multitude had been numbered and was drawn entirely from the tribes of Israel (v. 4). This second multitude **no**

one was able to number, and it was drawn from **all** the **tribes** of the earth.

Granted that the numbers describing the first multitude are symbolic, the image is still of a crowd that could be counted. This second multitude is specifically described as beyond counting. And granted that the Israelite identity of the first crowd is also symbolic (for the Church is drawn from many ethnic groups), its Jewish identity is still an integral part of the image, whereas the multi-ethnic nature of the second crowd is brought to the fore. Through the juxtaposition of these two images, the staggering diversity and size of this second multitude is stressed.

Those of this second crowd are all **standing before the throne and before the Lamb, clothed in white robes**, having **palm branches in their hands**. They cry out, **"Salvation to our God who sits upon the throne, and to the Lamb!"** They stand erect and triumphant, as victors before their King, arrayed in festal **white robes** (see 3:4–5 and comments), carrying **palm branches**, the emblems of victory (see 1 Macc. 13:51 for the use of palms as expressive of victory). In their joy, they describe their victory (their **salvation**) as entirely the work of **God who sits upon the throne** and **the Lamb**. (Compare Ps. 98:1–2 for the description of victory as salvation.) This vision also stresses the martyrs' victory over the enemy (see 15:2, which speaks of the martyrs as "conquering the beast"). Those who stand before God are victors over their foes indeed, but they know that all their victory comes from God, who strengthened them.

In response to their victory shout, **all the angels stood around the throne and around the elders and the four living *things***, surrounding God and His court, **and fell on their faces before the throne and worshipped God**. They cried over and over, **"Amen!"** to the shout of the white-robed multitude (the cry of **Amen!** comes twice in v. 12), acknowledging that the victory did indeed come from God. And they continued to pour out an abundance of praise, ascribing **the blessing and glory and wisdom and thanksgiving and honor and power and strength** to Him (piling up acclaim after acclaim, as did the angelic crowd of 5:12), extolling God as the God of the martyrs.

III. The Things Which Will Take Place   Revelation 7:13–14

> ☙ ☙ ☙ ☙ ☙
> 13 And one of the elders answered, saying to me, "These who are clothed in the white robes, who are they, and from where have they come?"
> 14 I said to him, "My lord, you *yourself* know." And he said to me, "These are the ones coming from the great tribulation, and they have washed their robes and whitened them in the Blood of the Lamb.

John is then approached by **one of the elders**, who questions him (in the classic rhetorical fashion of such visions; compare Zech. 4:5) and asks him, **"These who are clothed in the white robes, who are they, and from where have they come?"** John of course replies with a confession of ignorance, saying, **"My lord, you *yourself* know."** (The *you* is emphatic, meaning, "You are the one who knows, not I.") His angelic interpreter answers, **"These are the ones coming from the great tribulation."** He adds that **they have washed their robes and whitened them in the Blood of the Lamb.**

The image of washing robes in blood is not foreign to the Old Testament: In Isaiah 63:1–6, God is described as washing His robes in blood, as a warrior would stain his clothes in the blood of his foes on the field of battle. But such grim washing stains the clothes *red*; it does not make them white. Here, in a paradoxical reversal of the usual image, the **robes** of the saints are **whitened** by being **washed** in **the Blood of the Lamb**. White robes in the Apocalypse are always an image of festal worthiness to approach and worship God. Here the robes are made white through the Blood of Christ. It was through *His* Blood (received every Sunday in the Eucharist) that all their sin was cleansed (1 John 1:7); it was through *His* Blood that Satan was conquered (Rev. 12:11). It is through the Blood of Christ, the Lamb of God, that this triumphant multitude stands before God exulting.

What is the **great tribulation** of which the elder speaks? The term is used with the definite article—*the* **great tribulation**

(Gr. *tes thlipseos tes megales*). This would seem to indicate that this affliction from which the heavenly multitude emerged was well known.

The term is first used in the New Testament by Christ, in Matthew's version of the Olivet Discourse, to describe the catastrophic destruction of Jerusalem in AD 70 and its age-long aftermath. This Olivet prophecy provides much of the background to the Apocalypse, both conceptually and verbally. (Compare Matt. 24:6–9 with Rev. 6:1–11; Matt. 24:24 with Rev. 16:13–14; Matt. 24:29 with Rev. 6:12–13.)

In Matthew 24:21, Christ says that then (that is, after the abomination of desolation is seen standing in the holy place) "there will be great tribulation [Gr. *thlipsis megale*], such as has not happened since the beginning of the world until now, nor ever will." The description is taken from Daniel 12:1. This Old Testament prophecy describes the final time of crisis and judgment in Israel as "a time of tribulation [*thlipeos* in the Greek translation], such tribulation as has not been from the time that there was a nation on the earth until that time." Obviously the Matthean reference to "great tribulation" is based on the prophecy in Daniel.

This time of great tribulation seems to last throughout the age, for in Matthew 24:29 the Second Coming is said to occur "immediately after the tribulation of those days." The parallel version of this verse in Luke 21:24 seems to confirm this, for it describes what Matthew refers to as "great tribulation" as a time of "great distress upon the land . . . [the people] will fall by the edge of the sword and be led captive into all nations; and Jerusalem will be trampled underfoot by the Gentiles until the times of the Gentiles be fulfilled"—that is, until the end of the age. Even the original prophecy of Daniel 12 states that the "time of tribulation" will be followed by the resurrection of the dead, when "many of those who sleep in the dust will awake" (Dan. 12:2).

It would seem then that in Matthew 24 the "great tribulation" is the age-long time of suffering for Israel that began with the destruction of the Temple in AD 70. This time of distress becomes paradigmatic in the Apocalypse for the age-long suffering *of the Christians* at the hands of *their* pagan foes. Just as many concepts are transposed from a Palestinian Jewish key in the Olivet Discourse to a Gentile Christian key in the Apocalypse, so it is with the concept of Israel's "great tribulation": it becomes "*the* great tribulation" (note the definite article)—the time of unparalleled suffering, lasting throughout the age and ending only when the times of the Gentiles are fulfilled, when the kingdom of the world becomes the Kingdom of our Lord and of His Christ (Rev. 11:15).

(We note in passing how appropriate was the term "great tribulation"—without the definite article—to describe in 2:22 God's judgment on the false prophetess of Thyatira and her followers. For faithless Israel had to undergo "great tribulation"—Matt. 24:21, without the definite article—as God's unprecedented judgment for sin, and these faithless ones of Thyatira had to undergo a similar scourge. The term is retained, though transposed into a somewhat different key.)

This understanding of "the great tribulation" (7:14) as the suffering of the Church throughout the age explains too the difference in the two crowds mentioned in this chapter. In 7:1–8, John receives a vision of the Church on earth, sealed and protected by God in preparation for their entering the final time of conflict. It is the Church of the final days. In 7:9–17, however, John sees a vaster multitude. This crowd comprises, not just the Church of the final days, but the Church gathered throughout all the centuries, coming from "the great tribulation," the age-long struggle with the world. Unlike the former crowd, this multitude is vast beyond counting, stretching into the horizons of heaven. It is the Church glorified at last, fresh from its victorious struggle, an overwhelming testimony to the power of God.

---

15 "Therefore, they are before the throne of God; and worship Him day and night in His sanctuary; and He who sits upon the throne will *spread* His tent over them.
16 "They will not hunger anymore, nor thirst

> anymore; nor will the sun fall on them, nor any heat;
> 17 "for the Lamb in the middle of the throne will shepherd them, and will guide them to living fountains of waters; and God will wipe every tear from their eyes."

The elder continues to describe the reward of the victorious host. Because of their perseverance and faith, they are now **before the throne of God**, and they **worship Him day and night in His** heavenly **sanctuary** with a never-ending joy. **He who sits upon the throne**, the Most High God Himself, **will *spread* His Tent** (Gr. *skenoo*) **over them**.

This concept of finding rest in God's tabernacle, or tent (Gr. *skene*), has its roots in the Old Testament. In Isaiah 4:5–6, God promised that He would give His glorious Presence "for a canopy" to Zion, to "be a shelter to give shade from the heat by day." Even as He dwelt in glory among His people in His tabernacle (Ex. 40:34), so here He dwells among those who stand **before** His **throne**. His promises to provide for them and protect them, given long ago through Isaiah and the prophets, are fulfilled now. Far from their former suffering in the great tribulation, now His people **will not hunger anymore, nor thirst anymore; nor will the sun fall on them, nor any heat**. The privations of earthly life are no longer found. The Lamb, He who sits with God in the middle of the throne, **will shepherd them**; He will make them lie down in green pastures and lead them beside quiet waters (Ps. 23:2); He will **guide them to living fountains of waters** to slake their thirst. All the suffering of this parched life will be remembered no longer. Every tear they wept—tears shed because of persecution, sickness, bereavement, death—all are gone forever. **God** Himself **will wipe every tear from their eyes**.

Here is a vision to inspire the faithful of all ages and to steel them to endure any trial. This is the crowd of victors that awaits their arrival in heaven; these are the joys that are stored up for them in the Kingdom. David said a single day in God's courts was better than a thousand elsewhere (Ps. 84:10). How much greater

III. The Things Which Will Take Place — Revelation 8:1–2

will be the joy of standing in those courts forever, to ages of ages?

§III.5. The Opening of the Seventh Seal: Final Wrath Begins—The Seven Trumpets

The Seven Trumpets and the Language of the Apocalyptic Genre
At this point, it becomes even more crucial to be able to "read" or decode the peculiar language of the apocalyptic genre. The imagery of the coming trumpet judgments is drawn mainly from the story of the plagues of Egypt in Exodus 7—11. That was *the* archetypal outpouring of God's wrath upon men. In those plagues, waters become blood, hail and fire ravage the earth, thick darkness falls over the land, a plague of locusts swarms everywhere. These historic judgments form the paradigm for the trumpet judgments. God once again will war upon the earth as He did in ancient times.

This apocalyptic war is pictured in these classic terms. But, as with the seven seals, there is no one-to-one correspondence of this trumpet judgment with that historical disaster. The apocalyptic genre is aimed at the nerves, not the head. One is meant to read and tremble and repent—not to read and decide which historical event fulfills which trumpet. How literal will be the fulfillment is impossible to say, but the parallels with the judgments on Egypt should warn us not to expect too literal a fulfillment.

No doubt the disasters that will strike the earth (such as will cause men to "faint with fear and foreboding of what is coming on the world," Luke 21:26) are the result of His terrible and inscrutable judgment. God will judge the world as He once judged Egypt. But a chronologically detailed, step-by-step following of God's judgments is not provided.

---

8 1 And when He opened the seventh seal, silence occurred in heaven for about half an hour.
2 And I saw the seven angels who stood before God, and seven trumpets were given to them.

After such overwhelming events as accompanied the opening of the sixth seal (6:12–17), it might be expected that **when He opened the seventh seal** there would be an even greater upheaval. Instead, an unexpected and eerie **silence occurred in heaven for about half an hour**. This was the silence of dread anticipation, so terrifying was the seventh seal. (In this silence, which precedes the heavenly offering of incense in 8:3f, there is an echo of the silence that obtained in the earthly Temple on the Day of Atonement, when the incense was burned; compare Lev. 16:13.)

The judgment of the seventh seal was so mighty as to need seven more judgments to fully carry it out. This final seal therefore consisted of seven trumpets. And this final work of judgment was so important that it was entrusted to no one less exalted than **the seven angels who stood before God**, His inner court (1:4; 4:5). As the angels waited upon God, **seven trumpets were given to them**.

Why are these final judgments compared to trumpets? Trumpets warn of approaching battle. In the apocalypse of 2 Esdras 6:23, a trumpet is said to "suddenly terrify" all the earth. These judgments therefore are not merely punitive. They come to warn. They are aimed at the heart of man, that he may repent and be saved.

> ॐ ॐ ॐ ॐ ॐ
>
> 3   And another angel came and stood at the altar, having a golden censer; and much incense was given to him, that he might give *it* with the prayers of all the saints on the golden altar before the throne.
>
> 4   And the smoke of the incense, with the prayers of the saints, went up before God from the hand of the angel.
>
> 5   And the angel took the censer and filled it with fire from the altar, and cast it to the earth; and there occurred *peals of* thunder and sounds and *flashes of* lightning and an earthquake.

III. The Things Which Will Take Place   Revelation 8:3–5

Before the trumpets are blown, more prayer is offered in heaven. **Another angel came and stood at the** heavenly **altar, having a golden censer**. This reflected sacrificial practice in the old Jewish Temple—the priest standing at the altar would put incense upon the coals on the incense-altar to offer it as a pleasing odor to God (Ex. 30; Luke 1:9), symbolic of the acceptability of the sacrifices (Ps. 141:2). Here the angel, acting as priest, **stands at the altar, having a golden censer** or shovel pan, and **much incense was given to him, that he might give it with the prayers of all the saints on the golden altar before the throne**. That is, the angel offers **the prayers of all the saints** on earth, the prayers for vengeance, along with the **incense** of acceptability. Through the prayers of the angels, the Church's prayers on earth come **before the throne** of God. In 6:10 the martyrs cried out for vindication—now their prayers were about to be answered.

This answer is expressed briefly in terms of upheaval on earth. **The angel took the censer and filled it with fire from the altar, and cast it to the earth**. That is, the heavenly activity of intercession resulted in chaos below—in things such as *peals of* **thunder and** rumbling **sounds and** *flashes of* **lightning and an earthquake** (compare Ezek. 10:2). These last are mentioned as manifestations of God's power (they were last seen as coming from the throne of God; 4:5). They show that the seven trumpets that follow come as a result of God acting on behalf of His persecuted saints on earth through the prayers of those in heaven.

The concept of the heavenly intercession of the angels and saints is not foreign to Old Testament Judaism. The martyred high-priest Onias was seen in a vision praying for Israel during a time of crisis, as was the Prophet Jeremiah (2 Macc. 15:12–16). In Enoch 9:3, men on earth are said to "make their suit" to "the holy ones of heaven," saying, "Bring our cause before the Most High." The Archangel Raphael (in Tobit 12:15) says the angels "present the prayers of the saints" to the Holy One. The Apocalypse (and the Christian Faith) builds on this Old Testament foundation, asserting that those on earth are not alone in their struggle. Those in heaven see the plight of the saints on earth and make effective intercession for them.

※ ※ ※ ※ ※

6 And the seven angels who had the seven trumpets prepared themselves to trumpet *them*.

7 And the first *angel* trumpeted, and there occurred hail and fire, mixed with blood, and they were cast into the earth; and a third of the earth was burned up, and a third of the trees were burned up, and all the green grass was burned up.

8 And the second angel trumpeted, and something like a great mountain burning with fire was cast into the sea; and a third of the sea became blood,

9 and a third of the creatures having life in the sea died; and a third of the ships were destroyed.

10 And the third angel trumpeted, and a great star fell from heaven, burning like a torch, and it fell on a third of the rivers and on the fountains of waters.

11 And the name of the star is said *to be* Wormwood; and a third of the waters became wormwood, and many men died from the waters, because they were made bitter.

12 And the fourth angel trumpeted, and a third of the sun was struck and a third of the moon and a third of the stars, that a third of them might be darkened, and the day would not shine for a third of it, and likewise the night.

The seven angels who had the seven trumpets prepared themselves to trumpet *them*, dramatically bringing the trumpets to their lips. Like the silence mentioned in 8:1, this detail is meant to increase the sense of dramatic apprehension.

The first *angel* trumpeted, and there occurred hail and

fire, mixed with blood, and they were cast into the earth. This judgment echoed the seventh plague of Egypt, in which fire (that is, lightning) mixed with hail fell on the land (Ex. 9:24). This angelic judgment, however, came with greater ferocity, for it was **mixed with blood**, and it burned up fully a third of all the green things of the earth on which it fell.

The second angel trumpeted, and something like a great mountain burning with fire was cast into the sea. This second judgment echoed the first plague on Egypt, in which Moses turned the water of the Nile to blood (Ex. 7:17). Here, however, a great volcano explodes and falls upon the sea, and **a third** of the sea is destroyed, both the waters of **the sea** (which **become blood**) and its **creatures** within it and the **ships** that sail upon it. A third of all suffers God's wrath.

The third angel trumpeted, and a great star fell from heaven, burning like a torch, and it fell on a third of the rivers and on the fountains of waters. Here a meteorite falls to the earth and lands on the sources of water, **the rivers and fountains**, poisoning the drinking water. The **name of the star is Wormwood** (or "bitterness"; compare Lam. 3:19), and all the water became **bitter** and poisoned like the meteorite, so that **many men died from** drinking **the waters**. Water, normally life-giving, became deadly.

The fourth angel trumpeted, and a third of the sun was struck and a third of the moon and a third of the stars. All became darkened, echoing the ninth plague of Egypt, when darkness fell upon the land (Ex. 10:21). For **a third** of the day, total darkness prevailed.

We note the artistry of the first four judgments falling progressively against all the world: first on the earth, then on the sea, then on the drinkable waters, then on the powers of the heavens. The judgments become increasingly alarming, dangerous, and supernatural.

We note too the measured limitation of these judgments. This is not a total outpouring of wrath. It is here directed not upon men directly, but only upon the forces of nature. And even here, the destruction is not total, but only **a third** of the world is afflicted in each of these trumpets.

> ॐ ॐ ॐ ॐ ॐ
> 13 And I looked, and I heard a vulture flying in mid-heaven, saying with a great voice, "Woe, woe, woe to those who dwell upon the earth, because of the remaining sounds of the trumpet of the three angels who are about to trumpet!"

Soon, however, these judgments become more intense. As a sign of this increased severity, John **looked and heard a vulture flying in mid-heaven** (where the omen could be seen by all), and **saying with a great voice** (audible to all the world), **"Woe, woe, woe to those who dwell upon the earth!"** Now is the time for men to experience God's wrath. The vision of a circling vulture speaking with a human voice is part of the supernaturally eerie imagery of the apocalyptic genre.

The Greek word here translated *vulture* (Gr. *aetos*) is sometimes translated "eagle" and was used to denote both those birds. The word is used in Matthew 24:28, where it seems to mean "vulture," because a dead body brings a gathering of vultures, not of eagles. Here too the bird flying in mid-heaven is a sign of impending death (compare 9:15), just as the presence of vultures is. (If the word here be translated "eagle," then the image will be that of an eagle swooping down upon its prey.)

The vulture announces three **woes**, which are the final three trumpets. By grouping them together, with the triple repetition **"Woe, woe, woe!"** the messenger not only announces the final three trumpets (one for each "woe"), but also expresses the effect of these judgments on the earth—they will cause men to lament and cry over and again. For the previous trumpets only poured out the divine wrath upon the world—upon the earth, the sea, the waters, and the sky. In the coming woes, the judgments strike the bodies of men directly, bringing pain and death.

III. The Things Which Will Take Place — Revelation 9:1–12

9 1 And the fifth angel trumpeted, and I saw a star from heaven fallen into the earth; and the key of the shaft of the abyss was given to him.

2 And he opened the shaft of the abyss, and smoke went up from the shaft, as the smoke of a great furnace; and the sun and the air were darkened from the smoke of the shaft.

3 And from the smoke came out locusts into the earth, and authority was given them, as the scorpions of the earth have authority.

4 And it was told to them not to hurt the grass of the earth, nor any greenery, nor any tree; only the men, everyone who does not have the seal of God upon their foreheads.

5 And it was given to them that they should not kill them, but that they will be tormented for five months, and their torment *is* as the torment of a scorpion when it strikes a man.

6 And in those days men will seek death and will never find it; they will desire to die, and death will flee from them.

7 The likenesses of the locusts *were* like horses prepared for war; and upon their heads as *it were* crowns like gold, and their faces *were* as the faces of men.

8 And they had hair as the hair of women, and their teeth were as the teeth of lions.

9 And they had breastplates as breastplates of iron; and the sound of their wings *was* as the sound of chariots, of many horses running to war.

10 And they have tails like scorpions, and stings; and in their tails *is* their authority to hurt men for five months.

> 11 They have as king over them the angel of the abyss; his name in Hebrew *is* Abaddon, and in the Greek he has the name Apollyon.
> 12 The first woe is past; behold! two woes are yet coming after these things.

The **fifth angel trumpeted** (unleashing the first woe), and John **saw** in response **a star from heaven fallen into the earth**. This **star** was a spirit, an angel (compare 1:20 for stars representing angels). It would seem that this fallen (or shooting) star was a fallen angel, and in Enoch 21:6, the fallen angels are described as "stars of heaven which have transgressed the commandment of the Lord." It is possible that this angel is just another (unfallen) one of God's messengers who executes His judgments (as in 20:1). But the falling of the star from heaven to earth is portrayed here as a part of the judgment itself, as something evil and disastrous (like the falling star in 8:10), and so it is more likely that the falling of the star is here also a part of the judgment. That is, the judgment is that the malevolent angel was **given** the **key of the shaft of the abyss** to unleash the next plague on the earth.

The shaft leads down into the abyss, the underworld. This nether region is portrayed as filled with fire, so that when the **shaft** leading down to it was **opened, smoke went up from the shaft**, as thick **as the smoke of a great furnace**. There was so much smoke that **the sun and the air were darkened** and blotted from the sky. Here was a vast amount of smoke, as if all the underworld emptied its noxious fumes into the world above.

The judgment, however, was not the smoke itself—it was what emerged from it. For **from the smoke**, loosed from their subterranean prison, **came out locusts into the earth**, echoing the plague of locusts that struck Egypt (Ex. 10:12). And they were not locusts of the usual kind. That would be a bad enough plague, for locusts consume vegetation, which leads to famine. But these locusts were supernatural and demonic. **Authority** to hurt **was given to them**, even **as the scorpions of the earth** have such dreaded power.

The unnatural behavior of this locust plague is stressed. Locusts usually confine themselves to eating the grass of the earth and its vegetation, but **it was told** to these locusts **not to hurt the grass of the earth, nor any greenery, nor any tree**—that is, not to do what locusts usually do. With supernatural perversity, they were to do what locusts never do—to hurt **only the men** of the earth, **everyone who does not have** divine immunity from them, **the seal of God upon their foreheads** (compare 7:3). Authority **was given** to these locusts **that they should not kill** the men (however much the pain inflicted might cause men to **desire to die**). Rather, the locusts will cause men to **be tormented** with acute agony, like that caused by **a scorpion when it strikes a man.** This would last **for five months** (a limited time, and the normal life span of a locust), and during that time, **men will seek death** to escape the excruciating pain and **never find it**.

The **likenesses of the locusts** were terrifying, because they were unnatural, horrible, freakish things. Once again, one must understand the apocalyptic genre. The verbal description of the locusts cannot easily be translated into a visual medium without becoming comic. We are meant to recoil at the freakish combination of aspects and features: the locusts were like small **horses** (like little scorpion centaurs), but they had **crowns like gold** (as victorious agents of judgment) on their heads. The faces were horribly like the **faces of men** (full of intelligence and cruelty), but they had long hair **as the hair of women** (long hair being an image of vitality) and ferocious teeth, **as the teeth of lions**. They had **breastplates of iron**, like invincible soldiers, and **tails like scorpions**. Their wings roar **as the sound of chariots** as they go into battle. Normal locusts have no leader, no **king over them**, but these do: their king is Destruction itself, **in Hebrew, Abaddon**, the pit of death.

Lest St. John's hearers miss the point, he gives the Greek, **Apollyon**, "Destroyer." (Some think this is a backhanded reference to the pagan god Apollo, god of the sun. Certainly the locust was one of his symbols. If this is true, it is a very clever—and typically Jewish—rebuke. It is saying then that Apollo is the deity of death, not life—a demon, not a true god.)

At the conclusion of the horrifying description of the fifth trumpet, John announces that **the first woe is past**. But **behold!**—they cannot breathe easy yet. No sooner does this woe pass away than **two** more **woes** are **coming** hard at their heels.

What are these demonic locusts, and how will this woe be fulfilled? Of course we cannot say. But we can surmise that it is an image of plague, disease, pain, and pestilence unleashed upon the world. The ancient world did not know of germs or microbes, of bacteria or viruses. But it is interesting, perhaps, that the plague that brings pain is imaged by a living, mobile army of tiny, terrible things.

> ༃ ༃ ༃ ༃ ༃
>
> 13 Then the sixth angel trumpeted, and I heard a voice from the four horns of the golden altar before God,
> 14 saying to the sixth angel who had the trumpet, "Loose the four angels who have been bound at the great river Euphrates."
> 15 And the four angels were loosed, who had been prepared for the hour and day and month and year, to kill a third of men.
> 16 The number of the armies of the horsemen was twice myriads of myriads; I heard the number of them.
> 17 And I saw thus in the vision the horses and those who sat on them: they had breastplates *the color of* fire and hyacinth and sulfur; and the heads of the horses *are* as the heads of lions; and from their mouths proceed fire and smoke and sulfur.
> 18 By these three plagues a third of men were killed, by the fire and the smoke and the sulfur which proceeded from their mouths.
> 19 For the authority of the horses is in their mouths and in their tails; for their tails *are* like serpents having heads, and with them they hurt.

III. The Things Which Will Take Place   Revelation 9:13–19

The **sixth angel trumpeted** (announcing the second woe), and in response John **heard a voice from the four horns of the golden altar before God** (that is, from the place of prayer for judgment on the earth, 8:3). This voice said to the angel who blew the trumpet, **"Loose the four angels who have been bound at the great river Euphrates."**

It is difficult for us today to appreciate what **the great river Euphrates** was to those in the Roman Empire. For us, it is now simply a river, another body of water. But for those in the Roman Empire, it was a border, a bulwark, and it marked the dividing line between civilization and barbarism, between order and chaos, between law and the carnage of anarchy. That is, between Rome and the Parthian Empire. The Parthians were the only people Rome could not conquer, and they stood beyond the Euphrates like a standing threat to Roman existence. Romans lived in fear of them (one scholar spoke of "the Roman neurosis about Parthia"), and it was said by some of St. John's day that after his death, Nero would return again leading an army of Parthians to conquer the city of Rome and regain his crown. For the Romans, the Euphrates held at bay a mighty foe.

Thus, the loosing of **the four angels who have been bound at the Euphrates** was the signal for catastrophe. Like the angel who fell to the earth and unleashed the locusts (9:1–12), so these four angels unleashed a devastating invasion from beyond. These angels of punishment were intent on destruction; they **had been prepared** for this very **hour and day and month and year** to **kill a third of men**. Now they were released to do their terrible work. In the previous trumpets, a third of nature had been destroyed (8:7–12). Now a third of mankind was to suffer as well. (We note in passing the overruling sovereignty of God in human history: Kings of armies may think that all goes by their timetable, but God's inscrutable providence rules over all. God alone sets the day and hour for judging the earth with divine catastrophes.)

This invading force, however, is not the Parthian army, though that foreign empire forms the psychological background to this prophecy. This invasion did not come from Parthia, but from hell. For here was a host beyond counting. The **number of the armies of the horsemen was twice myriads of myriads**. The figure, of course, was not literally twice ten thousand times ten thousand, or two hundred million. When John says that he **heard the number**, he means that he heard it but does not relate it, since such a figure could have no real meaning. (Rather like our modern "trillions of billions"—the number is so large as to be essentially meaningless.) John uses this expression to show that the size of the army was such as to make counting unnecessary.

And it was not only the size of the cavalry force that was supernatural, but the horses themselves. In his **vision** of that army, the horses and their riders were **thus: they had breastplates *the color of* fire and hyacinth** (the color of dusky smoke) **and sulfur; and the heads of the horses *are* as the heads of lions; and from their mouths proceed fire and smoke and sulfur**. The breastplates on the riders therefore partook of the same quality as the fire and smoke and sulfur the lion-headed steeds breathed from their mouths. They were a unity of horror and destruction.

More than that, these horses were like scorpions as well. The **authority** and power **of the horses** was **in their mouths** (from which they breathed fire) and also **in their tails; for their tails *are* like serpents having heads, and with them they hurt**. That is, the tails of the horses were like the deadly, stinging heads of snakes, able to maim and kill.

This is a grotesque and revolting picture, with a countless hellish cavalry riding atop demonic horses, each horse freakish with the head of a fire-spewing lion on its neck and the lethal head of a serpent on its tail, and able to deal out death from both. One is not meant to reduce the image to a visual picture. Like all apocalyptic images, it is aimed at the nerves, not at the head. The spectacle is meant to revolt and terrify, as the forces of hell are let loose upon the earth. Through the **three plagues** of **fire**, **smoke**, and **sulfur** they breathe forth, **a third of men were killed**.

> ॐ ॐ ॐ ॐ ॐ
> 20 The rest of men, who were not killed by these plagues, did not repent of the works of their hands, so as not to worship the demons, and the idols of gold and of silver and of bronze and of stone and of wood, which are neither able to see, nor hear, nor walk;
> 21 and they did not repent of their murders, nor of their sorceries, nor of their fornications, nor of their thefts.

For all the horror of the preceding trumpets and woes, **the rest of men** (those **who were not killed by these plagues**) **did not repent of the works of their hands, so as not to worship the demons and the idols**.

Here St. John speaks as a Jew facing the idolatrous pagan world. Like all Jews, he was repelled by **the idols of gold and of silver and of bronze and of stone and of wood** that filled the pagan cities. (As was St. Paul when he walked through Athens; Acts 17:16.) The listing of all the materials from which these statues were made testifies to this Jewish impatience. It is as if there were idols made from every substance imaginable. And all this idolatry was so patently wrong and futile. The Gentiles treated these statues as if they were divine, but these images of their gods were manifestly unworthy of such treatment. They could not save those who called on them (compare Is. 45:20; Ep. Jer. 66). Indeed, they could not even do the works mere men could do; they were **neither able to see, nor hear, nor walk**—much less save their devotees from the wrath of the true God. And yet the world refused to repent of worshipping them or turn to the living God. They continued in the darkness of the Gentile world and **did not repent of their murders, nor of their sorceries, nor of their fornications, nor of their thefts**.

This is a frighteningly accurate description of our own society.

We too, in the secular West, have a culture characterized by **murders** (especially of the unborn) and **sorceries** (Gr. *pharmakeia*; compare our English word "pharmacy"), with our drugs to induce abortion and drugs to induce synthetic "highs." We too multiply **fornications** (Gr. *porneia*) with our rampant sexual immorality and multibillion-dollar pornography industry. We too delight in **thefts**, with dishonesty and corruption everywhere, even in the high levels of government. This is all because our society does not worship the true God, but rather Mammon, money, **the works of** our **hands**.

§III.6. Interlude: John Eats the Little Book and Measures the Temple; the Church Preaches the Gospel through Persecution

10 1 And I saw another strong angel coming down from heaven, clothed with a cloud; and the rainbow *was* upon his head, and his face *was* as the sun, and his feet as pillars of fire;
2 and he had in his hand an opened *little* book. He put his right foot upon the sea and his left upon the land;
3 and he cried out with a great voice, as when a lion roars; and when he had cried out, the seven thunders spoke with their voices.
4 When the seven thunders had spoken, I was about to write; and I heard a voice from heaven saying, "Seal the things which the seven thunders have spoken and do not write them."

After the blowing of the sixth trumpet, we have been brought closer still to the end of the age, for there remains only the blowing of the seventh trumpet, and then all will be done. Before this is narrated, St. John inserts a series of visions meant to encourage the

III. The Things Which Will Take Place Revelation 10:1–4

Church to persevere in preaching the Gospel and holding to the Faith, even in the face of martyrdom.

In the first of these visions, St. John saw another strong angel coming down from heaven. (As in 5:2, the designation of the angel as **strong** indicates a key event—in this case, the commissioning of the Church to preach the Gospel to the nations.) This angel was **clothed with a cloud**, traveling on the clouds from heaven to earth (compare Dan. 7:13, in which the Son of Man is brought on the clouds from earth to heaven). **The rainbow *was* upon his head** as a kind of heavenly turban, reflecting the glory of God, from whom he came (see Rev. 4:3 for the rainbow about the divine Throne). **His face** shone **as the sun**, reflecting his previous audience with God (compare Ex. 34:29 for the face of Moses shining with a similar radiance), and **his feet *were* as pillars of fire**. God had led Israel in the wilderness, shining by night from a pillar of fire (Ex. 13:21), and this angel also comes to lead the Church through the wilderness of suffering. The whole description of the angel recalls a similar angelic visitation in Daniel 10:5–6.

The angel had something for the Church—a *little* **book** (Gr. *biblaridion*). This was not a larger book or scroll (Gr. *biblion*) because it was meant to be portable and easily opened. It represented the Gospel the Church must carry into all the world and openly proclaim to the nations.

The angel who came with this gift and commission to the Church was of immense size, as he straddled both **land** and **sea**. Like a colossus, he stood tall above the earth so that his voice could reach all, and he **cried out with a great voice, as when a lion roars**, with great power. This leonine roaring was a challenge to the world and a call for the servants of God to proclaim their message. This roar hearkens back to the prophetic word of Amos 3:8: "A lion has roared! Who will not fear? The Lord God has spoken! Who can but prophesy?" The roaring of this angel is the signal for the Church to indeed prophesy to the nations.

It was also the signal for those in heaven to speak another word of prophetic warning to the earth. **When** the angel **had cried out, the**

seven thunders spoke with their voices. These seem to have been further words of heavenly warning to the earth, exhorting everyone to hear the Gospel written in the little book. Just as thunder in the heavens warns those on earth of a coming storm, so these seven thunders appear to have been meant as warnings for those on earth to heed the Church's Gospel.

John was **about to write** down these words of warning, but he was dissuaded from doing so. He **heard a voice from heaven saying, "Seal the things which the seven thunders have spoken and do not write them."** Further warnings were useless, since if the world refused to listen to the Gospel, there was no further hope. The seven thunders were the angelic echo of the Church's Gospel. But such a further echo was unnecessary; the proclamation of the Gospel was itself the authoritative and final warning to the world.

---

5 Then the angel whom I saw standing upon the sea and upon the land raised his right hand to heaven,
6 and swore by Him who lives to ages of ages, who created heaven and the things in it, and the earth and the things in it, and the sea and the things in it, that there will be time for delay no longer,
7 but in the days of the voice of the seventh angel, when he is about to trumpet, then the mystery of God is finished, as He preached the Gospel to His slaves the prophets.

As an encouragement to preach the Gospel even in such perilous times of persecution, **the angel raised his right hand to heaven** and, in a gesture of solemn oath-taking reminiscent of a similar encouragement in Daniel 12:7, **swore by Him who lives to ages of ages, who created heaven** and **the earth** and **the sea**, and all that they contained, **that there will be time for delay no longer**. (We note in passing the rebuke of pagan idolatry latent in this oath, and how it proclaims the eternal God as the only Creator.) According

III. The Things Which Will Take Place   Revelation 10:8–11

to this oath, the End was fast approaching, and the Church would be rewarded for its faithful perseverance in preaching the Gospel. **In the days of the voice of the seventh angel**, after that last trumpet judgment was done, **then the mystery of God is finished**.

God **preached the Gospel** (Gr. *euaggelizo*; cognate with *euaggelion*, "Gospel") **to His slaves the prophets** in the Old Testament, telling them of salvation and new life through Christ. This message was the **mystery of God** (Gr. *musterion*), hidden from the previous ages, but now revealed through the Church's preaching (Rom. 16:25; Eph. 3:4–6; Col. 1:26). Throughout all this long age the Church had labored at its holy task, bringing this mystery to the world. If it would labor but a while longer, after this final trumpet had been sounded, its labors would be over.

> ༄ ༄ ༄ ༄ ༄
>
> 8 And the voice which I heard from heaven was speaking with me again, saying, "Go, take the opened book *which is* in the hand of the angel who stands upon the sea and upon the land."
> 9 And I went up to the angel, telling him to give me the *little* book. And he says to me, "Take and eat it; it will make bitter your stomach, but in your mouth it will be sweet as honey."
> 10 I took the *little* book from the hand of the angel and ate it up, and in my mouth it was sweet as honey; and when I had eaten it, my stomach was made bitter.
> 11 And they say to me, "It is necessary for you to prophesy again about many peoples and nations and tongues and kings."

John **heard** a **voice from heaven** (the one that before had told him not to write what the thunders had spoken; v. 4) now speaking authoritatively and issuing an order: **"Go, take the opened book *which is* in the hand of the angel who stands upon the sea and upon the land."** John might well be reluctant even to approach such a towering and imposing figure without a prior word of command, much less to relieve that figure of the book he carried. But in obedience to the heavenly voice, he **went up to the angel** (with some trepidation?), **telling him to give** him **the *little* book**.

The angel is not reluctant to give John the book. Rather, he says to John, **"Take and eat it; it will make bitter your stomach, but in your mouth it will be sweet as honey."**

The whole scene reflects the prophetic vision of Ezekiel, who received from God a book containing God's word, which the prophet was to deliver. In Ezekiel 2:8—3:4, he was commanded to eat the scroll containing God's words (that is, to take them into his inmost being, making them a part of him) as a preparation for speaking God's message to Israel. God's words were found to be "sweet as honey in his mouth" (Ezek. 3:3).

Here St. John would find the Gospel message for the nations to be **sweet as honey** also, for it contained God's saving Word—the Word that was sweeter than honey (Ps. 19:10; 119:103). But after he **had eaten it**, it would **make** his **stomach bitter**. That is, though a joy to proclaim, it would lead to the bitterness of martyrdom.

John ate the little book and was told, **"It is necessary for you to prophesy again about many peoples and nations and tongues and kings."** This is a call to continue his work of receiving visions and proclaiming them as a prophet in the chapters to follow. But it is also a call to continue the work of preaching the Gospel. For John in this vision does not represent himself only. In his eating of the little book, he represents the whole Church. It is the Church that is to act as God's prophet to the world, bringing His Word to **many peoples and nations and tongues and kings**. It was **necessary** (Gr. *dei*) to do this. The Church may be tempted to shrink from this work of preaching during times of martyrdom, but it must persevere anyway. Whatever the bitterness of suffering it may entail, the Church must fulfill its sacred commission. As an expression of this sacred task, John is told that he must **prophesy again about** those **many peoples**. As the embodiment of the Church, he must not shrink from his own holy work of prophecy, but brace himself to receive visions of terrifying persecutions.

III. The Things Which Will Take Place   Revelation 11:1–2

> ꙮ ꙮ ꙮ ꙮ ꙮ
>
> **11** 1 And there was given me a reed like a rod, saying, "Rise and measure the sanctuary of God and the altar, and those worshipping in it.
> 2 "And cast outside the outer court of the sanctuary and do not measure it, for it has been given to the nations; and they will trample the holy city for forty-two months.

Next comes another vision, which begins with John being **given a reed** which is rigid **like a rod**. The imagery is drawn from Ezekiel 40—42 and Zechariah 2. In those visions, the prophets saw men with measuring lines, long reeds or bamboo-like canes that were long and stiff enough to be used to measure length. (They could be over ten feet long.) In those visions, the temple and the city of Jerusalem were being measured with a view to their protection by God. The same concept informs the image here: John is bidden to **rise** and use the reed to **measure the sanctuary** or temple **of God and the altar, and those worshipping in it**. But he is told to **cast outside** of his consideration and exclude from his measurements **the outer court of the sanctuary**. This is to be left unmeasured—and unprotected by God.

This is an image of the Church, which is the true Sanctuary and Temple of God (1 Cor. 3:16; Eph. 2:21–22). The layout described here is that of the second temple, built by Herod (and destroyed by the Romans in AD 70). Those temple grounds had an inner sanctuary with its altar. Jews alone could enter these areas to pray and worship. Around these courts lay an outer court, the Court of the Gentiles. Gentiles might enter this outer court and pray with their Jewish friends, but were permitted to go no further. No Gentile was permitted to accompany a Jew into the inner courts—the Court of Women, the Court of the Israelites, or the Court of the Priests. The inner sanctuaries were for the people of God alone.

Just as the Gentiles might tread the outer court, so in this vision **the outer court of the sanctuary** is **given** over to the persecuting **nations, and they will trample the holy city** down. That is, God will allow **the nations** to **trample** down and persecute the Church, the true and spiritual **holy city** of God, but only in its outer aspect. But not the inner life of the Church—that remains **measured** and known by God and under His protection. The true life of the Church remains remote from persecution and untouchable, abiding safely in the divine care. The persecutors may kill the bodies of the saints, but their true life remains hidden with Christ in God (Col. 3:3). The Christians may be put to death, but not a hair of their heads will finally perish (Luke 21:16–18). It is only the outer body of the Church that will suffer loss and waste away (2 Cor. 4:16).

This time of persecution is described here as **forty-two months.** In 12:6 it is described as "twelve hundred and sixty days" and in 12:14 as "time, times, and half a time" (i.e. one year, another two years, and half a year, for a total of three and a half years)—the same length of time is meant in all these instances. This temporal image comes from the Book of Daniel, where it describes the actual length of the brutal persecution of the faithful Jews under Antiochus Epiphanes, the "little horn" (Dan. 7:25; 12:7). This limited period from the Book of Daniel becomes in the Apocalypse a paradigm, an image of a period of short but savage persecution. This does not mean the actual historical period of the Church's persecution will last but three and a half years. The persecution begun by the Emperor Diocletian alone lasted about a decade. The number is a symbolic one, tapping into memories of the days of the Maccabees. The number tells us that the persecution may be harrowing, but that it will end.

---

3 "And I will give to My two witnesses, and they will prophesy for one thousand two hundred and sixty days, clothed in sackcloth."
4 These are the two olive-trees and the two lampstands that stand before the Lord of the earth.
5 And if anyone wants to hurt them, fire proceeds

> from their mouth and eats up their enemies; and if anyone wants to hurt them, it is necessary for him to be killed thus.
> 6 These have the authority to shut the heaven, that rain will not shower *down* during the days of their prophecy; and they have authority over the waters to turn them into blood, and to strike the earth with every plague, as often as they want.

John is told of the work of God's **two witnesses** or martyrs (Gr. *martus*, compare the English "martyr"). In this apocalyptic parable, they are said to **prophesy for one thousand two hundred and sixty days** (that is, throughout the duration of the forty-two months the Church is persecuted in the vision of 11:2) **clothed in sackcloth**. Clothed in the garments of mourning, they prophesy to the great secular city as Jonah did in Nineveh, proclaiming its overthrow unless it repents (Jonah 3:4).

And they are present as true prophets, having all the authority of the greatest prophets of old. God defends them as He defended Elijah, sending down fire from heaven upon those who want to arrest him (2 Kings 1:9–15). In this case, **fire proceeds from the mouth** of the two witnesses and **eats up their enemies,** who would destroy them before the time. **If anyone wants to hurt them, it is necessary for him to be killed thus**—this is the sure doom that awaits him.

Moreover, these two witnessing prophets have the power of Moses and Elijah, embodying all the authority of the Law and the Prophets. Like Elijah (see 1 Kings 17:1), they **have authority to shut the heaven, that rain will not shower *down* during the days of their prophecy**. The resulting torment of drought would thus witness to the truth of their message. Like Moses (see Ex. 7:20; 8—10), they also **have authority over the waters to turn them into blood, and to strike the earth with every plague**. These torments are meant to chastise, so that their hearers will repent and no longer "worship the demons, the idols of gold and silver" (Rev. 9:20).

The witnesses are said to have a greater significance also. They are **the two olive-trees and the two lampstands that stand before the Lord of the earth**. This image is drawn from Zechariah 4. There the Prophet Zechariah sees a golden lampstand, the olive oil to feed it coming from two olive-trees that stand beside it. In Zechariah's prophecy, this lampstand represents the Presence of God in Israel. This Presence is assured by Zerubbabel the governor and Joshua the high priest. As the lampstand was provided with an unfailing supply of olive oil from the olive trees beside it and so gave constant light, so these two men, Zerubbabel and Joshua, would give unfailing guidance and blessing to the new Jewish community.

In the prophecy of the two witnesses, this image from Zechariah's vision is freely adapted. **The two olive trees and the two lampstands** symbolize, not Zerubbabel and Joshua, but the two martyric witnesses of the Church. The martyrs of the Church are the true source of light and blessing. They were not criminals (as the world thought them), but the light of the world (Matt. 5:14).

---

7 When they have finished their witness, the beast coming up from the abyss will make war with them, and conquer them and kill them.

8 And their corpses *will be* in the street of the great city which spiritually is called Sodom and Egypt, where also their Lord was crucified.

9 Those from the peoples and tribes and tongues and nations will see their corpses for three and a half days, and will not let their corpses be laid in a tomb.

10 And those who dwell upon the earth will rejoice over them and be glad; and they will send gifts to one another, because these two prophets tormented those who dwell upon the earth.

The work of the two witnesses is brought to an end. **When they have finished their witness** (we note the sovereignty of God at work

III. The Things Which Will Take Place   Revelation 11:11–13

here—they are invincibly protected by God until their task is done), **the beast coming up from the abyss will make war with them, and conquer them and kill them**. This is the first time **the beast** is mentioned. He will be more amply described later (13:1f; 17:3f). Here he is simply described as coming from **the abyss**, from the pit of hell. He is an image of the Roman Empire, the great persecutor of the saints in St. John's day.

After the two witnesses are slain, **their corpses** are left to rot **in the street**—the ultimate indignity. The city in which their bodies are left is **the great city**, further described **spiritually** (that is, allegorically) as **Sodom and Egypt**. That is, the city (Rome is meant; compare 17:18) is the embodiment of all moral corruption (as **Sodom** was) and all oppression of God's people (as **Egypt** was). It is further described as the place **where also their Lord was crucified**. This does not indicate Jerusalem. (Christ was actually crucified *outside* that city; Heb. 13:12.) It means that these witnesses suffered the same fate from the Romans as their Master did, and by their martyrdom they follow in His steps.

Their death is cause for jubilation on the part of their enemies. They gawk at their corpses **for three and a half days, and will not let** them **be laid in a tomb**. Delighting in heaping these final insults on the **two prophets** who **tormented** them by their chastising miracles (from which they derived no benefit), **those who dwell upon the earth rejoice over them** and **are glad**, celebrating and sending gifts to one another. When the Jews triumphed over their pagan foes and averted national annihilation, they celebrated their triumph by **sending gifts to one another** (Esther 9:22). In horrible parody of this, the enemies of God do the same.

ॐ ॐ ॐ ॐ ॐ

11 But after the three and a half days, the spirit of life from God entered into them, and they stood upon their feet; and great fear fell upon those observing them.
12 And they heard a great voice from heaven saying to them, "Come up here." And they went

> up into heaven in the cloud, and their enemies observed them.
> 13 And in that hour a great earthquake occurred, and a tenth of the city fell; and seven thousand names of men were killed in the earthquake, and the rest were afraid and gave glory to the God of heaven.

But the secular city was not to triumph in the end. For after the three and a half days, **the spirit of life from God entered into them, and they stood upon their feet; and great fear fell upon those observing them.** Even as the dead and dry bones in Ezekiel's valley of death were given life and "stood upon their feet, a very great army" (Ezek. 37:10), so these two witnesses arose and stood erect also. Those who scorned their message and their God now were in **great fear**. And they **heard a great voice from heaven saying to them, "Come up here."** The witnesses **went up into heaven in the cloud**, even as Christ ascended thus (Acts 1:9), and this also was **observed** by **their enemies**. This was followed immediately by **a great earthquake** in which **a tenth of the city fell; and seven thousand names of men were killed in the earthquake. The rest were afraid and gave glory to the God of heaven**, acknowledging now that the two prophets had spoken the truth. God vindicated His prophets publicly and spectacularly.

What is the meaning of all this, and who are the two witnesses? In the image of two witnesses we are reminded that our Lord sent the disciples out in twos (Luke 10:1), and thus the image speaks of the witnessing Church. But these were not just any two witnesses. For especially imprinted on the mind and heart of the original hearers of this prophecy was the image of the two holy and beloved martyrs who died in the great city of Rome, St. Peter and St. Paul. They were, in some sense, the archetypical martyrs, whose blood was the seed of the Church. This does not mean that the two witnesses of this vision *are* St. Peter and St. Paul. Rather, in this parable of the Church's mission and suffering, these two apostles and martyrs form an image of the martyric Church, the embodiment and pattern for all the martyrs. The two witnesses therefore are a symbol of the Church as she witnesses with power in the midst of the world, and seals her witness with her own blood.

The story of the two witnesses here therefore constitutes a parable for the Church as she witnesses before all "peoples, tribes, tongues, and nations" (v. 9). The Church may fearlessly speak its message, for God will defend His witnesses as He defended these two prophets. Even should they be slain for their witness, God will vindicate them in the end. This vindication is here made a part of the parable, and as such is incorporated into the ongoing story of the trumpets and the woes. But in real life, their resurrection, exaltation to heaven, and final vindication will await the Lord's Coming.

---

14 The second woe is past; behold! the third woe is coming quickly.

It is now said that **the second woe** (that is, the sixth trumpet, consisting of the invading army of 9:13f) **is past**. Yet, as with the first woe, this one is scarcely past when the third and final woe comes upon the world.

It may be asked why this announcement of the passing of the second woe is delayed until after the story of the two witnesses. After all, a similar announcement about the passing of the first woe was made in 9:12, immediately after the first woe. Why insert the visions of chapters 10 and 11 after the second woe?

It would seem the intention was to locate the visions of persecution against a background of judgment. Even after the final woe and the seventh trumpet are announced in 11:15, the effects of this trumpet are not narrated until chapter 16, as more visions of Church persecution are given. It is true that the persecution of the Church is not confined to the end of the age, but rather the Church suffers persecution throughout the age. But these final judgments on the world *cannot be understood apart from these persecutions*, and so the story of the judgments is interspersed among the visions telling of that persecution.

❧ IV ☙

THE END OF ALL THINGS
(11:15—18:24)

§IV.1 The Blowing of the Seventh Trumpet:
The Last Outpouring of Wrath Begins

☙ ☙ ☙ ☙ ☙

15 And the seventh angel trumpeted; and there occurred great voices in heaven, saying, "The kingdom of the world has become the Kingdom of our Lord and of His Christ; and He will reign to ages of ages."

16 And the twenty-four elders, who sit on their thrones before God, fell on their faces and worshipped God,

17 saying, "We give thanks to You, O Lord God, the Almighty, who are and who were, because You have taken Your great power and have *begun* to reign.

18 "And the nations were angry, and Your wrath came, and the time *came* for the dead to be judged, and to give the reward to Your slaves, the prophets and the saints, even those who fear Your Name, the little and the great, and to destroy those who destroy the earth."

19 And the sanctuary of God in heaven was opened; and the ark of His covenant was seen within His sanctuary, and there occurred *flashes*

> *of* lightning and sounds and *peals of* thunder and an earthquake and great hail.

When **the seventh angel trumpeted, there occurred great voices in heaven**, a loud commotion of triumphant jubilation. For when the wrath of the seventh and last trumpet had been poured out, then **"the kingdom of the world has become the Kingdom of our Lord and of His Christ; and He will reign to ages of ages."** The sounding of the seventh trumpet was the signal that the End was at hand. In anticipation of this, **the twenty-four elders** of the heavenly court **fell on their faces and worshipped God**, overwhelmed at the majesty of God and the thought of His impending victory. They **give thanks** to their King, extolling Him as the **Lord God, the Almighty**, the Pantocrator who rules over all, the One who has all power and who always had all power (**who are and who were**). Formerly He was described as He "who is, who was, and who is coming" (1:4); the last attribute is now omitted, for the future has arrived. At last He has **taken** His **great power** and begun to reign on the earth, overthrowing the usurped authority of the godless. Reviewing the events of the final days of crisis, the elders announce that **the nations were angry, and** God's **wrath came** in response, **and the time *came* for the dead to be judged, and to give the reward to** God's **slaves** and faithful servants.

Undergirding this whole doxology is Psalm 2. That psalm is a celebration of God's power over the nations, a proclamation that the Messiah will overcome all the hostility of the nations and put down by force all godless resistance to Yahweh's reign. That psalm says the nations rebelled and plotted against God, taking their stand against Him and against His Christ. God, enthroned securely in heaven, spoke to them in His anger and made His Christ triumphant, so that He broke their power with a rod of iron (Ps. 2:1, 5, 9). For St. John, this final conflict of God with the rebels is now to begin.

Its outcome is assured: God will be victorious. The dead will be raised, and all will receive the justice due them. He will give the **reward** to His **slaves, the prophets** (such as John) and all His **saints, even those who fear** His **Name**, both **the little and the great**. None

IV. The End of All Things   Revelation 11:15–19

of His faithful will be overlooked. All will receive their reward.

The godless will receive their just recompense as well. **Those who destroy the earth** through their wars and sin God will **destroy**. The punishment will fit the crime, and the impenitent rebels will for once be on the receiving end of the suffering they previously gave out.

This final conflict is summarized by the image of God revealing Himself in power from heaven. **The sanctuary of God in heaven was opened**, so that **the ark of His covenant** within **was seen**. When the ark of God went forth to war in ancient days, Moses sang out, "Let God arise, let His enemies be scattered; let those who hate Him flee from before His face!" (Num. 10:35; Ps. 68:1). The ark was the Presence of God in the midst of Israel, and now that Presence is to be manifested in power. Now at last God will truly arise to judge the earth and possess all the nations (Ps. 82:8). God's wrath is to fall on them from heaven, signaled by *flashes of* **lightning and rumbling sounds and** *peals of* **thunder and an earthquake and great hail**. All the world's natural catastrophes combine as a prelude to the final wrath of God upon the earth.

§IV.2. Interlude: Signs in Heaven— The Church Is Persecuted by the World

Now follows another series of visions concerning the Church's conflict with the world, revealing the significance of the world's demand that all its citizens acknowledge the divinity of the emperor. As mentioned in the Introduction, the required ceremony of offering sacrificial incense to the emperor was intended only as a test of loyalty and had little or no theological significance. It was simply a demand that loyalty to the state be paramount.

It was the Church's refusal to participate in the cult of the emperor's divinity that brought about the promise of persecution from the state. And it also brought this question to the fore: What did burning a little pinch of incense matter? Shouldn't a Christian be prepared to grant this "small" civic demand? Did God really care if His people made this concession to the state?

The following visions reveal the eternal issues of this controversy.

God *did* care about this "small" concession, for it was not really a small concession at all, but involved the question of where one's fundamental loyalty lay. Which was most important, and who was the Christian's true Lord—Christ or Caesar?

These visions reveal that the state's persecution of the Church in this matter was not a question of the state legitimately insisting on its own rights. It was a part of the eschatological conflict, the eternal struggle between light and darkness, between Christ and Satan, between the Woman clothed with the Sun and the great Dragon, between the saints of God and the beast from the abyss. For the Christians to give in on this matter and to sacrifice to Caesar's divinity was an act of apostasy, which brought with it the damnation of their souls.

12 1 A great sign was seen in heaven: a woman clothed with the sun, and the moon under her feet, and upon her head a crown of twelve stars;
2 and she had *a child* in the womb; and she cried out, being in travail and in torment to give birth.
3 Then another sign was seen in heaven, and behold! a great red dragon having seven heads and ten horns, and upon his heads were seven diadems.
4 And his tail dragged *down* a third of the stars of heaven and cast them to the earth. And the dragon stood before the woman who was about to give birth, that when she gave birth to the child he might eat *the child* up.
5 And she gave birth to a son, a male, who is about to shepherd all the nations with a rod of iron; and her child was snatched *up* to God and to His throne.
6 And the woman fled into the wilderness, where

IV. The End of All Things   Revelation 12:1–6

> she had a place prepared by God, that there they might nourish her for one thousand two hundred and sixty days.

As St. John looked on, **a great sign** (Gr. *semeion*) **was seen in heaven**, a mighty omen and portent of the coming persecution—a **woman clothed with the sun**, having **the moon under her feet** and **upon her head a crown of twelve stars**. She is an image of the true Israel, the people of God from olden times. As the people of God who are destined for glory, she is radiant with divine glory, **clothed with the sun**; she is exalted above all the earth, so that **the moon** is **under her feet**, and she wears a heavenly **crown of twelve stars**, representing the twelve patriarchs of Israel. She is an image of celestial beauty and splendor, bearing in herself the majesty of heaven to which she is called.

Moreover, she **had *a child* in the womb**, and as the moment of childbirth drew near, she **cried out in travail and torment to give birth**. It was prophesied in Isaiah 66:7 that Israel would give birth to a male child (that is, give birth to its salvation). This sign shows the fulfillment of that prophecy as the woman, the people of God, gives birth to the Messiah. The travail of birth-giving is an image of the agony of controversy attending the life and ministry of Jesus Christ, to whom Israel gave birth.

The image of Israel's birth-giving coalesces with the image of the most-holy Mother of God. For if the Woman clothed with the sun is the People of Israel, nevertheless she wears the face of Mary the Theotokos, for Israel gives birth to the Messiah in her person. It is through her that Christ was born; it is she who is the true daughter of Zion (Zech. 2:10). She is the one "who is in labor to give birth" to the One born in "Bethlehem Ephrathah" (Micah 5:1–3). The heavenly glory of the woman clothed with the sun is therefore a reflection of her glory, as the image of the people of God coalesces with its antitype. This Marian picture of the Church is only to be expected from St. John, who had the care of Mary from the time of the Cross until her repose (John 19:27).

As St. John continued to look, **another sign was seen in heaven**.

Unexpectedly (the suddenness signaled by **behold!**), **a great dragon** appeared, **red** in color to signify its bloody and murderous intent. The dragon is an image of the devil (v. 9), who works through kings and men of power to accomplish his terrible work. Unlike other beasts, this dragon had **seven heads**, upon which were **seven diadems**, and **ten horns**. From 17:9f, we surmise that the **seven heads** are symbols of seven Roman emperors, reigning from the seven hills of Rome, and the **ten horns** are symbols of the nations of the Roman Empire. The **diadems** were **upon his heads** because the Empire's power was still centralized and had not yet devolved upon the kings of the nations (as would happen later; compare 13:1; 17:12). By identifying the dragon with Rome, the Apocalypse reveals that the state which opposes God is the instrument of the devil.

This dragon was so big and vast that its tail alone was able to **drag *down* a third of the stars of heaven and cast them to the earth**. This last detail echoes the persecuting power of Antiochus Epiphanes, whose persecution of the saints in the second century BC is described in Daniel 8:10 as causing "some of the host of heaven to fall to the earth." The great Roman dragon is similarly powerful in his arrogance. But whereas Antiochus caused some of the Jewish saints to fall to the earth (i.e. to suffer death), this dragon brings down the very angels from heaven (compare reference to the dragon's angels in v. 7). Satan is more powerful than any earthly ruler or persecutor, with power in heaven as well as on earth (compare his "war in heaven," v. 7).

The **dragon stood before the woman** in her hour of crisis, when she was **about to give birth**, poised and ready, that **when she gave birth to the child he might eat *the child* up**. The people of Israel, through Mary, **gave birth to a son, a male**, one virile and mighty with divine strength, One who is **about to shepherd all the nations with a rod of iron** (see 2:27). The dragon indeed wanted to devour the Son of Mary as soon as He was born, working at first through King Herod, as he schemed to destroy the infant Christ at Bethlehem (Matt. 2). But Jesus, through the protection of God, eluded all the stratagems of the Enemy and lived to full manhood.

IV. The End of All Things   Revelation 12:7–9

At length, at His glorious Ascension, He **was snatched *up* to God and to His throne**.

After Christ's Ascension, the persecution of His people the Church began (Acts 6f). The Church, the true Israel, fled into the wilderness. This image of the wilderness draws on such Old Testament traditions as Jeremiah 31:2 ("The people who survived the sword found grace in the wilderness"), Ezekiel 20:10 ("I brought them into the wilderness and gave them My statutes"), and Hosea 2:14 ("Bring her into the wilderness and speak kindly to her.") The wilderness here is not a place of desolation, but rather the place where God may be found, a place of safety, of divine provision. Elijah found refuge in the wilderness and was fed there by God's command (1 Kings 17:3–6). In the same way, the woman found her **place prepared by God**. In this place, which stood in readiness to receive her, she was to be **nourished** by God for **one thousand two hundred and sixty days**—that is, for all the days of persecution (see 11:2 and comments). When the persecution rages against the Church, the true Israel, God will protect her and sustain her. Though men may suffer martyrdom, the Church itself will survive.

> ॐ ॐ ॐ ॐ ॐ
> 7 And a war occurred in heaven, Michael and his angels warring with the dragon. The dragon and his angels warred,
> 8 and he was not strong *enough*, nor was there a place any longer found for them in heaven.
> 9 And the great dragon was cast out, the ancient serpent who is called the devil and Satan, who deceives the whole world; he was cast out to the earth, and his angels were cast out with him.

The reference in verse 6 to the flight of the woman (after the Ascension of her Son) was parenthetical. Upon the Ascension of the Son (in v. 5), **a war occurred in heaven**, in which **Michael** the Archangel (commander of God's forces and protector of His People; see Dan. 12:1), assisted by **his angels**, was **warring with the dragon** and **his angels**, the demons. The dragon **was not strong *enough*** to prevail against the forces of God, so that **a place** was no longer **found for them in heaven. The great dragon was cast out** from heaven down **to the earth**, and his **angels were cast out with him**. The rout of the evil forces was complete, and the heavenlies were cleansed of their evil presence. The ruler of this world was cast out (John 12:31).

John adds an explanatory note that the dragon was an image of **the ancient serpent**, the Tempter who brought death to the human race in the Garden (Gen. 3:1f), the one **who is called the devil** (Gr. *diabolos*, "slanderer") and **Satan** (Gr. *satanas*, "adversary"), the one **who deceives the whole world** with his lies, turning all from God to idols.

In saying that the slandering devil no longer had a place in heaven, St. John means that he can no longer stand before God and accuse us. In Job 1—2, Satan is portrayed as accusing Job before God, standing as Job's adversary before a heavenly court (see also Zech. 3:1f). The accuser of the Christian brothers (v. 10) is no longer able to do that, for the Presence of Christ the Savior at the right hand of God leaves no place for the devil's accusations. Through the Blood of Christ, all our sins have been forgiven, and Satan no longer has access to God, as he was portrayed as having in the story of Job. Now he has been once and for all cast from the heavenly court, all the way down to the earth.

> ꙮ ꙮ ꙮ ꙮ ꙮ
>
> 10 And I heard a great sound in heaven, saying, "Now the salvation and the power and the Kingdom of our God and the authority of His Christ have come, for the accuser of our brothers has been thrown down, who accuses them before our God day and night.
> 11 "And they *themselves* conquered him because of the Blood of the Lamb and because of the word of their witness, and they did not love their lives even unto death.

IV. The End of All Things | Revelation 12:10–12

> 12 "Therefore be glad, O heavens and you who tabernacle in them! Woe to the earth and the sea, because the devil has come down to you, having great wrath, knowing that he has only a little time."

This expulsion causes great joy to those in heaven. When Christ ascended on high and took His place at the Father's right hand, John **heard a great sound in heaven**, the triumphal shout of the angels there. The angels cried out, **"Now the salvation and the power and the Kingdom of our God and the authority of His Christ have come."** The rule of the messianic Kingdom had begun, and the angels were jubilant. For Satan, **the accuser** of the Christians, **has been thrown down**, and his ceaseless accusations, which went on **day and night,** have now come to an end. God has justified and forgiven sinners through the Blood of Christ—who will dare to condemn them (Rom. 8:33–34)?

Note that the angels refer to us as their **brothers**, since both angels and men fight in the same eschatological conflict. In that conflict, the Christians *themselves* (the pronoun is emphatic) **conquered** Satan **because of the Blood of the Lamb**, for they relied on Christ's Cross to silence Satan's accusations; they conquered him **because of the word of their witness**, for they refused to deny their Lord, even though it cost **their lives**.

Here our struggle with the devil is set forth. The Christian by his faith conquers Satan, who would overcome him with accusations of guilt, because the Lamb of God shed His Blood to buy his forgiveness and he relies on that Blood. He conquers Satan, who would separate him from Christ, because he confesses Christ through all manner of persecution, preferring death to apostasy. It may seem to the world that the martyrs were victims, that they were conquered by the invincible might of Rome. On the contrary, the angels know the truth—that the martyrs were the ones who conquered, defeating the dragon by Christ's **Blood** and their own enduring **witness** (Gr. *marturia*).

Though the expulsion of the dragon from the **heavens** is a source of joy to the angels **who tabernacle in them**, it is a source of **woe** and distress **to the earth and the sea**. For the devil **has come down** to this world **having great wrath, knowing that he has only a little time** left. Realizing that his expulsion from heaven means the end is drawing near, the devil is determined to do his worst. The wrath of the dragon, manifested through the persecution of the saints, does not mean that the dragon is victorious (as it might appear). Rather, it means that he is doomed. It is a sign of weakness, not of strength. The persecution ordered by the Roman state is shown to be the work of the devil—and a sign of his imminent end.

> ꙮ ꙮ ꙮ ꙮ ꙮ
>
> 13 And when the dragon saw that he was cast out to the earth, he persecuted the woman who gave birth to the male.
> 14 And there were given to the woman the two wings of the great eagle, that she might fly into the wilderness to her place, where she was nourished for a time and times and half a time, *away* from the face of the serpent.
> 15 And the serpent cast *water* as a river from his mouth after the woman, that he might cause her to be carried off by the river.
> 16 And the earth helped the woman, and the earth opened its mouth and swallowed up the river which the dragon cast from his mouth.
> 17 And the dragon was angry with the woman and went away to make war with the rest of her seed, those who keep the commandments of God and have the witness of Jesus.

John now narrates a vision of the dragon's ongoing conflict with the Church, the true Israel of God. Immediately upon his expulsion from heaven, the dragon **persecuted the woman**, the Church. The woman, however, was **given two wings of the great eagle** (compare Ex. 19:4) **that she might fly into the wilderness**. With her new wings, she was able to keep ahead of the pursuing dragon. That is, God provided the way of escape and survival for His Church. This flight was alluded to already, in verse 6. There in the wilderness she would remain and be **nourished** in a place of safety for **a time, times, and half a time**—i.e. the "one thousand two hundred and sixty days" referred to in 12:6 and the "forty-two months" of 11:2, the entire span of the persecution. God would not cease to care for His own. As Israel was nourished in the wilderness after escaping Pharaoh, so the new Israel was nourished by God and sustained, even in times of intense persecution.

The serpent, though, did not relent in his warfare. He pursued the woman and **cast *water* as a river from his mouth** after her, to drown her. Here is an image of complete destruction, of being overwhelmed by persecution (compare Ps. 124:4: "They would have swallowed us alive; the waters would have engulfed us, the raging waters would have swept over our soul"). But the Lord did not abandon His people. Miraculously, **the earth helped the woman** and **opened its mouth and swallowed up the river**, so that the dragon was foiled and **was angry with the woman**.

How are these images to be interpreted? To what historical realities do they refer? We have here an image of the intended persecution and destruction of the Church by the same demonic powers of the world that attempted to devour her child, Christ, soon after His birth (12:4). This initial attempt to devour found its historical fulfillment in the persecution of King Herod. Similarly, this persecution of the woman in the wilderness was fulfilled in the persecution of the Church by the Jews in the first century, as recorded in the Book of Acts. There Satan, through the Jews, attempted to sweep away the Church in a flood (see Acts 8:1; 21:30).

In those days of persecution, the Church's rescue came from the Romans (see Acts 21:31–32). The **two wings** of the Roman **eagle** enabled the Church to find its providential security. With these two wings, she was enabled to fly away and find peace so that all attempted Jewish plots eventually came to grief against the impartial and world-famous justice of the Roman legions. The dragon still did not give up, however. He **went away to make war with the rest**

of her seed—warring against the Church in the succeeding days to come. The progress of that war is revealed in the following chapters, as St. John is shown the rise of the beast.

ॐ ॐ ॐ ॐ ॐ

18 And he stood upon the sand of the sea.

13 1 And I saw a beast coming up from the sea, having ten horns and seven heads, and upon its horns *were* ten diadems, and upon its heads *were* names of blasphemy.
2 And the beast which I saw was like a leopard, and its feet *were* as a bear, and its mouth as the mouth of a lion. And the dragon gave it his power and his throne and great authority.

The connective sentence in 12:18, **And he stood upon the sand of the sea**, indicates that the events of chapter 13 follow in chronological sequence from those of chapter 12. The persecution by the beast follows the prior persecution by the dragon and represents a further phase of his ongoing war against the Church.

The dragon had been unable to devour the woman's Son, and had been foiled in his pursuit of the Woman herself. He is now intent on "making war with the rest of her seed" (12:17), the Christians. (Note that Christians are called "the rest of the Woman's seed": the devil's hatred of the Church is thus an extension of his hatred for Christ.) The dragon had been unable to kill the Church through Jewish persecution in the first days of the Church's life. He now tries something else.

The dragon therefore stands upon the sand of the sea, as if summoning up a new monster from its depths. John sees the result—a **beast coming up from the sea**. This beast was such as was never before seen on earth. It had **ten horns and seven heads** and **upon its horns *were* ten diadems, and upon its heads *were* names of blasphemy**. Moreover, it was not as the other beasts or animals of the earth, but was a supernatural and freakish amalgam of them. It was **like a leopard**, but **its feet *were* as a bear** and **its mouth as the mouth of a lion**. It was the dragon's masterpiece, and he **gave it his power and his throne and great authority** to carry out his will.

What is this beast? It is the Roman state at the time the Apocalypse was written, arising like a great Leviathan **from the sea**, drawing its strength from the waters of chaos, from "peoples, crowds, nations, and tongues" (17:15). (The sea for the Jews was always a place of restlessness, and therefore of evil, a remnant in creation of the primeval chaos.)

The image of the beast is drawn from Daniel 7. In those visions, Daniel saw four beasts arising to terrorize the earth. First came the three beasts/empires of his day: the Babylonian "lion," the Median "bear," and the Persian "leopard." Then came the nameless "fourth beast" with "ten horns," a symbol of the Greek Empire, out of which arose the Syrian power of Antiochus Epiphanes, "the little horn."

In the vision St. John sees, the beast symbolizing the Roman Empire is a composite, drawing images and power from all that have gone before it. It is **like a leopard** for swiftness in hunting its prey, but **its feet *were* as a bear** for crushing strength, and **its mouth** was **as the mouth of a lion**, able to roar after its prey with hungry ferocity.

Also, it has **seven heads** and **ten horns**. As with the image of the dragon in 12:3, the **seven heads** symbolize the seven hills of Rome and also the emperors who ruled from there, and the **ten horns** symbolize the many nations of the Empire itself. The **diadems** are now **upon** the ten **horns.** Formerly the crowns were upon the heads (12:3), as persecution was carried out from the seven hills of Rome (a reference to the local persecution in Rome under Nero). Now, however, the crowns are upon the ten horns, as the nations have received royal authority (17:12) to carry out the universal work of persecution.

The **seven heads** are not unadorned, however—upon them were **names of blasphemy**. These were the divine honors blasphemously claimed by the emperors. Augustus was proclaimed divine at his death; Nero was hailed as "Savior of the World" on his coins. Caligula demanded that everyone do homage to his image. All of these were bad enough. But the godless self-deification escalated with the Emperor Domitian, the ruler at the time the Apocalypse was written. He was addressed as "our Lord and God," and failure to worship him was, for the first time, a punishable offense.

The **dragon**, Satan, **gave** to this Roman beast **his power, throne, and great authority**. That is, the devil gave to the formerly beneficent Roman state all his energy and will to persecute. In the Church's struggle with demonic Jewish persecution up to that time, Rome had been a source of law, order, and rescue. Henceforth, Rome would be the instrument of Satanic will.

> ꙮ ꙮ ꙮ ꙮ ꙮ
>
> 3 I saw one of its heads as *if it had been* slaughtered to the death, and its death blow was healed. And the whole earth marveled *and followed* after the beast;
> 4 they worshipped the dragon because he gave *his* authority to the beast; and they worshipped the beast, saying, "Who *is* like the beast, and who is able to war with it?"

In his vision, John **saw one of its heads as *if it had been* slaughtered to the death**. One of its emperors was given, as it were, **a death blow**, a fatal wound. After its apparently miraculous recovery, **the whole earth marveled *and followed* after the beast**, in complete and submissive loyalty. From the miraculous healing, they concluded that the beast was truly invincible, and **they worshipped the dragon**. That is, **they worshipped the beast**, and *in so doing*, worshipped the dragon, for the dragon was inspirer of the beast, the one who **gave** it **his authority** and ruled through it. All the world was united in their adoration of the devil, bound together by the emperor cult. With fervent devotion, and in idolatrous parody of devotion to the true God (compare Ps. 71:19), they cried out, **"Who *is* like the beast?"** The beast had no rival on the earth. **"Who is able to war with it** and prevail?" No one. The beast was apparently invincible and worthy of worship. The Roman Empire indeed seemed

IV. The End of All Things   Revelation 13:5–8

unstoppable, the masters of the world, as they themselves proclaimed. The worship of the beast was, in fact, the worship of brute force.

The vision of the beast recovering from a fatal wound and rising from the dead echoes a myth then current about Nero. There was a fear and a rumor that the great persecutor who took his own life was not truly and finally dead, but would return from Parthia with an army to regain his lost dominion. Though the beast is not identified here with Nero, that fear forms part of the background. The beast, in a kind of demonic parody of Christ the slaughtered Lamb (v. 8), himself had been **slaughtered to the death,** and "yet came to life" (v. 14). Like a Nero risen from the dead, it was the embodiment of the worst and most impossible of fears.

> ༂ ༂ ༂ ༂ ༂
>
> 5 There was given to it a mouth saying great *things* and blasphemies, and authority was given to it to act *for* forty-two months.
> 6 And it opened its mouth in blasphemies against God, to blaspheme His Name and His tabernacle, *that is*, those who tabernacle in heaven.
> 7 It was also given to it to make war with the saints and to conquer them, and authority over every tribe and people and tongue and nation was given to it.
> 8 All who dwell upon the earth will worship it, whose name has not been written from the foundation of the world in the book of life of the Lamb who has been slaughtered.

The beast was **given** certain liberties by God. Though verse 2 says *the dragon* gave the beast his own "power and throne and authority," the passive **was given** here in verses 5–7 refers to *God* as the Giver. The phrase "was given" is used extensively throughout the Apocalypse to express the concept that events occur only because God allows them to. God remains sovereign upon His Throne, and all events serve *His* purposes. The beast was given **a mouth saying**

great *things* and blasphemies. This hearkens back to Daniel 7:8, where Antiochus Epiphanes blasphemes against God, claiming divine honors. Like the "little horn" of old, the Roman beast also speaks arrogantly against God and makes grandiose and blasphemous claims (see 13:1 and comments).

The beast is also given **authority to act *for* forty-two months**, and to further those claims by persecution. The duration of the persecution is set by God (as are all events in history). It could act for **forty-two months**, but no more. (The duration is once again a symbol for the short but savage time of persecution; see 11:2 and comments.)

Accordingly, **it opened its mouth in blasphemies against God** (unaware that its power came only because God allowed it), **to blaspheme His Name and His tabernacle**. John adds the explanation that by **His tabernacle** (Gr. *skene*) is meant **those who tabernacle** (Gr. *skenoo*) **in heaven**, the saints and martyrs there.

Reference to God's **tabernacle** or tent hearkens back to the place built by Moses according to God's instructions (Ex. 26f), so that God could dwell among His people. Here it refers to God's dwelling in heaven. Before, during the time of the Law, God dwelt in an earthly tent or tabernacle of curtains. Now He dwells in His people, the Christians. By identifying the Christians in heaven, the glorified saints and martyrs, as God's **tabernacle**, John shows their true dignity. The Christians persecuted by Rome were not criminals—they were the dwelling-place of the God of heaven. The Roman emperor's reviling and persecution of them were therefore all the more terrible.

But persecute them he did. He proceeded **to make war with the saints and to conquer them**, decimating the Church and shedding the blood of countless martyrs. The Church lost battle after battle as Rome seemed victorious. But this was not because God had abandoned His people. It was not evidence of Rome's strength, but of God's permissive decree. They could only succeed against the Christians because they were **given** this by God for the time being.

For now, though, it seemed their triumphs would go on forever, and **authority over every tribe and people and tongue and nation** was given to the beast. The beast's power spread over all, and it

IV. The End of All Things   Revelation 13:9–10

seemed as if there was nowhere the Christians could go to avoid the conflict. And **all who dwell upon the earth** were taken in by this display of brute force—at least all **whose name had not been written in the book of life of the Lamb**. Those not enrolled by God as His favored ones, His chosen people, would be deceived and would enthusiastically **worship** the beast, taking part in the emperor cult.

The image of **the book of life** is from the Old Testament (see Ex. 32:32, where Moses prays concerning being "blotted out of Your book") and has its roots in the ancient custom of kings keeping a register of favored persons, a kind of "roll of honor" (see Esther 6:1). The King of heaven is portrayed as also having a register of His own faithful and favored ones. To be enrolled in this book is thus to be one of God's friends, and the Lamb's **book of life** is the list of the true saints of Christ who will share in the life of the age to come. The Christians' names are said to have been written in this book **from the foundation of the world**, for John wants to show the eternal dimension of the struggle against the emperor cult. God had foreknown their decisions to serve Christ before the Roman Empire ever came into existence—let them not throw away such a salvation now by worshipping the emperor.

---

9   If anyone has an ear, let him hear!
10 If anyone *is destined* for captivity, to captivity he goes; if anyone is to be killed with the sword, with the sword he *must* be killed. Here is the perseverance and the faith of the saints.

Then follows an appeal to heed this warning of future persecution, recalling the words of Christ which He used during His ministry to urge men to hearken with their hearts: **if anyone has an ear, let him hear!** (see Matt. 11:15). And this is the message he must hear: **If anyone *is destined* for captivity, to captivity he goes; if anyone is to be killed with the sword, with the sword he *must* be killed**. The couplet is based on Jeremiah 15:2, and it stresses the inevitably of the coming contest. One cannot avoid **captivity** and suffering if it is God's appointed will. Thus **the saints** must show **perseverance and faith**.

There is some uncertainty about the second half of the couplet. Rather than the reading "if anyone *is to be killed* with the sword," some manuscripts read, "if anyone *kills* with the sword." If this latter reading is the correct one, the thought will then be that God will judge those who persecute the Church. Either way, the Church is called to endure the coming trial, confident in the final triumph of God.

> ### ❦ EXCURSUS
> #### On the Transformation of Rome and the Rise of the Beast
>
> Rome is the ally of the Church in the early parts of the New Testament. Though no Christian was a great lover of the Roman Empire (Rome was pagan, after all), yet the Christians knew it brought a stability and peace that aided them in spreading the Gospel. St. Paul writes that the existing Roman powers were established by God and to resist them is to resist God (Rom. 13:1–5). Paul could even say then that "rulers are not a cause of fear to good conduct, but to the wicked" (Rom. 13:3). The Christians therefore were to pray for "kings and all the ones in prominence" (2 Tim. 2:1–2). In fact, St. Paul had more than once been rescued by Roman might from unjust persecution (Acts 21:32; 23:18f). He could confidently appeal to Caesar, knowing he would receive a fair and just hearing (Acts 25:11).
>
> St. Peter too (1 Pet. 2:13–17) tells the Church to obey the Roman power, "being submissive, for the Lord's sake, to the king or to governors as sent by him." They are told to fear God and honor the King. For "who is there to harm you if you are zealous for what is right?" (1 Pet. 3:13). This represents an early attitude to Rome, when she was the helper and ally of the Church. At this point, in terms of

IV. The End of All Things   Revelation 13:11–15

Apocalyptic imagery, the earth was still helping the woman (Rev. 12:16), and the Christians in their trouble could turn to Rome for rescue in the same way citizens in trouble today look for help from the police.

But there soon came a transformation, and with the growth and enforcement of the cult of emperor worship, the Roman state was no longer friend, but foe. She was no longer a beneficent power, but a ravening beast—brutal, irrational, deadly. The unthinkable had happened, and the far-famed justice of Rome had turned to injustice and oppression. It is this stage of Rome's dreadful metamorphosis that is reflected here in the Apocalypse. The Christians now had to make a sudden and inward paradigm shift regarding the state, and the Apocalypse urgently invites them to make that shift.

༄ ༄ ༄ ༄ ༄

11 And I saw another beast rising up from the earth; and it had two horns like a lamb and spoke as a dragon.
12 It exercises all the authority of the first beast before its *presence*. And it makes the earth and those who dwell in it to worship the first beast, whose death blow was healed.
13 It does great signs, so that it even makes fire come down from heaven to the earth before *the presence of* men.
14 And it deceives those who dwell upon the earth because of the signs which it was given it to do before *the presence of* the beast, telling those who dwell upon the earth to make an image to the beast who had the blow of the sword and *yet* came to life.
15 And it was given to it to give breath to the image of the beast, that the image of the beast

145

> would even speak and make as many as do not worship the image of the beast to be killed.

As St. John looked, he **saw another beast**. As the first beast arose like Leviathan from the sea, so this beast rose just as supernaturally **from the earth**. That is, if the first beast had an international origin (as the sea is international), so this beast was more local. In fact, the cult of emperor worship had its stronghold in local Asia Minor.

This second beast **had two horns like a lamb**, but it did not act like a lamb. It acted and **spoke as a dragon**, raging and threatening like the monster it was. It **exercised all the authority of the first beast before its *presence***, functioning as its deputy, and compelling the earth and its inhabitants to **worship the first beast**. This second beast did **great signs** and miracles, **so that it even makes fire come down from heaven to the earth**.

Who was this second beast? As suggested above, it was the religious priesthood responsible for enforcing emperor worship. Elsewhere in the Apocalypse it is called "the false prophet" (16:13; 19:20). As a false prophet, it of course disguises itself, appearing **like a lamb.** For the Lord warned that false prophets would come in sheep's clothing (Matt. 7:15). Like supernaturally demonic false prophets, it even performs lying "signs and false wonders" (compare 2 Thess. 2:9), bringing **fire from heaven**, aping the true wonders of Elijah.

Foremost among these demonic miracles was the bringing to life of a statue of the emperor, so **that the image would even speak**. The roots of this are deep in the Old Testament. The self-deifying Nebuchadnezzar had an image of himself constructed, and he commanded all to worship it, on pain of death (Daniel 2). There was a mystical and intimate connection between the gods and their statues, so much so that the statues were held by some even to eat (see Bel and the Dragon v. 6). The ancients thought of statues coming to life as one of the great proofs of power and divinity. Simon Magus was widely reputed to have brought a statue to life, and others in ancient times who pretended to divinity were said to do this. This Satanic miracle, with its roots deep in the ancient psyche, is the crowning wonder of the false prophet, and the means whereby he compelled the worship of the emperor. If any (such as the Christians) would refuse to worship, the bestial false prophet would have him **killed**.

What is the fulfillment of this in history? Certainly the pagan priesthoods enforced emperor worship in St. John's day, compelling all, on pain of death, to worship the emperor's image. But there is no record of them performing demonic miracles, such as bringing the statue to life. It would seem here that this detail borrows from St. Paul's description of the final Antichrist in 2 Thessalonians 2:9–10, where the coming of the lawless one "will be according to the working of Satan, with all power and signs and false wonders and with all the deceit of unrighteousness." The false prophet is painted with such lurid colors as these to show the truly demonic nature of the cult. The vision also leaves room for an extension of the miraculous in the final days before the Lord's Coming.

> ༄ ༄ ༄ ༄ ༄
>
> 16 And it makes all, the little and the great, and the rich and the poor, and the free and the slaves, to be given a brand upon their right hand or upon their forehead,
> 17 that no one will be able to buy or to sell, except the one having the brand, either the name of the beast or the number of its name.

The second beast enforced something else upon the general population—it required all people, without exception, to **be given a brand upon their right hand or upon their forehead**. The word rendered here *brand* is the Greek *charagma*, which can mean any mark that is engraved or imprinted. It is used for stamps on documents and impressions on coins. It is also used for brands on horses, and that seems to be its meaning here. As slaves were sometimes branded, so it is with the people living under the beast. The beast would make them its slaves, and without this brand no one was able to buy or sell. Integration into society and life itself within it depended on capitulation to the beast and receiving the brand, **either the name of the beast or the number of its name**.

The origin of this vivid image of spiritual conformity to the world is perhaps found in the practice of tattooing in the ancient world. Religious tattooing was especially common, as devotees would often brand themselves to show their devotion to their deity. (This is reflected in Isaiah 44:5, where the faithful will write "Belonging to Yahweh" on their hand.) It is this widespread practice that forms the basis for the mark or brand of the beast, described here with classic apocalyptic imagery.

In interpreting the meaning of this brand, reference must be made to similar marks in the Apocalypse. All those who worshipped the beast received its mark on their hand or upon their forehead. But others in the Apocalypse received marks upon their foreheads too: Christ will write upon the faithful the Name of His God, and the name of the city of His God, and His own new Name (3:12). In the beginning of the next chapter, the one hundred and forty-four thousand have Christ's Name and the Father's Name written upon their foreheads (14:1). Like these marks, it would seem that this mark or brand of the beast finds its fulfillment in a *spiritual* mark, not a literal one. There is no reason for thinking the godless will receive a literal tattoo of sorts, any more than for thinking that Christians will literally have the Name of Christ, His Father, the new Jerusalem, and Christ's new Name written on *their* foreheads.

In describing how the beast will brand the population with its own mark, John shows how the beast will give to its followers a mark that identifies them as belonging to it. By all they do (the brand **upon their right hand**) and all they think (the brand **upon their forehead**), they proclaim to the world that they belong to the beast. Without this spiritual compromise and act of loyalty to the Roman beast, one will simply not be able to survive and cope in society, or even be able **to buy or sell** with one's neighbors. The Christians were thus not able to assimilate themselves to pagan society, for such conformity, predicated on spiritual betrayal of Christ, was impossible for them.

IV. The End of All Things Revelation 13:18

> ৯৮ ৯৮ ৯৮ ৯৮ ৯৮
> 18 Here is wisdom. Let him having understanding count the number of the beast, for the number is that of a man; and its number is six hundred and sixty-six.

St. John now identifies the beast, as clearly as is possible, given the difficulties and the risks involved in denouncing the beast directly. He calls for **wisdom** and says that the one **having understanding** of such matters should **count the number of the beast** to identify which **man** is meant. **Its number is six hundred and sixty-six.**

The method of using numbers to indicate a name is called *gematria*, and it was quite common in the ancient world. (Indeed, in the graffiti found in Pompeii, archaeologists have uncovered one saying, "I love her whose number is 545.") It is here used because it was too dangerous to name the emperor himself, clearly and plainly, as the beast and enemy of God.

In like manner, St. Paul, in writing to the Thessalonians, shrinks from clearly saying, "The emperor and his empire is that which hinders the final revelation of the man of lawlessness. The emperor must be removed before this can happen." To write so clearly about the "removal" of the emperor would be to risk a charge of treason. Instead, he says in a roundabout way, "Do you not remember that while I was yet with you, I said these things to you? You know what holds [the Antichrist] back now [viz. the Roman Empire]. . . . He who presently holds him back [viz. the presence of the emperor] will do so until he is taken out of the way" (2 Thess. 2:5–7). Paul writes in such an elusive way so as to be understood by the faithful, but not by others.

It is the same here. The practice of *gematria* (whereby one adds up the numerical equivalents of a word and substitutes the number for the name) serves as a cover for the faithful. The Church is meant to understand the riddle, whereas the hostile pagan world will not.

The number is **the number of a man**, that is, of a specific individual. But which one? Many guesses have been made. St. Irenaeus made several, including "LATEINOS," "the Latin one." I would suggest that the Emperor Domitian himself is indicated, the emperor who exiled St. John and began the persecution in earnest. His full Latin title was, in Greek, "AUTOKRATOR KAISAR DOMETIANOS SEBASTOS GERMANIKOS." These various titles were abbreviated on the coins of that day as "A. KAI. DOMET. SEB. GE." The numerical equivalents of this add up to 666 as follows:

A	=	1
K	=	20
A	=	1
I	=	10
D	=	4
O	=	70
M	=	40
E	=	5
T	=	300
S	=	200
E	=	5
B	=	2
G	=	3
E	=	5
		666

Thus, safely hidden from hostile Roman understanding, St. John was being told that the emperor was the beast, the instrument of the devil, blaspheming against the true God and those in heaven, and that to offer him the worship he commanded was to apostatize from Christ.

Domitian as an historical figure has long been dead, so it must be asked what significance this can have for us today. It is true that

Domitian—and all the Roman emperors—have long since perished. But the Apocalypse was not warning merely about Domitian *as an individual*, but about Domitian *as an eternal principle*. In identifying the Roman emperor of his day as the beast from the abyss, St. John warns Christians of all generations of the brutal power of the godless state. And though Domitian is gone, the threat from the godless state remains, whether that state be Roman, Turkish, Soviet, Chinese—or American. The state, previously beneficent, had in John's day lately become brutal, and began a persecution of the Church which would long continue. Persecution from the world remains the standard and usual experience of the Christian. In this world, we have tribulation, for if the world hated Christ, it will also hate us (John 15:19–20; 16:33). In revealing the conflict of the Church with the Roman beast, the Apocalypse steels us for that conflict throughout the age.

❦ EXCURSUS
On the Beast of the Apocalypse and the Final Antichrist

The term "Antichrist" does not in fact occur in the Apocalypse. It is drawn from the Epistles of St. John (1 John 2:18; 4:3; 2 John 7) and refers to certain heretical movements of his day, such as the so-called "Docetists"—teachers who denied the reality of the Incarnation and said that Jesus only "seemed" (Gr. *dokeo*) to have a real body. Heretical teachers were deemed by John "antichrists," for they offered a rival Christ, one different from the Christ proclaimed by the apostles and ultimately opposed to Him.

The concept of the final and personal Antichrist, the individual who will arise at the End to deceive the world and persecute the Church, is found in St. Paul's second Epistle to the Thessalonians. He writes there of "the man of lawlessness" who would come at the end of the age with all the power of Satan, and do signs and false wonders (2 Thess.

3—4; 6—10). Paul said that he had given them this teaching before, when he was with them (2 Thess. 2:5). Thus, it is a part of the apostolic deposit of the Faith, and Christians have always expected a final arch-persecutor to arise as part of the climactic events heralding the End.

The Apocalypse deals directly with neither of these two themes. Though it warns of heretical movements (such as the Nicolaitans), its main focus is not the threat of heresy. Neither is its main focus the final Antichrist, the man of lawlessness, a single individual whose rise will be a precursor of the End.

What the Apocalypse *does* focus on directly is persecution by the state, a persecution that would begin soon and continue until the end of the age. This is apparent from an examination of 17:10–11 and 19:11f: the chronology of chapter 17 anchors the persecution of the beast in the first century, while the culmination and deliverance from this persecution comes with the Second Coming, described in chapter 19. Thus, the persecution of the beast in some way spans the age. As we have suggested, though the beast manifested itself in St. John's day through the Roman emperor, its persecution and rage can be felt whenever the state usurps the place of God and wars upon God's Church. The beast was in this way bigger than the historical Roman Empire and would outlive it, for state persecution of the Church did not cease with the historical fall of Rome.

St. John does, however, make the rise of the beast a sign of the final days, of the time after great signs and wonders would be seen in the heavens as precursors of the End (6:12f; compare Luke 21:25f), and he sets the stage for the contest with the Roman beast against that background. This is because the Church had been warned that the final man of lawlessness would arise at the End (2 Thess. 2:3f). For John, that last hour had come (1 John 2:18) and was even then casting its long eschatological shadows over the conflicts of

IV. The End of All Things   Revelation 14:1–5

his day. That is, St. John invites his contemporary readers to see in their first-century conflict the same moral urgency that would characterize the conflict with the final man of lawlessness. The final eschatological conflict had begun, whether or no this or that emperor was the final Antichrist. For the suffering Christians, the struggle was one and the same, whether one faced the beast in the first century or the Antichrist at the End.

There are, therefore, two ways of viewing the Apocalypse. One way is to view it as being primarily about the struggle of the state with the Church throughout this age, and to see the final struggle with the Antichrist at the End as the culmination of this. Another way is to see the struggle portrayed in the Apocalypse as the final one against the Antichrist and then to project it back in time, so that the persecutions St. John's churches were to undergo were seen as the foretaste and prelude to this eschatological climax. Both ways are valid, and both produce the same result. Like all apocalyptic writers, St. John was less interested in historical chronology and fulfillment than he was in the persevering courage of those who would have to endure the eschatological struggle that was then beginning.

༄ ༄ ༄ ༄ ༄

14 1 Then I looked, and behold! the Lamb standing upon Mount Zion, and with Him one hundred and forty-four thousand, having His Name and the Name of His Father written upon their foreheads.
2 And I heard a sound from heaven, as a sound of many waters and a sound of great thunder, and the sound which I heard *was* as harpers harping on their harps.

> 3 And they sing a new song before the throne and before the four living *things* and the elders; and no one was able to learn the song except the one hundred and forty-four thousand who had been bought from the earth.
> 4 These are the ones who have not been defiled with women, for they are virgins. These are the ones who follow the Lamb wherever He goes. These have been bought from *among* men *as* first fruits to God and to the Lamb.
> 5 And a lie was not found in their mouth; they are blameless.

As the counterpoint to the slaves of the beast prostrate in worship before it with its name and number written upon their foreheads, John sees **the Lamb standing upon** the heavenly **Mount Zion** (compare Heb. 12:22f) with His own mustered army of **one hundred and forty-four thousand, having His Name and the Name of His Father written upon their foreheads**. God sealed them on their foreheads (7:3; 9:4) and this seal, consisting of the Name of the Father and the Son, protected them from spiritual defeat at the hands of the beast. (We note in passing John's customary pairing of the Father and the Son; see 1 John 1:2–3; 2:22–23; 4:13; 2 John 3, 9.)

This vision echoes the prophecy of 2 Esdras 2:42–48: "I saw on Mount Zion a great multitude that I could not number, and they all were praising the Lord with songs. In their midst stood a young Man of great stature, and on the head of each of them He placed a crown. ... He is the Son of God whom they confessed in the world." After the vision of the beast boasting of its invincibility, St. John sees the hosts that are *truly* victorious—the army of the martyrs in heaven.

This heavenly location is called **Mount Zion** in order to show the futility of the world's resistance to the coming reign of Christ. In Psalm 2:6–9 (LXX), Messiah says, "I was established as King by God on Zion, His holy mountain. ... The Lord said to Me, 'You are My Son. ... You will shatter the nations like a potter's vessel.'" The reference to heaven as the heavenly Mount Zion is a promise

IV. The End of All Things   Revelation 14:1–5

of ultimate victory. On Mount Zion those who are saved will be gathered (Joel 2:32 LXX).

The roar of acclaim for the beast on earth had been impressive, as every tribe and people and tongue and nation worshipped it, exclaiming, "Who is like the beast and who is able to war with it?" (13:4, 7). Here was a mightier roar of acclaim, **a sound from heaven as a sound of many waters**, a deafening cataract of jubilation, **a sound of great thunder**, filling the ears and swelling the heart. It was a sound like **harpers harping on their harps**, an overwhelming outpouring of praise. The army of the Lamb **sing a new song before the throne and before the four living *things* and the elders**, standing before the inner court of heaven, boldly approaching the unapproachable God.

Their gift of praise was the new song. In the Psalter, David often exhorts his hearers to "sing to Yahweh a new song" (Ps. 96:1; 98:1; 144:9). In its Old Testament context, this meant a song commemorating the new and recent victories given by Yahweh, when He rescued His people from their foes. In its apocalyptic context, it is a song praising God for giving His martyrs victory over the beast. Through the strength God provided, they had kept their faith and conquered the world (compare 1 John 5:4). Though pitied by the apostate world as pathetically deluded and wretched, they were actually the privileged ones. The new song that was theirs to sing could be sung by no one else—**no one was able to learn** that **song except** them. Separation from the world and suffering for the Lamb, who by His Blood had bought them from the earth for God (5:9), qualified them to sing that song before the Presence of the Throne of heaven.

Their separation from the world and their faith are further described, so that the readers may follow their example. They are described as **the ones who have not been defiled with women, for they are virgins** (Gr. *parthenoi*). This does not mean they were celibates. Rather it means they retained their spiritual purity of devotion to Christ, which kept them from fornication and the sexual immorality that was the way of the world (compare the sexual laxity of the Nicolaitans in 2:14, 20).

Also, they **follow the Lamb wherever He goes**, following in His footsteps, being faithful witnesses even unto death. St. Peter called the Church to such suffering, saying that Christ suffered, leaving us an example so we could follow in His steps (1 Pet. 2:21). These have followed in those steps, having been **bought from *among* men *as* first fruits to God and to the Lamb**. In their suffering and deaths, these martyrs offered themselves as holy sacrifices upon the altar of their confession.

Furthermore, they are **blameless** in that **a lie was not found in their mouth**. The **lie** referred to is the lie of idolatry. (Compare Is. 44:20: The idolater does not say to himself, "Is there not a lie in my right hand?" St. Paul also uses this customary Jewish term for idolatry in Rom. 1:25.) The idolatry denounced here is that of emperor worship and the worship of other pagan gods. These martyrs will have nothing to do with such lies, being true followers of Jesus Christ, the Truth.

❦ EXCURSUS
On the Apocalyptic Church as Martyric

In this passage as in others in the Apocalypse, it seems to be supposed that all in the Church will be martyrs. The two witnesses image the Church in chapter 11, and they are martyrs. It is explicitly stated in chapter 13 that all the world must worship the beast and those who refuse will be killed. This seems to say that every Christian must therefore be killed and that only those who apostatize will survive. Yet we know that *some* will be alive at the Second Coming to be caught up to meet the Lord in the air (1 Thess. 4:17). Is it really the case that the Book of Revelation says all Christians will be martyred? Or, to put it another way, that only the martyrs are the true Christians?

There is a difference between being martyric and being an actual martyr. An actual martyr is someone who is physically killed for his faith in Jesus Christ. But the Church can be *martyric* without being actually martyred, in that the

Church is always *ready for martyrdom*. It suffers persecution and confesses Christ, and its members are prepared to pay the final penalty and lay down their lives for Him. Whether or not they actually do so depends on the circumstances. Oftentimes in the past, Christians have been tortured and imprisoned and have awaited execution, only to be unexpectedly released as political circumstances changed. The Church has always considered these Christians to be true confessors and (in this sense) martyrs.

The Apocalypse was written for a Church that daily would face the threat of martyrdom. It was written to steel them for this task and to encourage them to persevere in confessing the Faith. Martyrdom is presupposed throughout, if only because it was always a real possibility for them all. In those days (as in ours), the Church is called to be martyric as the price of true devotion to the Lord.

---

6 And I saw another angel flying in mid-heaven, having an eternal Gospel to preach to those sitting upon the earth, even to every nation and tribe and tongue and people;

7 and he said with a loud voice, "Fear God, and give Him glory, for the hour of His judgment has come; worship Him who made the heaven and the earth and sea and fountains of waters."

After the vision of Christ and His mustered army on Mount Zion, St. John sees a vision of three angels flying past, soaring **in mid-heaven**, where they can be seen by all the earth. The messages are all urgent, since the time for the final outpouring of wrath has come. Each angel has a different message, and together they constitute God's call to those who dwell on the earth in the final days.

The first **angel** cries out, calling the world to repentance. Echoing the Church's message of the **eternal Gospel**, he **preaches** (Gr. *euaggelizo*, "to preach the Gospel") to those who were **sitting upon the earth**. The verb *sitting* (Gr. *kathemai*) is used deliberately. It is not just used as a synonym for "dwelling," but has the flavor of one sitting down in despair, "sitting in darkness and the shadow of death" (Luke 1:79). These pagans are urged to cast aside their idols and only **worship Him who made the heaven and the earth and sea and fountains of waters**. They are to **fear** the living **God** of Israel and **give Him glory**. The **hour of judgment had come**, and this was the last chance for repentance and salvation.

> ॐ ॐ ॐ ॐ ॐ
>
> 8 And another angel, a second one, followed, saying, "Fallen, fallen is Babylon the Great, she who has made all the nations drink of the wine of the indignation of her fornication."

The second angel followed hard on the heels of the first, for his message also was urgent. He calls out that **Babylon the Great**, mighty Rome (see 1 Pet. 5:13 for "Babylon" as a code name for Rome), has completely **fallen**. The greatness of its fall is expressed in the double use of the word **fallen, fallen**, and echoes a similar announcement concerning ancient Babylon in Isaiah 21:9. The Roman Babylon of John's day had **made all the nations drink of the wine of the indignation of her fornication**, but the hour of judgment for such sins had come at last. Why should those who sit upon the earth persist in loyalty to her and her sins when judgment was at hand?

The phrase *the wine of the indignation of her fornication* is an unusual one. In 17:2 it is said that Rome made those who dwell upon the earth drunk with "the wine of her fornication." This has obvious echoes of the denunciation of Babylon of old in Jeremiah 51:7 ("Babylon has been a golden cup, intoxicating all the earth; the nations have drunk of her wine") and of the denunciation of Israel in Ezekiel 23:5f (Israel "played the harlot; she lusted after her

IV. The End of All Things   Revelation 14:9–11

lovers, after the Assyrians and her neighbors"). The thought in 17:2 is of the nations committing spiritual fornication with Rome by participating in her sins. What is unusual here is the description of the wine as that of **the indignation** (Gr. *thumos*; compare its use in Rom. 2:8) **of her fornication**. The thought is that this fornication leads to the **indignation** and wrath of God. The wine offered by Babylon is heady and may seem to lead to the joy of intoxication and pleasure, but it finally leads to divine wrath.

> 9 And another angel, a third one, followed them, saying with a great voice, "If anyone worships the beast and its image, and receives a brand upon his forehead or upon his hand,
> 10 "he *himself* also will drink of the wine of the indignation of God, which is mixed undiluted in the cup of His wrath; and he will be tormented with fire and sulfur before *the presence* of the holy angels and before *the presence* of the Lamb.
> 11 "And the smoke of their torment goes up to ages of ages; they do not have rest day and night, those who worship the beast and its image, and whoever receives the stamp of its name."

The third angel also followed the first two angels, since his message was essentially the same as theirs. It too was a warning to the earth-dwellers: **If anyone worships the beast and its image**, thereby drinking of the wine of fornication (mentioned in v. 8), that same one (the *he* is emphatic in the Greek) **also will drink** another cup of wine—**the wine of the indignation** (Gr. *thumos*) **of God, which is mixed undiluted in the cup of His wrath**. If one drinks from one cup, he will also drink from the other.

The image of being judged as drinking a cup of wine is a very old and obvious one. Just as drinking too much wine from a cup causes one to stagger and fall, so one will also stagger and fall when the divine judgment strikes him down (see Ps. 75:8; Is. 51:17; Jer. 25:15–16).

If one did not worship the beast and its image, there were terrible consequences, for one would be put to death (13:15). But there were worse consequences if one *did* worship it. The pain of death that came from refusing to worship the beast would last but a moment. But the pain that came from worshipping the beast would last forever—for such a one would **be tormented with fire and sulfur** (i.e. with the fires of Gehenna) and **the smoke of** that **torment** would **go up to ages of ages**. The fire of God's wrath would be eternal and unquenchable (Mark 9:44), and they would **not have rest day and night**. This torment would be **before *the presence* of the holy angels and before *the presence* of the Lamb**. That is, those tormented would see the blessedness of heaven, but would not be able to partake of it; they would know that such joy was lost to them forever.

Some have quailed before these severe words (as the author intended), and have even suggested that such ferocity is unworthy of the Christian Faith, which proclaims a God of love. But this is to forget the Lord's words of judgment. It is the Lord who first told the Church that the fires of Gehenna were terrible and unquenchable (Mark 9:44); it was the Lord who spoke of a fire of judgment so painful that one would be in agony in the flame (Luke 16:24); it was Christ Himself who warned of the eternal furnace in which men would weep and gnash their teeth (Matt. 13:42). Such sentiments as we have here in the Apocalypse cannot be unworthy of the Christian Faith if they were first uttered by Christ.

Granted this, we must still ask ourselves why the horrors of Gehenna are described so vividly here. Is it just that the Christians, suffering from the Roman authorities, are consoling themselves with the thought of pain inflicted on their tormentors?

Such is not the case. It must be remembered that, although the messages of these three angels are addressed to *the world*, the Apocalypse in which they are found would be read by *Christians*. That is, the "target audience" for these warnings is not the pagan population, it is the Church. The intended message is not "look at how these

IV. The End of All Things   Revelation 14:12–13

tormenting pagans will one day suffer"; it is "look at how *you Christians* will suffer if you apostatize." It is meant as a Christian dissuasive to apostasy under torture, and that is how it was used. Christians about to undergo torture and martyrdom often steeled themselves against the possibility of apostasy by reminding themselves of the eternal punishment awaiting them if they denied their Lord.

> 🙰 🙰 🙰 🙰 🙰
>
> 12 Here is the perseverance of the saints who keep the commandments of God and the faith of Jesus.
> 13 And I heard a voice from heaven, saying, "Write, 'Blessed *are* the dead who die in the Lord from now *on*!'" "Yes," says the Spirit, "that they may rest from their labors, for their works follow with them."

These warnings St. John adds were a call to **the perseverance of the saints**; it was a challenge to endure, to **keep the commandments of God** (refusing idolatry), and to keep **the faith of Jesus**, clinging to the Faith that confessed His Name (compare 2:13, where Christ speaks of "My faith," i.e. the Faith regarding Him).

After these angelic messages from mid-heaven, John **heard a voice from heaven**, confirming them and promising heavenly rewards for those who would indeed persevere and keep the Faith. He was commanded to **write** the beatitude, **"Blessed *are* the dead who die in the Lord from now *on*!"** That is, the persecution brought with it the possibility of great blessing in the age to come. The Christians should not regard the Roman persecution as a catastrophe so much as the opportunity to acquire a greater reward. It was as the Lord had promised: "Blessed are you when they reproach you and persecute you; rejoice and be glad, for your reward is great in heaven" (Matt. 5:11–12).

After this **voice from heaven** had sounded, **the Spirit** added His promise also. He adds the assurance that the martyrs will **rest from their labors, for their works follow with them**. After their deeds of heroism, they will have their rest, serving God forever in His sanctuary, guided by the Good Shepherd to springs of the water of life (7:15f). Their works will not be forgotten but will have their eternal reward.

This special word from the Spirit recalls the earlier messages from the Spirit to the churches in chapters 2 and 3. In those chapters, John saw a vision of the glorified Christ speaking a word to each of the churches of Asia, and each of those messages was described as "what the Spirit says to the churches" (2:17, 11, etc.). That is, the Spirit within John enabled him to receive the words of Christ, so that what John was transmitting was true prophecy.

It is the same with the voice of the Spirit here. The Spirit does not speak to John as one of the characters in his vision. He is not one of the speaking *dramatis personae* of the visions, along with angels, elders, and living creatures. Rather, the Spirit speaks from within John, even as He "spoke through the prophets" of old (as the Creed says). Thus, St. John **heard a voice from heaven**, telling him to write down a message of God's blessing on the dead, and then **the Spirit** within him (who before enabled him to receive the vision of Christ in chapters 2 and 3) spoke within his heart, giving this confirming word about the dead receiving God's reward.

༄ ༄ ༄ ༄ ༄

14 And I looked, and behold! a white cloud, and sitting on the cloud was one like a son of man, having upon His head a golden crown, and a sharp sickle in His hand.

15 And another angel came out from the sanctuary, crying out with a great voice to the one sitting upon the cloud, "Send your sickle and harvest, for the hour to harvest has come, for the harvest of the earth is dried."

16 And the one sitting upon the cloud cast His sickle over the earth, and the earth was harvested.

IV. The End of All Things — Revelation 14:14–16

After the three angels, St. John continues to look and beholds visions of the final judgment. He sees **a white cloud**, and **sitting on the cloud one like a son of man**. The description of the one sitting as not just "a son of man" but **like a son of man** brings the reader back to Daniel 7:13.

In that passage, Daniel sees someone coming "with the clouds of heaven" who looked "like a son of man." The phrase "a son of man" originally meant simply "a human being" (its use in Ezek. 2:1). In the visions of Daniel 7, it was an image of the Kingdom of God, which was differentiated from all the pagan kingdoms that went before it. Those kingdoms were brutal, bestial, and fittingly symbolized by ravening beasts (the lion, the bear, and the leopard). In contrast, the coming Kingdom was humane, rational, and gentle, bearing the image of God as men do, and it meant that the Kingdom of God was as different from all the kingdoms that went before it as man is different from the beasts. Thus it was fittingly symbolized by a human being, "a son of man."

In time, the phrase "Son of Man" became a title for the Messiah, the One who brings in this final Kingdom. (This later development is reflected in the *Book of Enoch*.) The Lord Jesus used it as His favored messianic self-designation. The usage in this passage reflects this. Thus the One **like a son of man** is the Messiah, fulfilling the prophecy of Daniel, bringing in the Kingdom of God. He has **a golden crown**, the symbol of eternal sovereignty, and **a sharp sickle**, the symbol of God's judgment. He sits in heaven with sovereign authority, ready to judge.

In this vision, an angel **came out from the sanctuary**, as from the Presence of God, with the command to reap (that is, to judge), **for the harvest of the earth is dried** (i.e. ready for reaping). The Father's timing of the End is thus revealed, and the Son, in this as in all things, fulfills the will of the Father. (We are reminded of Christ's word that the time of the End was known to the Father alone; Mark 13:32.) The time to harvest the souls of men had come. The Son swung the sickle, and **the earth was harvested**. All the souls of men were reaped at the Second Coming and brought before the judgment of God.

The Judgment has often in the Scriptures been compared to the reaping of a harvest, for in the harvest, all the things that were sown before have finally come to maturity and are gathered and evaluated. Thus the Lord compared the Last Judgment to the final harvest in His parables (Matt. 13:39; Mark 4:29). Throughout this age, we have sown the seeds of our words, thoughts, and deeds. They grow up and mature throughout our life. At the end, we will see the final result and what kind of fruit they have borne (Mark 4:20).

> ❧ ❧ ❧ ❧ ❧
>
> 17 And another angel came out from the sanctuary in heaven, and he *himself* also had a sharp sickle.
> 18 And another angel, the one who has authority over the fire, came out from the altar; and he called with a great voice to him who had the sharp sickle, saying, "Send your sharp sickle and gather the clusters from the vine of the earth, because her grapes are ripe."
> 19 And the angel cast his sickle to the earth and gathered the vintage of the earth, and cast *it* into the great winepress of the indignation of God.
> 20 And the winepress was trodden outside the city, and blood came out from the wine press, up to the horses' bridles, for sixteen hundred stadia.

There is another aspect of this final judgment. The End did not merely mean that God would harvest and gather to Himself all the souls of men. It also meant that He would harvest all the deeds of men and all the wickedness of the earth. It is this aspect that is represented here.

Thus **another angel came out from the sanctuary in heaven,** and this angel **also had a sharp sickle,** for he also was involved in the final judgment. He stood ready to judge, and **another angel,**

IV. The End of All Things — Revelation 14:17–20

the one who **has authority over the fire** (that is, over the judgment of the earth; compare the fire of judgment in 8:5), **came out from the altar**. The saints under the heavenly altar had cried to God for vengeance, and here that vengeance was to be seen at last. This second angel **called with a great voice** (that is, with effective authority) to the first, saying, **"Send your sharp sickle and gather the clusters from the vine of the earth, because her grapes are ripe."** The vintage of the earth's wickedness had reached its full, and the time for divine judgment had come. At the time of the End, the evil of men will have reached its limit.

In response, the angel of judgment cast his sickle to the earth, wielding the sickle of judgment with power, and he gathered the vintage of the evil of the earth and **cast *it* into the great winepress of the indignation of God**. All the evil deeds done by the children of men come before the Face of God, and at the Second Coming will be avenged. The image of divine wrath as treading a winepress is drawn from Isaiah 63:1–6. Even as treading a winepress purples one's garments, so, it is said, will Yahweh make His garments purple with the blood of His adversaries. It is this image which is used here for the final Judgment. The blood of men will flow as God avenges their evil and their oppression on the helpless of the earth.

And what a flow of vengeance this will be! The resultant blood of men is said to be **trodden outside the city** of Jerusalem. It will be so plentiful as to come **up to the horses' bridles, for sixteen hundred stadia** (or about two hundred miles). That the winepress will be **trodden outside the city** means that this vengeance will come outside the safety and security of the Holy City. Those who spiritually dwell in the city of Jerusalem (that is, under God's protection) are preserved from such wrath.

For those with no such immunity as the living God will give to His people, the judgment will be full and overwhelming. The depth is said to be **up to the horses' bridles**. This image is found in other apocalyptic literature also, such as the Book of Enoch (100:3), where it is said that on the day of judgment, "the horse will walk up to the breast in the blood of sinners."

The distance mentioned is **sixteen hundred stadia**, the approximate length of the Land of Palestine. This is a way of saying that the wickedness of the earth is so great that the resultant flow will fill the length of the whole land. Thus the judgment will be of horrifying proportions.

---

15 1 And I saw another sign in heaven, great and marvelous, seven angels who had seven plagues, the last ones, because in them the indignation of God is finished.
2 And I saw as *it were* a glassy sea mixed with fire, and those who had conquered the beast and its image and the number of its name, standing on the glassy sea, having harps of God.
3 And they sing the song of Moses, slave of God, and the song of the Lamb, saying, "Great and marvelous *are* Your works, O Lord God, the Almighty; righteous and true *are* Your ways, King of the nations!
4 "Who will not fear, O Lord, and glorify Your Name? For *You* only *are* holy; for all the nations will come and worship before You, for Your righteous acts have been manifested."

In 12:1, St. John saw a great sign in heaven, and here he **saw another sign in heaven**, one that was **great and marvelous**, to make him gape and wonder: **seven angels who had seven plagues**. As God once threatened sinners with "plagues seven times according to their sins" (Lev. 26:21), so He would now plague the sinful earth. These were the **last** plagues, **because in them the indignation of God** was **finished**. They were, in fact, the seventh trumpet, the third and last woe.

As well as the seven angels with their seven bowls of wrath, he saw as *it were* a glassy sea mixed with fire, and those who had conquered the beast standing on it, having harps of God. This vision of triumph forms the background for the coming judgments, for it will come as divine vengeance for these martyric hosts.

The **glassy sea mixed with fire** is an image of the holiness of God, which separates sinful man from His holy Presence even as the sea separates one from another on earth (4:6). Here St. John sees the martyrs standing on the water, having drawn near to the very Throne of God, ready to hymn His wonders.

In saying that the martyrs have conquered the beast, we see a paradox typical of the Christian Faith. Christ's Cross is viewed by the world as His defeat, yet the Church proclaims it as His eternal victory. In the same way, the martyrs seemed to have been defeated by the beast who slew them, yet here it is proclaimed that they have **conquered** it.

The harps they have are the **harps of God**, for their song of victory comes from Him. And the song they sing to this divine accompaniment is **the song of Moses** and **the song of the Lamb**. The **song of Moses** is the hymn of triumph found in Exodus 15. Liberated from Egypt and victorious over Pharaoh's drowned hosts, the Israelites sing of Yahweh's power, by which He is glorified in the sight of the watching nations. This is the song the martyrs sing now to God, the **King of the nations**. For **who will not fear, O Lord, and glorify Your Name?** In the age to come, God's power will be acknowledged by all the earth, so that **all the nations will come and worship** before Him, bringing their glory into His City (21:24), for His **righteous acts** of outpoured judgment **have been manifested**.

This song of Moses is also called **the song of the Lamb**, for the martyrs' victory and triumph is from Him. They conquered the beast and its image, but only through their testimony and the Blood of the Lamb (12:11). Like Moses and the children of Israel, they stand in freedom, having been saved from the persecuting tyrant Pharaoh. But this freedom is through the Lamb, Jesus Christ. The song of freedom is His song.

§IV.3. The Seven Bowls: The Final Plagues of Judgment

> ꕤ ꕤ ꕤ ꕤ ꕤ
>
> 5 After these things I looked, and the sanctuary of the tabernacle of witness in heaven was opened,
> 6 and the seven angels who had the seven plagues came out from the sanctuary, clothed in linen, clean and bright, and girded around their breasts with golden belts.
> 7 And one of the four living *things* gave to the seven angels seven golden bowls full of the indignation of God, who lives to ages of ages.
> 8 And the sanctuary was filled with smoke from the glory of God and from His power; and no one was able to enter the sanctuary until the seven plagues of the seven angels were finished.

The outpouring of the final bowls is narrated with great drama. John looked and saw that the sanctuary of the tabernacle of witness had been opened. God was about to manifest His Presence in wrath upon the world. Out of that sanctuary came **the seven angels who had the seven plagues** (the seven bowls of wrath), and they were clothed as priests (**clothed in linen, clean and bright, and girded around their breasts with golden belts**; compare the priestly descriptions in Ezek. 9:2; 44:17; Dan. 10:5). As priests ministered to God and carried out His will, so these angels also carried out His will for judgment. **One of the four living *things*** (who had earlier invited judgment on the earth; 6:1f) now gave to the seven angels the bowls of God's wrath, to be poured out on the sons of men. Even as boiling water was poured out on the besieging enemy by those besieged, so heaven would pour out from its high battlements the wrath of God upon the world.

The heavenly **sanctuary was filled with smoke from the glory of God and from His power**. Even as the earthly sanctuary was once filled with the glory of God so that no one could enter there (2 Chr. 7:2), so God's heavenly sanctuary was filled with the **smoke** from the **glory** of His Presence (compare Is. 6:4, where the smoke of incense filling the Temple imaged the glory of God). This **glory** that shone forth and forbade entry was the majesty of God, who arose to judge all the nations (Ps. 82:8). One could no longer enter His sanctuary to make intercession for the world (see Jer. 7:16). Time had run out for the nations. The wrath of God had begun.

---

16 1 And I heard a great voice from the sanctuary, saying to the seven angels, "Go and pour out into the earth the seven bowls of the indignation of God."

St. John next **heard a great voice from the sanctuary** (the voice of God?) **saying to the seven angels** to **go** forth from the sanctuary where they stood and **pour out into the earth the seven bowls** they had been given (15:7), which were full of **the indignation of God**. This phrase about the **voice from the sanctuary** recalls a similar prophecy in Isaiah 66:6, in which the prophet heard "a voice from the sanctuary—the voice of the Lord rendering recompense to His enemies." This voice from the heavenly sanctuary is the signal for God to render recompense to all on earth who had defied Him and persecuted His people. Earlier the seventh trumpet and the third woe had been announced (in 11:14–15). Here that judgment comes to pass in the form of the seven bowls.

The Seven Bowls of the Final Wrath
In the vision of the seven bowls, we see the same artistic structuring and literary precedents as with the seven seals and the seven trumpets. The initial structure repeats that of the first four trumpets, in that the judgments are poured out successively upon the earth (8:7; 16:2), sea (8:8; 16:3), waters (8:10; 16:4), and heavens (8:12; 16:8).

The seven bowls also share with the seven trumpets the same literary precedents of the plagues of Egypt. As with that classic outpouring of wrath on the land of Pharaoh, so with this eschatological judgment. In Egypt, the waters turned to blood. So, in this outpouring, the sea became blood (16:3), as did the fountains of waters (16:4). In Egypt, boils and sores broke out upon man and beast (Ex. 9:10). So here, loathsome sores broke out upon those who had the mark of the beast. In Egypt, darkness fell over all the land (Ex. 10:22). So here, darkness fell upon the throne of the beast and his kingdom (16:10). In Egypt, hail fell upon the land (Ex. 9:25). So here, huge hail fell from heaven upon men (16:21). In Egypt, a swarm of frogs came up and invaded all. Even here, there are literary parallels, as from the mouths of the dragon, the beast, and the false prophet "unclean spirits like frogs" came forth (16:13). This tells us that God again judges the earth with power, as He did when He once liberated His people from the tyranny of Pharaoh. Pharaoh hardened his heart, and so judgment fell. Mankind also hardened its heart, refusing to repent at the preaching of the Church, making this judgment inevitable.

Further, we notice an escalation when the bowls are compared with trumpets. This is contained in the very name of the judgments themselves, for trumpets warn, but bowls of wrath (like bowls of boiling water poured out on the heads of besieging invaders) give no chance for repentance and surrender. Thus, the trumpets were unleashed typically upon "a third" of the world, but the bowls upon the totality. (Compare the judgment on the sea: with the trumpets, "a third" of the sea creatures died, 8:9; but with the bowls, "every living thing in the sea" died, 16:3.) This escalation is apparent in the timing of the bowls as compared with the trumpets. There was a brief delay between the fifth and sixth trumpets (9:12) and between the sixth and seventh trumpets (11:14). There is no such delay between any of the bowls. Indeed, those who are judged are still suffering the effects of the first bowl (sores; 16:2) when the fifth bowl strikes (darkness; 16:10–11).

Finally, we note that, as with all such apocalyptic details, one should not expect a one-to-one correspondence of vision to historical fulfillment with these bowls, any more than with the trumpets or seals. One cannot assert that this bowl finds specific and exhaustive fulfillment in that historical disaster. The bowls may find

IV. The End of All Things   Revelation 16:2–7

their fulfillment in many historical disasters at the actual time of the End.

> ꙮ ꙮ ꙮ ꙮ ꙮ
>
> 2 And the first angel went and poured out his bowl into the earth; and it became a bad and evil sore upon the men who had the stamp of the beast and who worshipped its image.
> 3 And the second *angel* poured out his bowl into the sea, and it became blood as that of a dead *man*; and every living soul in the sea died.
> 4 And the third *angel* poured out his bowl into the rivers and the fountains of waters; and they became blood.
> 5 And I heard the angel of the waters saying, "Righteous are You, who are and who were, O Holy One, because You judged these things;
> 6 "for they poured out the blood of saints and prophets, and You have given them blood to drink. They are worthy *of it*!"
> 7 And I heard the altar saying, "Yes, O Lord God, the Almighty, true and righteous are Your judgments!"

As mentioned above, the bowls recall the plagues of Egypt. The first bowl recalls the boils that broke out on man and beast (Ex. 9:10). The **first angel** poured out his judgment **into the earth**, and **those who worshipped the beast** and **its image** were afflicted with **bad and evil sores** on their bodies.

Immediately after the **second *angel*** poured out his wrath **into the sea**, the sea **became blood**, coagulating and rotting **as that of a dead *man***. Naturally, **every living soul** (that is, everything living) **in the sea died**.

The **third *angel*** poured out his bowl **into the rivers and the fountains of waters**, the sources of drinkable water for mankind, and these also **became blood**. In Egypt, Moses had turned the waters of the Nile into blood (Ex. 7:20), and here God strikes the world with a similar plague.

Those in heaven rejoice at such judgments, applauding the divine justice. God had decreed in His Law that there should be punishments equal to the crime, and that the loss of an eye should be punished with the loss of an eye (Ex. 21:24). Here we see that same principle worked out. **The angel** assigned to care for earth's **waters** (the same one pouring out God's wrath upon the waters in v. 4?) himself acknowledged the poetic justice of God's judgment on the waters he was to care for. He cried out that God was **righteous** in this act, for the persecutors **poured out the blood of** God's **saints and prophets**, and God **had given them** nothing but **blood to drink**. Since they were so bloodthirsty, let them drink the blood they thirsted for! They were **worthy** and deserving of such a judgment. Those martyred souls under the **altar** (last heard demanding such justice in 6:9–10) added their acclaim also, declaring that God's **judgments** were **righteous and true**. Those in heaven had long desired to see before their eyes God's vengeance for the outpoured blood of His servants (Ps. 79:10). Now they had been vindicated at last.

---

8 And the fourth *angel* poured out his bowl upon the sun, and it was given to it to burn men with fire.

9 And men were burned with great heat; and they blasphemed the Name of God, who has the authority over these plagues, and they did not repent so as to give Him glory.

10 And the fifth *angel* poured out his bowl upon the throne of the beast, and its kingdom became darkened; and they gnawed their tongues from the pain,

11 and they blasphemed the God of heaven because of their pains and their sores; and they did not repent of their works.

IV. The End of All Things — Revelation 16:12–16

The **fourth *angel*** poured out his wrath **upon the** very **sun** itself, and the sun scorched all those on the earth, to **burn men with** its **fire**. Scorched with such **great heat**, men **blasphemed the Name of God**, who was avenging His servants. Once again, they did **not repent so as to give Him glory** (as in 9:20); in vain they experienced His rebuke.

The **fifth *angel*** poured out his bowl **upon the throne of the beast**, the city of Rome, and its **kingdom became darkened**. Just as those of Egypt experienced a darkness that could be felt (Ex. 10:21), so earth's apostates now groped in the darkness. Since they had rejected the spiritual light, they were now deprived of the physical light as well. The darkness made them prisoners in their homes, where they "lay as captives of darkness and prisoners of long night" (Wisdom 17:2), and they sat in their prisons alone with the pain from their sores. They were in such fear and agony of mind and body that they **gnawed their tongues from the pain** and once again **blasphemed the God of heaven**. Their blaspheming is related to show their helplessness before God's mighty judgments—there was nothing they could do to relieve themselves of the plague or to strike back at God. They were reduced to impotent blaspheming.

---

12 And the sixth *angel* poured out his bowl upon the great river, the Euphrates; and its water was dried up, that the way might be prepared for the kings from the rising of the sun.

13 And I saw *coming* from the mouth of the dragon and from the mouth of the beast and from the mouth of the false prophet three unclean spirits as frogs;

14 for they are spirits of demons, doing signs, which go out to the kings of the whole world to assemble them for the war of the great day of God, the Almighty.

15 ("Behold, I am coming as a thief. Blessed *is* the one who keeps alert and keeps his garments,

> lest he walk naked and they see his shame.")
> 16 And they assembled them to the place which in Hebrew is called Armageddon.

The **sixth** *angel* poured out his judgment **upon the great river, the Euphrates**, the protecting eastern boundary of the civilized (i.e. Roman) world (see 9:14 and comments). The **water** of that boundary **was dried up**, leaving the world exposed to invasion from **the kings from the rising of the sun**. The image recalls fears of invasion from the dreaded Parthian Empire in the east, but the thought here is more cosmic.

This battle would not be a simple Parthian invasion, dreaded as that prospect was. The **kings** from far away, from the very **rising of the sun** in the furthest east, were to serve as catalyst for the final conflict, the ultimate conflagration. Just as the drying up of a river leaves the frogs, so here the drying up of the Euphrates brings demonic frogs. For from the **mouths** of the trinity of evil, **the dragon, the beast,** and **the false prophet** (as the second beast of 13:11 is now called), come **three unclean spirits**, appearing as unclean **frogs**, croaking out their lies. They are the **spirits of demons**, and they **do signs**, deceiving the **whole world to assemble them for the war of the great day of God, the Almighty**. The place to which they are assembled is **the place which in Hebrew is called Armageddon**.

This was the Hebrew *Har-Magedon* or "Hill of Megiddo," the tableland surrounded by hills near the city of Megiddo. It was the scene of many decisive battles in the history of Israel (Judg. 5:19; 2 Kings 9:27; 23:29), and thus it gives its name to this final and bloody conflict. In saying that all were assembled to **Armageddon**, St. John tells us that all the world was united for the last battle.

We have here the apocalyptic description of what St. Paul refers to as the final end-time deceit of the man of lawlessness, the Antichrist (2 Thess. 2). The *Didache* (a church manual dating from about AD 100) spoke of this as the time when "the world-deceiver will appear as the Son of God, working great signs and wonders," and when "all created mankind will come into the fire of testing." Here

IV. The End of All Things   Revelation 16:17–21

was this final crisis, when all the world assembled for a definitive rebellion against God, **the war of the great day of God,** when He will strike down His foes.

In the midst of this description and without prior warning, the voice of Jesus is suddenly heard (the suddenness of this message from Christ mirroring the suddenness of His Coming). He says, **"Behold, I am coming as a thief,"** that is, without warning (compare Matt. 24:43–44). And He pronounces a blessing on the one who is ready for His Coming, saying, **"Blessed *is* the one who keeps alert and keeps his garments."** This beatitude refers to the practice of keeping vigil in the Jerusalem Temple. Should one of the guards be caught by his captain sleeping on this watch, that one was punished by having his garments set aflame and burned. He would have to **walk naked** and shamed away—having learned his lesson. The Lord's people must keep awake spiritually, and not be unconscious of the spiritual peril of sin and apostasy (see Luke 21:34–36).

> ॐ ॐ ॐ ॐ ॐ
>
> 17 And the seventh *angel* poured out his bowl upon the air, and a great voice came from the sanctuary from the throne, saying, "It has happened!"
> 18 And there occurred *flashes of* lightning and sounds and *peals of* thunder; and a great earthquake occurred, such as had not occurred since man came to be upon the earth, so mighty and great an earthquake was it.
> 19 And the great city was split into three parts, and the cities of the nations fell. And Babylon the Great was remembered before God, to give her the cup of the wine of the indignation of His wrath.
> 20 And every island fled, and the mountains were not found.
> 21 And a great hail, *each* as a talent *in weight,*

> came down from heaven upon men; and men blasphemed God because of the plague of the hail, because its plague was extremely great.

The **seventh *angel* poured out his bowl upon the air**, in an unprecedented display of power. God had formerly poured out His wrath upon earth, sea, and rivers (8:7–11; 16:2–7), even upon the sun and moon and stars (8:12; 16:8), but never before upon something as all-covering as the air itself. In these other judgments, the powers of nature warred against man; now the very air around him is full of judgment, and there is no escape. After this, **a great voice came from the sanctuary, from the** very **throne** of God, declaring that all of God's wrath had been poured out. The Greek has a single dramatic word—*gegonen*—it has **happened**, it is done! There occurred ***flashes of* lightning and** rumbling **sounds and *peals of* thunder** as the air was filled with the power of God to bring low the children of men. There was even a **great hail**, each hailstone weighing **a talent** (that is, about a hundred pounds). Everything under the sky was battered and destroyed; there could be no escape. No place was safe, no place offered refuge from this final outpouring of anger. Men could only **blaspheme God** once more **because of the plague of the hail**.

It is important to understand the significance of this hail. It was not, as with us today, just another form of precipitation. It seemed to the ancients to represent the anger of heaven, as if God were pounding in fury, smashing everything beneath the clouds. It is thus uniquely a symbol of divine wrath (see Josh. 10:11; Is. 30:30; Ezek. 38:18–23).

A part of this climactic convulsion was **a great earthquake**, one **such as had not occurred since man came to be upon the earth**. **The great city** of Rome was **split into three parts** (that is, split entirely), and all **the cities of the nations fell**, collapsing from the earthquake. **Every island fled**, submerged in the seas, **and the mountains were not found**, having fallen flat. This was how **Babylon the Great**, fatally exalted in her pride, was **remembered before God**, so that God would **give her the cup of the wine of**

the indignation of His wrath. This last description of the cup of judgment is a long one: the wine is not just "the wine of His wrath," but rather **the wine of the indignation of His wrath**. Word is piled upon word in an attempt to express the divine anger, poured out at last upon the world.

§IV.4. The Judgment of Babylon the Great

17 1 And one of the seven angels who had the seven bowls came and spoke with me, saying, "Come, I will show you the judgment of the great prostitute who sits upon many waters,
2 "with whom the kings of the earth committed fornication, and those who dwell upon the earth were made drunk from the wine of her fornication."
3 And he carried me away in the Spirit into a wilderness; and I saw a woman sitting on a scarlet beast, full of names of blasphemy, having seven heads and ten horns.
4 The woman was clothed in purple and scarlet, and gilded with gold and precious stones and pearls, having in her hand a gold cup full of abominations and of the uncleanness of her fornication,
5 and on her forehead a name was written, a mystery, "Babylon the Great, the mother of prostitutes and of the abominations of the earth."
6 And I saw the woman drunk from the blood of the saints and from the blood of the witnesses of Jesus. When I saw her, I marveled with great marveling.

After this final outpouring of wrath upon the world and upon Babylon the Great (16:19), **one of the seven angels** responsible for this outpouring **came and spoke** with John, to reveal how God's **judgment** would finally fall upon Babylon. She had been mentioned earlier, in 14:8, as "Babylon the Great, she who made all the nations drink of the wine of the indignation of her fornication." Now she is referred to more fully as **the great prostitute who sits upon many waters, with whom the kings of the earth committed fornication,** and as the one with whom **those who dwell upon the earth were made drunk from the wine of her fornication**. Unlike the Church, the woman clothed with the sun (12:1), undefiled and virginal (14:4), this woman is thoroughly immoral, the very image of luxurious decadence and sinfulness.

She **sits** like a queen, enthroned like Babylon of old **upon many waters** (Jer. 51:13)—that is, enthroned upon "peoples and crowds and nations and tongues" (v. 15). But though claiming to be a queen, she was as debased as a **prostitute**. Nineveh was compared to a prostitute in the days of her power (Nah. 3:4), as was ancient Tyre (Is. 23:17). Babylon the Great (that is, Rome) had surpassed them, for she had seduced all the nations with her spiritual fornication, causing them to fall into idolatry and the worship of the beast.

With this, the angel **carried** John **away in the Spirit into a wilderness**. The **wilderness** was always in Israel's history a place free of worldly distractions, where one could better hear the voice of God, and it was preeminently the place for receiving revelation (compare Ex. 3:1f, 1 Kings 19:4f). John was again in the state of prophetic ecstasy and able to receive such a great revelation.

What he saw was horrifying and revolting. He saw a **woman sitting** astride **a scarlet beast**. The beast was **full of names of blasphemy,** and it had **seven heads and ten horns**. (A simpler description of this beast had already been offered in 13:1f.) The beast represented the Roman Empire, and it was **scarlet** in color, as befits such a bloodthirsty and murderous creature. Its **names of blasphemy** were the claims to divinity advanced by its emperors (see 13:1 and comments).

Horrifying as it was to see someone astride such an unnatural and freakish creature, the woman herself was equally appalling. She was **clothed in purple and scarlet, and gilded with gold and precious stones and pearls**, decadent in her amassed wealth. (Purple and scarlet were expensive and a sign of luxury.) **In her hand** was **a gold cup**, not filled with delightful wine but **full of abominations and of the uncleanness of her fornication**. The contents of her chalice were sickening and brought corruption and impurity. (One thinks of such passages as Lev. 18:19.) Her sins were plain for all to see, as if **written** in bold letters **on her forehead**. All the world could see her for what she was: the great **mystery** of iniquity, long hidden but now revealed, **Babylon the Great, the mother of prostitutes and of the abominations of the earth**. All the immorality and impurity of the world found its source in her.

Moreover, she lolled about atop the animal in a drunken stupor, being **drunk** not from wine, but **from the blood of the saints and from the blood of the witnesses of Jesus** (*martus*; compare the English word "martyr"). The image of drinking literal blood was revolting enough, and she had drunk cup after cup of this precious fluid, as Christian after Christian allowed his blood to be shed for his Lord. John looked at this unnerving sight and **marveled with great marveling** (that is, marveled greatly), at a loss to take it all in.

> ꙮ ꙮ ꙮ ꙮ ꙮ
>
> 7 And the angel said to me, "Why do you marvel? I will tell you the mystery of the woman and of the beast that carries her, which has the seven heads and the ten horns.
> 8 "The beast that you saw was, and is not, and is about to come up from the abyss and go to destruction. And those who dwell on the earth, whose name has not been written in the book of life from the foundation of the world, will marvel when they see the beast, that it was and is not and will come.
> 9 "Here *is* the mind which has wisdom. The seven

> heads are seven mountains where the woman sits,
> 10 "and they are seven kings; five have fallen, one is, the other has not yet come; and when he comes, it is necessary for him to remain a little *while*.
> 11 "The beast which was and is not, is itself also an eighth and is of the seven, and it goes to destruction.

The angel asks John **why** he **marvels**, as if at a loss to understand, for he **will tell** him **the mystery of the woman and of the beast that carries her** (that is, of the city of Rome sitting astride the empire). **The beast** is described as both past and future: it **was** (i.e. it existed in the past, persecuting the Church under Nero), and now **is not** (i.e. is not now actively persecuting the Church with that Neronian zeal), and **is about to come up from the abyss** (i.e. it will arise in persecuting zeal from the pit of hell itself)—and **go to destruction**. The furious persecution the Church experienced under Nero was, at the time of St. John's first writing the Book of Revelation, a thing of the past. There had been a lull. But only for a while. The persecution was about to begin again, as the beast arose again to continue its persecuting career. When this happens, all **those who dwell on the earth** who are not warned from such deception by their Christian faith **will marvel**. There will be a universal capitulation to the power of the beast.

St. John is then called to apply his **mind** to **wisdom** and to solve the puzzle of **the seven heads**. They are both **seven mountains where the woman sits** and also **seven kings**. The **seven mountains** are, of course, the seven hills of Rome. But they were also **seven kings** or emperors who dwelt there. John is called to count the kings of Rome in order to get the intended answer.

We are reminded again of the need for discretion and secrecy in these documents (see the similar reluctance to state such political things openly in 13:18). John is given the numbers and expected to work out the answer for himself. He is told that **five** kings **have fallen**. These would be Augustus (who ruled from 27 BC to AD 14), Tiberius (14–37), Caligula (37–41), Claudius (41–54), and Nero

IV. The End of All Things   Revelation 17:12–18

(54–68). (This leaves out of the reckoning a brief succession of pretenders to the throne, Galba, Otho, and Vitellius, whose combined imperial adventures only lasted from 68–69.) **One** king currently **is**—Vespasian, whose reign was from 69 to 79. Then there is another **who has not yet come; when he comes, it is necessary for him to remain a little *while*.** This would be Titus, who ruled only from 79 to 81. The **beast** who would come to persecute **is an eighth**. This would be Domitian, the very emperor under whom John was exiled, and who was beginning to enforce the emperor cult. (Not unexpected, since his number had been worked out in 13:18.) He is said to be **of the seven**, in that he is an emperor like his predecessors and continues their self-glorifying work—even though it finally leads him **to destruction**.

As with other apocalyptic writers, St. John casts himself back in time and looks ahead (as it were) to the present (see 2 Esdras 14:11, where it is said that all of history is divided into twelve parts, of which nine and a half have already past). The apocalyptist wants to make clear that history has just about run its course, and the final crisis is at hand. In this case, the message is that the line of good Roman emperors has all but run out. The persecuting beast from the abyss is about to arise.

> ॐ ॐ ॐ ॐ ॐ
> 12 "And the ten horns which you saw are ten kings who have not yet received a kingdom, but they receive authority as kings with the beast *for* one hour.
> 13 "These have one resolve, and they give away their power and authority to the beast.
> 14 "These will war against the Lamb, and the Lamb will conquer them, because He is Lord of lords and King of kings, and those who are with Him *are* called and chosen and faithful."
> 15 And he says to me, "The waters which you saw where the prostitute sits are peoples and crowds and nations and tongues.

> 16 "And the ten horns which you saw, and the beast, these will hate the prostitute and will make her desolate and naked, and will eat her flesh and will burn her up with fire.
> 17 "For God has put it in their hearts to do His resolve by having one resolve, and by giving their kingdom to the beast, until the words of God will be finished.
> 18 "And the woman whom you saw is the great city which reigns over the kings of the earth."

The angel continues his explanation. **The ten horns are** the **ten kings** or nations that make up the Roman Empire. The number **ten** is drawn from Daniel 7:24 and is here symbolic (as with apocalyptic numbers generally) of all the multitude of nations that make up the empire. These member nations **receive authority as kings with the beast** *for* **one hour** (that is, for a short time) to carry out its imperial policy of persecution. They connive and reach **one resolve**—to **give away their power and authority to the beast** and support Rome in its policy, waging war against the Church.

They thereby also **war against the Lamb** Himself, who rules from heaven. In this they cannot succeed, for He is the true Sovereign and Master of the World, **the Lord of lords and King of kings**. His army also shares His invincibility, for they are **called and chosen and faithful**, the picked troops of heaven, worthy of such a Captain. Rome's policy of persecution will prove utterly futile.

The heavenly Lord works to overrule all the contrary purposes of men. By His plan, the nations that make up **the beast** will eventually rebel against **the prostitute** who rides them, **hating** and destroying her, leaving Rome **desolate**. They will make her **naked** and defenseless; they **will eat her flesh and will burn her up with fire**. (These images of destruction are drawn from Ezek. 23:25–29.)

Thus God's plan will be carried out in the world. The nations **have one resolve** (to **give their kingdom to the beast** to do the beast's will). But that is only because **God has put it in their hearts to do** what is in reality **His resolve**. Their power to persecute will last

IV. The End of All Things   Revelation 18:1–3

only **until the words of God** are **finished** and fulfilled. After this, the harlot will be destroyed. And should anyone still somehow miss the identity of **the woman**, she is identified at last (by a circumlocution) as Rome, **the great city which reigns over the kings of the earth.**

---

18 1   After these things I saw another angel coming down from heaven, having great authority, and the earth was enlightened from his glory.
   2   And he cried out with a strong voice, saying, "Fallen, fallen *is* Babylon the Great! She has become a dwelling of demons and a prison of every unclean spirit, and a prison of every unclean and hateful bird.
   3   "For all the nations have drunk from the wine of the indignation of her fornication, and the kings of the earth have committed fornication with her, and the traders of the earth have become rich by the powers of her luxury."

After these things had been revealed to John in the wilderness by the angel (17:3f), John saw **another angel coming down from heaven**, as from the very Presence of God. This angel had **great authority**, for it was to announce the destruction of Babylon the Great, and it needed the power of God to make its voice heard through that vast empire. Since it came straight from God's Presence, it reflected His **glory**, and this radiance was brilliant enough that **the earth was enlightened** from it. The earth had long sat in the darkness of bondage and sin, but now its liberation from the tyranny of Babylon was at hand.

The angel **cried out with a strong voice** (strong enough to reach the far corners of the earth) and declared, **"Fallen, fallen *is* Babylon the Great!"** The great oppressor had entirely fallen and been overthrown. Like Babylon of old, **she has become a dwelling of demons and a prison of every unclean spirit, and a prison of**

every unclean and hateful bird (compare Is. 13:20–22). Just as only the demons dwelt among the tombs (Mark 5:2–5), so the great city was to be ruined and desolate, inhabited only by forlorn **birds** of the desert and by **unclean spirits.**

This was her due, for all the nations had drunk from her immoral cup and been seduced into the idolatry of emperor worship. All **the kings of the earth** had committed this spiritual **fornication** with her, and their **traders** and wholesalers (Gr. *emporos*, used in contrast with a retailer) had **become rich by the powers** and resources of **her luxury** and sensually decadent living. Rome had led astray the whole world, both political and economic, and had not paid the price.

---

4 I heard another voice from heaven, saying, "Come out from her, My people, lest you co-share in her sins and receive of her plagues;

5 "for her sins have touched *the height of* heaven, and God has remembered her unrighteous *acts*.

6 "Render to her as she also has rendered, and *repay* her double according to her works; in the cup which she has mixed, mix double for her.

7 "To the *measure* that she glorified herself and *lived in* luxury, to that *measure* give her torment and mourning; for she says in her heart, 'I sit as a queen and I am not a widow, and will never see mourning.'

8 "For this *reason* in one day her plagues will come, death and mourning and famine, and she will be burned up with fire; for strong *is* the Lord God who judges her.

John **heard another voice from heaven**, that of an angel bearing a message from God Himself, saying, **"Come out from her, My people, lest you co-share in her sins and receive of her plagues."** Christians the world over were to flee from the city, as Lot fled from Sodom. This was a spiritual flight more than a physical one;

IV. The End of All Things   Revelation 18:4–8

the Christian, even in Rome, was to live differently from his pagan neighbors. He was to "come out from their midst and be separate" (2 Cor. 6:17), living as a citizen of Jerusalem. For if he **co-shared** (Gr. *sugkoinoneo*) in the sins his neighbor indulged in as a partner with him, then he would also share in **the plagues** the neighbor received. For God judges sin impartially in all.

And these plagues would be severe indeed, for Rome's **sins have touched** *the height of* **heaven**. The image is that of sins piling up so high as to reach into heaven itself, attracting the notice of those who dwell there. Therefore **God has remembered her unrighteous acts**. The Judge of all the earth must do justly (Gen. 18:25) and judge her for her sins. All those murdered and robbed, all those oppressed and beaten, all those children aborted in the womb or exposed after their births—all the downtrodden of the earth would now be judged and avenged. Babylon's unrighteous acts would be remembered before God.

The angel with the message cried out to God to judge these sins. Let God **render to her as she also has rendered** to others and *repay* **her double** for her sins. **In the cup** of suffering **she mixed** for others to drink, let God **mix double for her**. (This **double** measure of suffering here means "abundantly, fully"; compare such a use in Is. 40:2.) Let her know what the suffering was like that she inflicted on the helpless.

And let the measure of her pride be also the measure of her humiliation: to the degree that **she glorified herself and** *lived in* **luxury** and wanton sensuality, to that same degree **give her torment and mourning**. She had greatly exalted herself above others; let her be just as greatly humbled (see Luke 18:14). She had boasted of her invincibility—others might fall, but never she. Her riches made her immune to the common lot of men. **She says in her** secret **heart, "I sit as a queen** and **will never see mourning"** (compare Is. 47:8). Deep down inside, she believes herself secure from judgment and disaster. Let her now know that she is not stronger than God, nor beyond His power to judge. **In one day** (that is, suddenly and unexpectedly), **her plagues will come—death** (that is, pestilence) **and mourning and famine**. The city will be **burned up with**

Revelation 18:9–19   APOCALYPSE OF ST. JOHN

fire, set ablaze by her foes (17:16), **for strong *is* the Lord God who judges** through them. Rome had thought the God of the deluded Christians powerless to act. She would learn the truth.

> ✥ ✥ ✥ ✥ ✥
>
> 9 "And the kings of the earth, who committed fornication with her and *lived in* luxury, will weep and lament over her when they see the smoke of her burning,
>
> 10 "standing far off because of the fear of her torment, saying, 'Woe, woe, the great city, Babylon, the strong city! For in one hour your judgment has come.'
>
> 11 "And the traders of the earth weep and mourn over her, because no one buys their cargo anymore—
>
> 12 "cargo of gold and silver and precious stones and pearls and fine-linen and purple and silk and scarlet, and every *kind of* scented wood and every *kind of* ivory vessel and every *kind of* vessel of precious wood and bronze and iron and marble,
>
> 13 "and cinnamon and spice and incense and perfume and frankincense and wine and oil and *fine* flour and wheat and beasts and sheep, and horses and chariots and bodies, even souls of men.
>
> 14 "The fruit of the desire of your soul has departed from you, and all things that were luxurious and bright perished from you, and *men* will never find them any more.
>
> 15 "The traders of these *things*, who became rich from her, will stand far off because of the fear of her torment, weeping and mourning,
>
> 16 "saying, 'Woe, woe, the great city, she who was clothed in fine-linen and purple and scarlet, and

IV. The End of All Things   Revelation 18:9–19

> gilded with gold and precious stones and pearl;
> 17 "'for in one hour such great wealth has been desolated!' And every pilot and every passenger and sailor, and all who work on the sea, stood far off,
> 18 "and were crying out as they saw the smoke of her burning, saying, 'What *city* is like the great city?'
> 19 "And they cast dust upon their heads and were crying out, weeping and mourning, saying, 'Woe, woe, the great city, in which all who had ships at sea became rich by her wealth, for in one hour she has been desolated!'

As a measure of the greatness of Babylon's fall and the completeness of her desolation, all the earth is portrayed as lifting up a lamentation for her in the classic forms of old. (It is modeled especially after the lamentation over the fall of Tyre in Ezekiel 27.) In this lament, three classes of men raise the cry of **Woe, woe, the great city!**—the **kings of the earth** (vv. 9–10); the **traders of the earth** (vv. 11–16); and **every pilot and passenger and sailor** (vv. 17–19).

Each had their own reasons for mourning. The **kings of the earth** mourned because they too *lived in* **luxury**, and they feared for their own overthrow. The **traders** (or wholesalers, Gr. *emporos*) mourned because **no one buys their cargo anymore**. The **pilots** and other seafarers mourned because **all who had ships at sea became rich by her wealth**. All had profited by her immorality and oppression. All alike were united in a great solidarity of corruption. Thus all alike wept and lamented over her judgment (18:9, 11, 15), **casting dust upon their heads and crying out**.

The passage is remarkable for the great inventory in verses 12–13 of goods of which the traders would now be deprived. The list is given to show the great decadence of the city, and how great was the wealth it had amassed in its luxurious sensuality.

The inventory ends with **bodies** (that is, slaves). For the secular city, slaves were just another commodity to be bought and sold, like any other. John, however, cannot resist adding a correction—these slaves were **souls of men** (Gr. *psuxas anthropon*)—that is, human souls, human beings. They were not just *animate* (i.e. "souls"; compare the use of the word in 16:3 to describe animate water life); they were animate *men*. The world might consider them as simply objects—valuable, but only as objects were valuable, like any other cargo. John knew these were more than that—they were men for whom Christ died, and they had a value beyond any other cargo on those ships. As a Christian, John was incapable of listing that final item without also registering the Christian protest against the theology of slavery.

> ༄ ༄ ༄ ༄ ༄
>
> 20 "Be glad over her, O heaven, and you saints and apostles and prophets, because God has judged against her for your judgment."
> 21 Then a strong angel took up a stone as a great millstone and cast *it* into the sea, saying, "Thus will Babylon, the great city, be cast with violence, and will be found no longer.
> 22 "And the sound of harpers and musicians and flutists and trumpeters will never be heard in you any longer; and every craftsman of every craft will never be found in you any longer; and the sound of a mill will never be heard in you any longer;
> 23 "and the light of a lamp will never shine in you any longer; and the voice of the bridegroom and bride will never be heard in you any longer; for your traders were the great *ones* of the earth, because all the nations were deceived by your sorcery.
> 24 "And in her was found the blood of prophets and of saints and of all who have been slaughtered upon the earth."

IV. The End of All Things   Revelation 18:20–24

But if the earth mourned over her fall, there was jubilant rejoicing in heaven. Babylon has slain the **prophets** and **saints**—indeed, **all** the unjust blood of those **slaughtered upon the earth** was **found in her** (v. 24). She was the source of all injustice and tyranny. Therefore those **saints and apostles and prophets** could **be glad** and rejoice over her fall, for **God has judged against her**, vindicating at last those who were unjustly slain. Here at last was the longed-for justice.

Babylon was to sink without a trace of her former glory. As Jeremiah had cast a stone into the waters as a sign that Babylon would sink down, not to rise again (Jer. 51:63), so **a strong angel** (indicating a key event; compare 5:2; 10:1) **took up a stone** and **cast it into the sea**. (The prophets of old enacted such prophetic parables; see Jer. 13:1f; Ezek. 12:3f.) This stone was **as a great millstone** (that is, of tremendous weight), and it instantly sank with a mighty splash. **Thus** also **will Babylon, the great city**, **be cast** down and sink **with violence**, with a mighty noise, and **be found no longer** among the cities of men.

All in the ruined city would be deserted and eerily quiet. All the sounds of festivity—**the sound of harpers and musicians** at feasts, the sound of **flutists** at dinners (and funerals), the sound of **trumpeters** announcing games and theatre performances—all would be forever gone. **Every craftsman** engaging in commerce would **never be found** in her, nor the creaking and prosperous **sound of a mill** grinding grain for food. Every ruined house would be dark and silent, with no **light of a lamp** giving signs of life within. The joyful **voice of the bridegroom and bride** would never **be heard** uplifted in song and merriment. The wanderer would look in vain for any of the signs of a living city within Babylon's burnt-out shell. The city's **traders** had strutted through the world in arrogance and pride, as **the great ones of the earth**, and their **sorcery** (that is, their seductive worldliness) had **deceived all the nations** into supporting them. (The word rendered *sorcery* is the Greek *pharmakeia*; it often denoted the making of love potions and spells used to incite lust. The metaphor here is that of the traders' ability to seduce the nations and bend them to their will.) God's judgment had fallen on such pride at last. All the slain of the earth had been finally avenged.

⁐ V ⁐

THE NEW BEGINNING
(19:1—22:21)

§V.1. The Second Coming of Christ: The Final Victory

19 1 After these things I heard as it were a great voice of a great crowd in heaven, saying, "Alleluia! Salvation and glory and power be to our God;
2 "for His judgments *are* true and righteous; for He has judged the great prostitute who was corrupting the earth with her fornication, and He has avenged the blood of His slaves against her hand."
3 And a second *time* they said, "Alleluia! Her smoke goes up to ages of ages."
4 And the twenty-four elders and the four living things fell and worshipped God, who sits upon the throne, saying, "Amen! Alleluia!"
5 And a voice came out from the throne, saying, "Praise our God, all you His slaves, you who fear Him, the little and the great."
6 And I heard *something* like the voice of a great crowd and like the sound of many waters and like the sound of strong *peals of* thunder, saying, "Alleluia! For the Lord our God, the Almighty, has become king!

> 7 "Let us rejoice and exult and give the glory to Him, for the wedding of the Lamb has come and His bride has prepared herself."
> 8 It was given to her to clothe herself in fine-linen, bright *and* clean; for the fine-linen is the righteous *acts* of the saints.
> 9 Then he says to me, "Write, 'Blessed *are* those who are called to the wedding supper of the Lamb.'" And he said to me, "These are true words of God."

As the stunning contrast and counterpoint to the sound of lamentation over Rome's fall (18:19), heaven erupts in jubilation, so that the sound of joy in heaven drowns out the sound of sorrow on earth. John heard a **great crowd in heaven**, all the saints and angels, crying out, **"Alleluia!"**

This shout of acclamation is from the original Hebrew *halleluYah*, (that is, "Praise Yahweh"). In the worship of the synagogue, it had changed from an invitation to praise God to the shout of praise itself, and as this acclamation it became part of the Church's liturgy.

This ecstatic joy erupts because God, whose acts are always **true and righteous**, faithful and just, has now acted to **judge** Rome, **the great prostitute who was corrupting the earth**, leading all into idolatry, and pouring out the **blood** of God's **slaves**, the Christians. All **salvation** (or victory; compare 7:10) and **glory** and **power** belong to Him. He alone, and not the seemingly invincible Roman Empire, has been proven to be almighty. By overthrowing that immoral city, He has pronounced judgment against her on behalf of His martyrs.

The cry of **Alleluia** was heard **a second *time***—that is, repeatedly. Heaven's jubilation over her destruction cannot be restrained, but sounds over and over again. Those of the inner court, **the twenty-four elders and the four living things**, **fell** down in adoration **and worshipped God**, overcome with joy. The **smoke** from the ruin of Rome **goes up to ages of ages**, for she shall never be rebuilt, nor the persecution of the saints renewed (compare Is. 34:10).

All joy is expansive, and of its own nature seeks to include others

V. The New Beginning   Revelation 19:1–9

in its bliss. Thus heaven calls to earth to echo its praise. An angelic **voice came out from the throne**, inviting the **slaves** of God on earth to join in this **praise** to **our God**. The moment of liberation had come at last.

As St. John listened, it was as if he was swallowed up in a mighty roar of praise. It sounded as it were **like the voice of a great** roaring **crowd**, or **like the sound of many** thundering **waters** over a waterfall, or **like the sound of strong *peals of* thunder**. All alike shouted out, "**Alleluia! For the Lord our God, the Almighty, has become king!**" His authority at last had been manifested upon the earth.

John dwells at length on this deafening cataract of praise (the word **alleluia** is repeated four times in five sentences) in order to lift the hearts of the suffering Church on earth in his day. They had all experienced vast crowds shouting out their acclaim for the Roman emperor, and had felt that their own liturgical chanting of Alleluia was somewhat pathetic and poor in comparison. Here was the antidote to such temptations to discouragement. Their present liturgical cry of Alleluia was but the forerunner to the final shout of triumph that would resound throughout heaven.

The overthrow of the prostitute meant that the time had arrived for another Woman. God's saints were to **rejoice and exult and give the glory to Him** because **the wedding of the Lamb had come and His bride had prepared herself** for that wedding feast.

We have here the classic image of the Kingdom of God as a marriage feast (Matt. 25:1–13). A marriage supper was one of the great joys of life in the ancient world. Marriages always took place at night. Among the Jews, the bridegroom would come with his attendants to "surprise" the bride at her home on the appointed day and take her home to be with himself. All the family and friends were invited to celebrate with them as they then began a weeklong feast, with plenty of wine, food, and joyful song. Thus it was a fitting image for the eternal joy shared by Christ and His Church on the last day.

In preparation for the wedding, all brides spent much time in adorning themselves in costly and elaborate wedding garments. The bride of the Lamb, the Church, also had been **given** by God the gift of adorning herself in beautiful attire. She was to **clothe herself in** fine-linen, bright *and* clean (and contrasting with the decadent attire of the prostitute; 17:4). These garments were symbolic of **the righteous *acts* of the saints** (Gr. *dikaiomata*), their obedience to God's commandments (compare 12:17; 14:12; and the use of *dikaiomata* in Rom. 2:26).

John was then given another commandment to **write** a beatitude: **"Blessed are those who are called to the wedding supper of the Lamb."** This blessing is pronounced upon the martyric Church. As the invited wedding guests of the great King considered themselves fortunate to be invited to such a feast, so the Christians are blessed to take part in that final eschatological wedding supper. If the merriment and joy at an earthly wedding supper were wonderful, how much more the joy at this nuptial feast? For there "the voice of those who feast is unceasing, and the gladness of those who behold the goodness of God's countenance is unending" (from a thanksgiving prayer after Holy Communion).

By insisting that these were the true words of God, the voice declares that this prophecy of final joy would surely be fulfilled, for by the words of God is meant "*prophetic* words of God" (compare similar usage in 17:17; 21:5; 22:6).

> ॐ ॐ ॐ ॐ ॐ
>
> 10 And I fell before his feet to worship him. But he says to me, "See *that you do* not *do that*! I am a fellow-slave of you and your brothers who have the witness of Jesus; worship God. For the witness of Jesus is the spirit of prophecy."

At this, John **fell before his feet to worship him**, only to receive a rebuke. **"See *that you do* not *do that*,"** the angel said, for **"I am a fellow-slave of you and your brothers who have the witness of Jesus. Worship God."**

This presents us with something of a dilemma, for how could a Jew, and an apostle at that, think one could lawfully give to an angel the worship due God alone? Whose was this voice that spoke to John, telling him to write this beatitude? It is possible that one should simply look for the answer to the immediate grammatical antecedent (which would be the "voice from the throne" in v. 5), but with the multitude of other "voices" sounding in the Apocalypse (the word rendered *voice*, Gr. *phone*, also means simply "sound"; compare such a use in 16:18), it may not be as simple as this.

We are on firmer ground if we look to the voice that told John to write the other messages. In 14:13, it is described as "a voice from heaven," and it tells John to write a beatitude which the Spirit confirms; in 10:4, this same voice (as we think) commands John *not* to write something. In 1:10f, it is the voice of Christ Himself, in His initial revelation to John, commanding him to write what he sees and to send it to the churches. Could this voice be somehow the voice of Christ?

This supposition finds some confirmation in examination of other verses. As said above, in 14:13 the voice that commands John to write is described as "a voice from heaven." Are there other instances in the Apocalypse of such "a voice from heaven" speaking?

There are. In 18:4 John hears "a voice from heaven saying, 'Come out of her, My people.'" Though clearly an angelic voice and not the voice of God Himself (the next verse refers to God in the third person, not the first person), it is noteworthy that this angel speaks in a divine voice, calling God's people "*My* people." In 10:4, the voice that commanded John not to write something is also described as "a voice from heaven." In 10:8, this same voice tells John to overcome his fear and go take the book from the angel who stood astride earth and sea. In 11:12, a loud "voice from heaven" tells the two witnesses to "come up here." This is the same command given in 4:1, and it would seem the same voice gives this command. In 4:1, however, this voice is explicitly said to be the voice of Christ, "the first voice which [John] had heard, speaking with [him] as a trumpet."

It would seem then that this "voice from heaven" is the same voice that told John to write his messages, and that this voice is the voice of Christ. John fell down to worship, therefore, because he thought he was worshipping Christ. How then can it be that what appeared to be Christ was actually just an angel?

I would suggest that Christ's angel sent by Him with His

revelation for John (1:1) resembled Christ Himself. Certainly in the case of guardian angels generally, it would seem they bear an outer resemblance to those whom they guard. Thus, when St. Peter was released from prison and stood at the door of Mary's house in Jerusalem seeking entrance, some thought it was not Peter himself but "his angel" (Acts 12:15). Apparently one's "angel," then, looks rather like oneself.

Not, of course, that Christ our God has a guardian angel as we do. Rather, this angel would be a special servant, sent to carry His message and His Presence, and as such looked like Christ, whose Presence he carried.

Granted that this was the cause of John's mistake, why does he relate it here? It is a matter of some importance, for he later narrates a second instance of the same mistake in 22:8–9. The answer is that John was concerned to check the growth of an unlawful adoration of angels present in Asia Minor, and he uses his own experience to impress upon the Church at large that such worship of angels was unorthodox.

This angel-worship was indeed a problem to the early Church, especially in Asia Minor. In Isaiah 9:6 (LXX), the Messiah is referred to as "the Angel of Great Counsel"—i.e. as the Messenger (Gr. *angelos*) who carried out the divine will. Such angelic titles were used for Christ in certain centers of Jewish Christianity.

This need not have been a problem, but some drew unwarranted conclusions from it. For some groups, with gnostic tendencies, suggested that the Messiah was, in fact, an angel—that is, a created being. Exalted above all others, to be sure, but a created being nonetheless. This was heretical and not a valid conclusion from the (admittedly ambiguous) Jewish title for the Messiah in Isaiah 9:6. It was in flagrant contradiction to the apostolic deposit of the Faith, which asserted in no uncertain terms the full deity of Jesus Christ.

Nonetheless, this teaching continued to spread in Asia Minor. The Epistle to the Hebrews rebukes the idea that Christ is an angel (see Heb. 1:5f, "To which of the angels did He ever say, 'You are My Son'?"). St. Paul rebukes the teaching in his Epistle to the

V. The New Beginning   Revelation 19:11–16

Colossians (see Col. 2:18, "Let no one disqualify you by delighting in the worship of angels").

Because of the prevalence of this heretical practice, John records his own mistake as a kind of enacted rebuke of the heresy. None in the churches may follow the heretics in the adoration of angels; such worship is for God alone. One may not give the worship due the Father and the Son (such as is given in 5:13) to created angels. The Church must take care not to reduce Christ to the status of an angel. For **the witness of Jesus is the spirit** and essence of all true **prophecy**. The Church is called to hold to the witness about Jesus (12:17) and must do nothing that does not exalt Him. True Christian prophecy will always glorify Christ.

> ༄ ༄ ༄ ༄ ༄
>
> 11 And I saw heaven opened, and behold! a white horse, and He who sat upon it is called faithful and true, and in righteousness He judges and wars.
> 12 His eyes *are* as a flame of fire, and upon His head *are* many diadems; and *He has* a name written *on Him* which no one knows except Himself.
> 13 And He is clothed with a garment dipped in blood, and His name is called the Word of God.
> 14 And the armies which are in heaven, clothed in fine-linen, white *and* clean, were following Him upon white horses.
> 15 And from His mouth proceeds a sharp sword, that with it He may strike the nations, and He will shepherd them with a rod of iron; and He treads the wine press of the indignation of the wrath of God, the Almighty.
> 16 And upon His garment and upon His thigh He has a name written, "King of kings and Lord of lords."

Now comes the climax of the entire Apocalypse. In the opening verses of 1:7, the heart of the reader had been set on the time when He would be "coming with the clouds," and here the Lord is seen at last. St. John **saw heaven opened**, splitting apart that its warrior King may ride forth to war with His hosts. Introduced by **behold**, the final Coming is sudden and dramatic. The actual Second Coming will of course be ineffable and beyond description. St. Peter speaks of a day when "the heavens will pass away with a roar, and the earth and its works will be burned up" (2 Pet. 3:10).

Here that day is described in classic apocalyptic terms: The conquering Lord sits upon **a white horse**, the emblem of victory. (Horses were not the usual means of transportation. Its appearance here speaks of the rider's military speed and power.) He is **faithful and true** to His promises to judge and redeem His people, and **in righteousness He judges and wars** to fulfill those promises. **His eyes *are* as a flame of fire**, seeing all men's works, consuming in a fiery blaze their excuses and lies (see 1:14). **Upon His head *are* many diadems**, including those falsely usurped by the beast, for all earthly sovereignty belongs by right to Him. He has **a name written *on Him* which no one knows except Himself**. In the ancient world, a person's name embodied his true self, his inner essence. To know a person's name therefore was to exercise some degree of power over him. (Thus the Lord asked the name of the "Legion" demon in Mark 5:9.) But Christ is all-powerful, and no one can know His Name or exercise power over Him. He is the uncreated and infinite God.

He is clothed with a garment dipped in blood. As Yahweh of old purpled His robes in the blood of His enemies (Is. 63:1–6), so Christ's garments are similarly seen as **dipped** in the **blood** of His foes. As He rides forth, His adversaries will know His Name and feel His power. For **His name is called the Word of God**, the eternal and creative power of God Himself (John 1:1–3). Those who know that Name will put their trust in it (Ps. 9:10), and all the nations of the earth will fear it when they see His glory (Ps. 102:15).

The King does not ride without His army. His **armies** are **in heaven**, and they are **clothed in fine-linen, white *and* clean**. That is, they are clothed in the purity of their righteous acts (v. 8), in

V. The New Beginning Revelation 19:17–18

festal **white**, their purity showing the justice of the divine retaliation. They **follow** their King riding, like Him, **upon white horses**, sharing His victory.

When He comes, He will **strike the nations** with the **sharp sword** of His **mouth** (1:16, compare Is. 11:4), issuing words of judgment upon them. He will **shepherd them with a rod of iron** (compare Ps. 2:9 LXX), **treading the winepress of the indignation of the wrath of God, the Almighty**. As harvesters trod grapes and purpled their robes with the juice, so God would tread the overflowing winepress of His anger at men's sins (14:18f; Is. 63:3). Christ would manifest this judgment and bring this divine wrath upon the world. The Father's **indignation** for the sins of men would find expression in Christ's Second Coming.

Finally, **upon His garment**, on the **thigh** of it, **He has a name written**, expressing His absolute sovereignty over all the earth. Caesar may have imagined himself to be Master of the World, but he was not. It is Jesus Christ, the crucified carpenter, who is the true **King of kings and Lord of lords**. Why the thigh? It seems most probable that the garment clothing the thigh was chosen because the thigh was always the ancient symbol of vitality and life, being near the generative loins. Thus did Abraham's servant place his hand on his master's thigh when he took an oath, swearing (as it were) by the vital life of his master (Gen. 24:2). This image there declares that the life and power of the coming Lord is that of the most exalted Sovereign.

༄ ༄ ༄ ༄ ༄

17 Then I saw one angel standing in the sun, and he cried out with a great voice, saying to all the birds flying in mid-heaven, "Come, assemble for the great supper of God,

18 "that you may eat the flesh of kings and the flesh of generals and the flesh of strong *men* and the flesh of horses and those sitting upon them and the flesh of all *men*, both free *men* and slaves, and little and great."

John then **saw one angel standing in the sun**, where he could be heard by all on the earth. He **cried out with a great voice**, summoning **all the birds flying in mid-heaven**, all the carrion-eaters who inhabit the heights, to **the great supper of God**. God was providing them with a sumptuous feast—let them all gather. For rich fare was provided—**the flesh of kings and the flesh of generals and the flesh of strong *men* and the flesh of horses** and their riders **sitting upon them**. Indeed, they could come feast upon the flesh of **all *men*, both free *men* and slaves**, both **little and great**. All would be there without distinction. After the final battle, the carnage would be universal and would stretch out across the earth.

This grisly image is drawn from the apocalyptic part of Ezekiel's prophecies. The prophecies of Ezekiel 38—39 describe the Kingdom of God in terms of a final assault of the nations upon Israel, and of God's defense of His People. It describes the greatness of the opposing force ("like a cloud covering the land," Ezek. 38:9) in order to show the might of God, who acts to defend His People. That opposing host was so great that its overthrow would provide the vultures with an unparalleled meal from the resulting corpses (Ezek. 39:17–20).

This image is used here to show how great will be the overthrow of God's foes at the Second Coming. The image uses the symbolism of the apocalyptic to make its point, and does not suggest that after the Coming, vultures will literally feed on the slain. (Indeed, St. Peter speaks of the whole earth dissolving before the fire of God's Presence—including, presumably, the flesh of the slain and of the vultures alike; 2 Pet. 3:12.) Like all apocalyptic images, its appeal is to the nerves and the emotions. The **kings** of the earth and **generals** and **strong *men*** and mounted riders were presently warring upon the Church—but their time would come.

༄ ༄ ༄ ༄ ༄

19 And I saw the beast and the kings of the earth
and their armies assembled to make war against

V. The New Beginning — Revelation 19:19–21

> Him who sat on the horse and against His army.
> 20 And the beast was taken hold of, and with it the false prophet who did the signs before its *presence*, by which he deceived those who had received the stamp of the beast and those who worshipped its image; these two were cast alive into the lake of fire which burns with sulfur.
> 21 And the rest were killed with the sword which proceeded from the mouth of Him who sat upon the horse, and all the birds ate their flesh to the full.

The overthrow of powers hostile to God is described symbolically in terms of the seizure of the leaders of the rebellion and the slaying of their armies. Though **the beast and the kings of the earth and their armies** were **assembled to make war** against Christ and His army, their concerted stand was all in vain. "The kings of the earth and the rulers gathered together against the Lord God and His Christ" (Ps. 2:2), but their opposition was useless. It was all over for them, and the actual battle is not even narrated. **The beast** and **the false prophet** (the leaders of the enemy armies) were **taken hold of**. Like kings who flee in terror after their armies are defeated, but are nonetheless captured and brought to justice, so the beast and the false prophet faced their final fate. That is, all the worldly powers which opposed the reign of God were finally destroyed.

They suffered no common punishment, but a truly horrifying end and a fate fitting to their deeds. As Dathan and Abiram of old went down alive to Sheol (Num. 16:30–33), and thus were swallowed up by sudden terror, so with these personified images of Roman power. There was no time for them to plead for mercy. The wrath of God overtook them suddenly and **cast** them **alive into the lake of fire**, giving them no time for even a final word of defiance. **The rest** of the rebel host were **killed** also, slain by Christ's word of judgment, the **sword which proceeded from** His **mouth** to smite all the nations (v. 15).

❧ ❧ ❧ ❧ ❧

20

1 And I saw an angel coming down from heaven, having the key of the abyss and a great chain in his hand.

2 And he seized the dragon, the ancient serpent, who is the devil and Satan, and bound him for a thousand years;

3 and he cast him into the abyss, and shut and sealed *it* over him, so that he should not deceive the nations any longer, until the thousand years were finished; after these things it is necessary *for* him to be loosed for a little time.

4 And I saw thrones, and they sat upon them, and judgment was given to them. And *I saw* the souls of those who had been beheaded for the witness of Jesus and for the Word of God, and those who had not worshipped the beast or its image, and had not received the stamp upon their forehead and upon their hand; and they came to life and reigned with Christ for a thousand years.

5 The rest of the dead did not come to life until the thousand years were finished. This *is* the first resurrection.

6 Blessed and holy *is* the one who has a part in the first resurrection; over these the second death does not have authority, but they will be priests of God and of Christ and will reign with Him for a thousand years.

7 When the thousand years are finished, Satan will be loosed from his prison,

8 and will come out to deceive the nations in the four corners of the earth, Gog and Magog, to

V. The New Beginning   Revelation 20:1–10

> assemble them for the war; their number *is* as the sand of the sea.
> 9 And they came up upon the breadth of the earth and encircled the camp of the saints and the beloved city, and fire came down from heaven and ate them up.
> 10 And the devil who deceived them was cast into the lake of fire and sulfur, where the beast and the false prophet were; and they will be tormented day and night to ages of ages.

We come now to a very controversial part of the Apocalypse, the so-called Millennium (or "thousand years"), for which there are three main interpretations.

First there is the *premillennial* view (the name indicating that Christ returns *before* the Millennium). This is the plain, "common sense" reading of the text. It seems to have been the earliest view, and was certainly held by St. Justin the Philosopher and martyr (see his *Dialogue with Trypho*, ch. 81). In this view, Christ returns to earth, and the saints are then raised from the dead to reign in Jerusalem with Him for a thousand years. Only after that are all men judged as eternity begins.

There are problems, however, with this view. First of all, it asserts that the Last Judgment of the dead does not occur at the Second Coming, but rather a thousand years later. This is in stark contradiction to the rest of the New Testament, which clearly teaches that all the dead, righteous and unrighteous alike, are judged when the Lord returns (e.g. John 5:28–29).

Also, this view distorts the clear meaning of the text. For according to the premillennial view, **the first resurrection** (v. 5) is the resurrection of *all* the Christian dead at the Second Coming. Premillennialists assume this because it is the clear teaching of the rest of the New Testament (e.g. 1 Thess. 4:13–17). But the text here clearly says the opposite: the first resurrection is only of **those who had been beheaded** by the beast (v. 4). **The rest of the dead**—including presumably the rest of the Christian dead—**did not come to life until the thousand years were finished** (v. 5). Thus this view fails to read what the present passage actually says.

Then there is the *amillennial* view (meaning "no millennium"). St. Augustine of Hippo popularized this view as an alternative to a previous and overly literal premillennial view (see his *City of God*, Book 20). In the amillennial view, there is no actual thousand-year period on earth. After Christ returns, the eternity of the new heaven and earth begins. Rather, the period of a thousand years refers to the saints living in heaven, reigning there with Christ throughout this present age.

There are problems with this view as well. It assumes that the thousand-year reign of the martyrs is their continuation of life in heaven, but the text does not say this. Rather, it clearly describes the *bodily resurrection* of these saints, saying in v. 4 that **they came to life** (Gr. *ezesan*, compare its use in 2:8 to describe Christ's resurrection). To make absolutely clear that this coming to life is the resurrection of the dead, the text compares it to the resurrection of the dead for the rest of mankind.

Making the period of a thousand years contemporaneous with this age, as a sort of parallel existence in heaven, is ruled out by the text itself. For the passage begins by describing the binding of Satan after the Second Coming. There were no chapter divisions in the original, and it is apparent that the defeat of the beast at the end of the age in chapter 19 is followed by the account here in chapter 20 of Satan's binding in the abyss. The binding of Satan thus *follows sequentially* the Second Coming. Therefore, the thousand-year reign of the saints which follows that binding cannot be the saints reigning during this age. It is clear their reign is meant to begin *after* the Second Coming.

Finally, there is the *postmillennial* view. In this view, the events of chapter 19 refer not to the Second Coming, but to a great worldwide diffusion of the Gospel and a mass conversion of the world. It is only *after* this thousand-year period of unprecedented faith and earthly utopia that Christ will return. The reign of the saints in chapter 20

V. The New Beginning — Revelation 20:1–10

refers to the Church's ascendancy during this age after that end-time diffusion of the Gospel.

This view is the least satisfactory of them all. It is apparent that the Lord's coming upon a white horse from the opened heaven (in 19:11) is a description of the Second Coming, not (as suggested by the postmillennial view) a utopian diffusion of the Gospel throughout all the earth. This event heralds the wedding of the Lamb, for which His Bride has prepared herself (19:7). This consummation is clearly the bliss of the age to come—which, all agree, immediately follows the Second Coming. If this central event of chapter 19 is not the Second Coming, then that Coming *is never described in the Apocalypse*, but is left to be inferred as having happened at the end of the Millennium. This is untenable, given that the Second Coming is the climax to which the entire book has been building.

These three classic views of the Millennium, despite their differences, all have one thing in common. The common thread uniting them all (and disqualifying them all as adequate explanations of the passage) is that they understand the passage *as literal events pertaining to all the Church* and not as *a parable about the martyrs and their reward*.

All of these views fail because they try to interpret the literal events of chapter 20 in such a way as to make this text harmonize with the rest of the New Testament teaching about the Second Coming. As we have seen, this cannot be done without distorting the clear meaning of the text. As a recitation of literal events, this text *does not fit*. I suggest, though, that it is not to be taken literally, but as a parable.

What we are given here is not an answer to the question, "What happens to the Church after the Second Coming?" Everyone knew that answer already: the Kingdom of God and the Wedding of the Lamb, the bliss and joy of the age to come. What we are given here, in chapter 20, is a parable answering the question, "What reward shall the martyrs have, those who have paid the supreme sacrifice that others have not paid?"

This was no theoretical or merely academic question. Families and church communities in the early centuries would see their members—men, women, young teens—taken away, tortured, and publicly killed. The question of the reward of the martyrs was of urgent and heartbreaking pastoral concern. The parable of the Millennium gives the answer.

After the Second Coming, **an angel having the key of the abyss and a great chain**, the authority to render Satan powerless and inactive, came down from heaven. **He seized the dragon** who had persecuted the saints (12:17) and **cast him into the abyss**, so that Satan **should not deceive the nations any longer**. Through the devil's deception, the nations had been deceived into worshipping the beast and martyring the saints. Now he could do so no longer. The saints were safe.

John then **saw thrones** and those who **sat upon them**. The persons who previously stood in the dock as condemned criminals now **came to life** and sat upon the throne as judges of the world. (The term *souls* refers to living beings, not just the inner and bodiless spirits of the martyrs; compare the use of the term "soul" in 16:3 and 18:13.) These shared Christ's authority on earth **for a thousand years**, during which Satan was bound. They were **blessed and holy** and served with special privileged access as **priests of God and of Christ. The rest of the dead**, those who did *not* die as martyrs, **did not come to life** until after the reign of the martyrs was finished.

Thus, those who die for the Lord shall reign with Him, with a glory, radiance, intensity, and closeness not shared by others who were not called upon to pay this price. This extra reward is envisioned in this parable *in temporal terms*—as a kind of thousand-year "head start."

It is only after this that **Satan will be loosed from his prison** and will once again **deceive the nations** as he did before. There will be one final assault upon **the camp of the saints and the beloved city**. This final war against the City of God is called the assault of the far-distant **Gog and Magog** from **the four corners of the earth**. Using the apocalyptic image found in Ezekiel 38—39, St. John describes this last attempt of the nations to wipe out the people of God. As in the prophetic parable of Ezekiel, God defends His own

V. The New Beginning — Revelation 20:11–15

(Ezek. 39:6). **Fire came down from heaven and ate them up.** The devil **who deceived** the nations and orchestrated the final assault on the saints was **cast into the lake of fire**, even as **the beast and the false prophet** had been, and together they will be **tormented day and night to ages of ages** (compare 14:10–11).

What is this final rebellion and the loosing of Satan? Why would God loose him after he had been bound in the abyss? The answer is that the parable pictures this final war against the Church because *the Last Judgment was inconceivable without it*. All of the eschatological teaching in the Church presupposed that the Last Judgment would be preceded by a final outpouring of evil and an assault upon the Church. In the parable of chapter 20, a thousand-year reign of the martyrs is posited as a way of expressing the reward given them for their extraordinary suffering. But to preserve the Church's teaching that the Last Judgment is preceded by a time of crisis, it becomes necessary to posit a fresh release of Satan to precipitate this crisis. Thus the loosing of Satan is part of the overall parable and is necessitated by it. Its message is the same as the message of the persecution by the beast and of the final Armageddon: The Church may be surrounded by her foes, but the Lord will rescue her at the End and destroy all evil.

---

೫ ೫ ೫ ೫ ೫

11 And I saw a great white throne and Him who sat upon it, from whose face earth and heaven fled, and a place was not found for them.

12 And I saw the dead, the great and the little, standing before the throne, and books were opened; and another book was opened, which is the book of life; and the dead were judged from the things which were written in the books, according to their works.

13 And the sea gave *up* the dead in it, and death and Hades gave *up* the dead in them; and they were judged, each one, according to their works.

> 14 And death and Hades were cast into the lake of fire. This is the second death, the lake of fire.
> 15 And if anyone was not found written in the book of life, he was cast into the lake of fire.

Here, after the description of the Second Coming (and the parable of the martyrs' reward), is a description of the Last Judgment. John sees **a great white throne and Him who sat upon it, from whose face earth and heaven fled** away. The world would vanish like a dream before the unveiled Presence of the Judge. All the universe will flee in fear from before that countenance. But even so, that flight will be in vain, for His Presence will fill every corner of the cosmos. The throne is **great**, for its Judge will pass sentence on all who have ever lived. It is **white** because of the irreproachable purity of His judgment and the justice of His verdicts.

The image of the world fleeing from before God's face echoes Psalm 68:1. In this psalm, God is bidden to rise in judgment upon Israel's enemies, scattering them, so that those who hate Him flee from before His face. Here the whole universe seeks to flee from before that Face. The world would evade His scrutiny and avoid His judgment. But that is not possible. **A place** of escape will **not be found for them**. There will be no flight from the justice of God.

This image of final justice would have been very comforting and precious to a martyric Church that saw so little justice during its earthly sojourn. The martyrs saw many men, exalted Roman judges, sitting upon their earthly thrones, dispensing what passed for justice, condemning the Christians to death. The image of the great white throne declares to the martyrs that one day they will receive the justice denied them on earth, and that a higher Judge than the Roman ones will reopen their cases. Then the earthly judges will find themselves judged and will themselves stand in the dock.

And not just the Roman judges, but all **the dead, the great and the little**, must one day find themselves **standing before that throne**. None will be lacking. **The sea** will **give *up* the dead in it**, even though men thought such were irretrievably lost. **Death and Hades** will **give *up* the dead in them** too, as everyone who descended

V. The New Beginning   Revelation 20:11–15

to the land of the dead will come forth to face God's justice.

Then **books** will be **opened**, containing the truth about their works. All will be **judged**, each one, **according to** those **works**. If they kept the commandments of God (see 12:17), this will be disclosed. If their works were those of idolatry, murders, sorceries, fornication, and theft (see 9:20–21), this will be disclosed too. The books contained an accurate account of all their deeds, and all will be **judged from the things which were written in** those **books**. That is, there will be no bribery affecting the verdict, no favoritism. Justice will be absolutely impartial.

Another book will be **opened** as well—**the book of life**, containing the record of God's favorites and those destined for life (see 13:8 and comments). All upon whom God would have mercy were written in the heavenly register. The faithful Christians certainly were enrolled there (3:5), as were the righteous of the nations who persevere in doing good, thereby seeking for glory and honor and immortality (Rom. 2:6–7). In being assured that **the book of life** will be **opened**, the Christian readers are assured that God will not forget His promise to give them eternal life. Their reward is sure.

At the end, **death and Hades**, all the land of the dead, will be **cast into the lake of fire**. Indeed, **if anyone was not found written in the book of life, he was cast into the lake of fire** too. There will be only two fates awaiting all the children of men at the last—eternal life with Christ or eternal punishment. The only alternative to the lake of fire was to be enrolled in the book of life of the Lamb who was slaughtered (called this in 13:8). A Christian tempted to apostatize might imagine a place of rest in eternity even if he fell away from Christ and was erased from the register of His people. It was not to be so. If apostasy caused one to be erased from that book, one could not be saved.

This is the purpose of these terrifying verses. Its purpose is not a bloodthirsty one, as if the author were delighting in the prospect of how a great multitude of souls would be damned. It is rather a pastoral one, encouraging those tempted to fall away from Christ to hold onto the faith.

§V.2. The New Jerusalem: The Church's Inheritance and Reward

ॐ ॐ ॐ ॐ ॐ

21 1 And I saw a new heaven and a new earth; for the first heaven and the first earth passed away, and the sea is no longer.
2 And I saw the holy city, new Jerusalem, coming down from heaven from God, prepared as a bride adorned for her husband.
3 And I heard a great voice from the throne, saying, "Behold! the tabernacle of God *is* with men, and He will tabernacle with them, and they will be His peoples, and God Himself will be with them,
4 "and He will wipe away every tear from their eyes; and death will be no longer; neither shall there be mourning, nor clamor, nor pain; the first things have passed away."
5 And He who sits upon the throne said, "Behold, I am making all things new!" And He says, "Write, for these words are faithful and true."

As John continued looking, he **saw a new heaven and a new earth**. Isaiah had long ago prophesied that God would thus heal the sorrows of His people and "create Jerusalem for rejoicing" (see Is. 65:17–19). In Christ this new creation is manifested in the world. For after His Second Coming, there will be a renewed cosmos, and this present creation will be "freed from the slavery of corruption into the freedom of the glory of the children of God" (Rom. 8:21). St. Peter had written that the very heavens will be destroyed by burning and the elements will melt with the intense heat (2 Pet. 3:12). The new heaven and the new earth will rise up like a phoenix from the ashes of the old creation, and in this new world, "righteousness will find a home" (2 Pet. 3:13). This is because heaven will come to earth, uniting earth with heaven. God, who dwells now in

V. The New Beginning   Revelation 21:1–5

heaven, will then dwell on the earth, making His home among men.

In this renewed cosmos, **the sea** will be **no longer**. The sea represented restlessness and chaos for the ancient world. It was as if the primeval waters which once engulfed the earth in the flood were always straining at the world's edges, threatening to swallow it up again. It was only by the constant vigilant mercy of God that its proud waves were stopped (Job 38:11) and that it was restrained from once again drowning all. In the new world, such things as restlessness and chaos would find no place.

And John **saw** another sight, of breathtaking beauty: **the holy city, new Jerusalem, coming down from God**. Jerusalem was the city where God dwelt in power from the days of David, and it was thus the joy of the whole earth (Ps. 48:2). His tabernacle was there, a source of blessing to all in the city, making His saints to sing aloud for joy (see Ps. 132:13–16). All that Zion meant to Israel would be now eternally fulfilled, as God would finally dwell in the midst of His people. His dwelling-place or **tabernacle** (Gr. *skene*) would be **with men**, and He **will tabernacle with them** (Gr. *skenoo*). Israel was often promised by God that they "would be His people" and that He "would be their God" (e.g. Lev. 26:12; Jer. 31:33; Ezek. 37:23). That age-old hope now finds its complete and satisfying fulfillment. In the new city, God will draw close to all men in an intimate communion of love, and all the nations **will be His peoples**. We note that *peoples* is in the plural. Formerly, under the Old Covenant, Israel alone was called to be God's holy and chosen people. Now in Christ, at the consummation of the age, all the nations of the earth share that privilege and saving status.

The indwelling Presence of God among men meant the final glorification of His bride, a triumphant *theosis* and transformation for all His creation. In the days of John, brides were prepared for their wedding celebrations by being beautified with fine apparel. The Bride of Christ is also thus **prepared**, **adorned** with her righteous acts (19:8), ready and eager to meet her divine **husband**. The joy of an earthly wedding reflects something of the eternal bliss of the final indissoluble union of the Church with Christ.

In that day, as was prophesied of our return to Zion, "sorrow and sighing will flee away" (Is. 51:11). Now, in this age, our days are marked by pain, frustration, and sorrow. Years fly by, and happiness slips like sand through our fingers. Loved ones sicken and die before our eyes; hearts are loaded down with sorrow, tried by suffering, broken by grief. The youthful beauty of children turns too soon into decay and corruption; all men hasten to the hour of death. But all these things will vanish as a dream vanishes in the morning sun. While we look on, God will **make all things new.** He **will wipe away every tear** from the **eyes** of His children and banish from their world all things that had made them weep. **Death will be no longer**, nor will there be **mourning** from disaster, nor **clamor** and crying from bereavement, nor **pain** from disease and loss. These **first** and former **things** that now darken the world will have **passed away** forever. Such promises are almost too good to be believed, but John is told to **write** them down. The prophetic **words** are **faithful and true**, and will surely be fulfilled.

> ꙮ ꙮ ꙮ ꙮ ꙮ
>
> 6 And He said to me, "It has happened! I *Myself* am the Alpha and the Omega, the beginning and the end. I *Myself* will give to the one who thirsts from the fountain of the water of life freely.
> 7 "He who conquers will inherit these things, and I will be God to him, and he himself will be a son to Me.
> 8 "But for the cowardly and faithless and abominable and murderers and fornicators and sorcerers and idolaters and all liars, their part will be in the lake that burns with fire and sulfur, which is the second death."

God then said to John, **"It has happened!"** This is the single Greek word *gegonen*, "It is done!" (literally "*they* are done," referring to the making of all things new, v. 5). The announcement rings like a single note of triumph from a trumpet. God is the One who is **the Alpha and the Omega** (the pronoun **I** is emphatic), **the beginning**

(Gr. *arche*) **and the end** (Gr. *telos*). (The letters *alpha* and *omega* are the first and last letters of the Greek alphabet.) God had proclaimed of old that He was the first and the last (Is. 41:4), and so He will prove Himself to be. He is the source of all creation and its final goal; all things began through His command, and all will find their consummation, meaning, and fulfillment in Him as He recreates them. Just as "He who sits upon the throne" (v. 5) is the Creator of all (compare 4:10–11), so is He also the "re-Creator" of all, healing and transfiguring the cosmos after the image of its original beauty. The world lost its primordial beauty when we fell into sin. Now this divine beauty is restored afresh.

God is the One (again the pronoun **I** is emphatic) who will **give to the one who thirsts from the fountain of the water of life**, and will do this **freely**, without charge. Through the prophet Isaiah, God had long ago invited "everyone who thirsts" to "come to the waters," to slake their thirst "without money and without cost" (Is. 55:1). In Christ these promises find their eternal Yes, their everlasting fulfillment (2 Cor. 1:20). The soul who "thirsts for God" will finally "behold His power and His glory" (Ps. 63:1–2).

The invitation here is not so much to the unbelieving world as it is to the believing Christian, who is nonetheless tempted to fall away in the persecution and worship the beast. Such a one is encouraged to hold onto his faith and thus slake his thirst in the Kingdom of God. If he would **conquer** the world through his faith (1 John 5:4), he would indeed **inherit** all **these things**. The Father would **be God to him**, giving him protection and provision, and he would **be a son** to Him, receiving all that He had to give.

If he did *not* hold onto his faith, another fate awaited him. If, under pressure of persecution, he was **cowardly** and apostatized to save his neck, if he proved **faithless** to Christ and renounced Him, if he worshipped pagan abominations and became **abominable** himself—then he would not receive his promised inheritance. If he joined the ranks of the pagan **murderers and fornicators and sorcerers and idolaters** (compare 9:20–21), if he accepted the lie that the beast was to be worshipped and joined **all** the other **liars** (that is, those who accepted the lies of the beast), then he would share their fate. And **their part would be in the lake that burns with fire and sulfur**. Such idolaters might have thought that if they died peacefully in their beds, they were safe from divine justice. But God is not mocked (Gal. 6:7), and a **second death** awaited those whose works deserved the wrath of God.

> ॐ ॐ ॐ ॐ ॐ
>
> 9 And one of the seven angels who had the seven bowls full of the seven last plagues came and spoke with me, saying, "Come, I will show you the bride, the wife of the Lamb."
> 10 And he carried me away in the Spirit to a great and high mountain and showed me the holy city, Jerusalem, coming down from heaven from God,
> 11 having the glory of God.

Then one of the seven angels who had the seven bowls full of the seven last plagues came to John. As one of those who had judged the great prostitute, he had shown John the degraded harlot he had judged (17:1). Once before John had been carried away in the Spirit into the wilderness to behold the harlot (17:3); now he was similarly carried away in the Spirit to a great and high mountain to behold a very different woman. For this was no harlot, but the spotless bride of Christ, the wife of the Lamb. Even as one needs distance to fully see a mountain, so John had need of such an exalted location to see such an exalted sight.

The image of the bride coalesces into an image of a city—**the holy city, Jerusalem, coming down from heaven from God**, radiantly lit up with **the glory of God**. Jerusalem was always, from the days of King David, the dwelling-place of God, and the prophet Ezekiel prophesied that at the end it would be so in truth. It would be known finally as *Yahweh-shamma*—"Yahweh is there" (Ezek. 48:35). St. John saw that this too would be fulfilled in Christ, and that at the end, God would manifest His unveiled glory in the midst of His people.

V. The New Beginning — Revelation 21:11–21

❧ ❧ ❧ ❧ ❧

11 Her light *was* like a precious stone, as a stone of crystal-clear jasper.

12 *It* had a great and high wall, having twelve gates, and at the gates twelve angels; and on the gates were written the names of the twelve tribes of the sons of Israel.

13 There were three gates on the east and three gates on the north and three gates on the south and three gates on the west.

14 And the wall of the city had twelve foundations, and on them were the twelve names of the twelve apostles of the Lamb.

15 The one who spoke with me had a gold measuring reed that he might measure the city, and its gates and its wall.

16 And the city lies foursquare, and its length is as much as the breadth; and he measured the city with the reed, twelve thousand stadia; its length and breadth and height are equal.

17 And he measured its wall, one hundred and forty-four cubits, by the measure of man, which is also *that* of the angel.

18 The material of the wall *was* jasper; and the city *was* pure gold, like pure glass.

19 The foundations of the city wall were adorned with every precious stone. The first foundation was jasper; the second, sapphire; the third, chalcedony; the fourth, emerald;

20 the fifth, sardonyx; the sixth, sardius; the seventh, chrysolite; the eighth, beryl; the ninth, topaz; the tenth, chrysoprase; the eleventh, jacinth; the twelfth, amethyst.

21 And the twelve gates *were* twelve pearls; each one of the gates was from one pearl. And

> the street of the city *was* pure gold, like clear glass.

There follows a symbolic description of the holy city. Her **light** and brilliance was **like a precious stone**, sparkling like **crystal-clear jasper**, shining with the radiance of the divine Presence. It **had a great and high wall**, showing that the redeemed remain secure, protected by God from any harm. Those walls were **one hundred and forty-four cubits** high (v. 17). This symbolic number was previously used in 7:4, being the product of twelve times twelve. Twelve is the number of completion, so that one hundred and forty-four is the number of perfect completion. Thus nothing is lacking in God's provision of security in the age to come.

Moreover, the twelve walls between the twelve gates had **twelve foundations** (that is, a foundation stone under each wall), and on these were written **the twelve names of the twelve apostles of the Lamb**. The apostles were foundational to the Church (Eph. 2:20), and therefore their names are inscribed on the foundations of the heavenly city. It is upon their witness that our salvation is built.

Those unbreachable walls were nonetheless pierced by **twelve gates** (compare Ezek. 48:31–34). At each of the four directions, there were **three gates**, for the Kingdom stood open to all. Men would come "from east and west, and from north and south to recline at table in the Kingdom of God" (Luke 13:29). Men were called to bring all their honor and glory into it (Rev. 21:26), and an abundance of gates stood ready to receive them. **At the gates** stood **twelve angels**, for the power of God guarded the saints; and **on the gates were written the names of the twelve tribes of the sons of Israel**, for the Kingdom of God fulfilled all the divine promises to the chosen people.

The angel who spoke with John **had a measuring reed that he might measure the city, and its gates and its wall**, to survey all and praise all that God had done. The reed was **gold**, for the city it measured was precious and eternal. As Ezekiel in his vision saw Jerusalem measured (Ezek. 40:42), and as Zechariah in his vision saw an angel going to measure the holy city (Zech. 2:1f), so St. John also saw an angel measure the heavenly Jerusalem. That this **measure of man** is **also *that* of the angel** who spoke with John (v. 17) means that the city is to be home to both angels and men.

The measurements were all deeply symbolic. **The city lies four-square**, with its **length and breadth and height** all **equal**, for in the thought of the ancients, the cube was the perfect shape. (We note that the inner sanctuary in Solomon's Temple was of cubic shape; 1 Kings 6:20.) Each of these measurements was **twelve thousand stadia**, the number twelve being the image of completeness and the number thousand that of vastness (compare such numerical significance in 7:5). The city is thus vast enough to hold all the redeemed and contains their complete number. There is room for all; none need fear there will be no place left for him. (To translate *twelve thousand stadia* into the English "fifteen hundred miles" is thus to miss the point of the symbolism.)

All the material of the heavenly city reflected its preciousness. The **wall** was of **jasper**, a translucent rock crystal, sparkling with the divine glory; the **city** itself and its **streets** were of **pure gold**, shining **like clear glass**, without any impurity or flaw, timeless and eternal (for gold does not rust). Its **twelve gates** were each from **one** single **pearl**, of breathtaking beauty (for beaming pearls are of captivating beauty; compare the man in Matt. 13:46 who sold all that he had to possess such a treasure). The **foundations of the city wall were adorned with every** kind of **precious stone** known to man, reflecting the stones on the breastplate of the high-priest (Ex. 28:17–20), for the city contained the Presence of God, which Presence that high-priest also was called to serve. Such precious stones once belonged to the high-priest alone, but now the privileged communion he alone once enjoyed is given to all the people.

> ༃ ༃ ༃ ༃ ༃
> 22 I saw no sanctuary in it, for the Lord God the Almighty and the Lamb are its sanctuary.
> 23 And the city does not have need of the sun or of the moon to shine on it, for the glory of God has illumined it, and its lamp *is* the Lamb.

> 24 And the nations will walk by its light, and the kings of the earth will bring their glory into it.
> 25 And its gates will never be shut by day (for there will be no night there);
> 26 and they will bring the glory and the honor of the nations into it;
> 27 and no unclean thing, and no one who does abomination and lying, will ever enter into it, but only those whose names are written in the Lamb's book of life.

In all that eternal city, there was but one thing missing that one could find in any earthly city of man: John **saw no sanctuary** or temple there, no place to worship God. Indeed, it had need of none. Earthly sanctuaries were places for God to dwell in, localities where His Presence could be accessed. One built an altar and a temple *here*, in this or that place, so that one might find God there, and God was to be found in that temple as He could not be found elsewhere. It marked the division between holy ground and common ground (compare Gen. 28:16–17 and Ex. 3:5–6 for the concept of God being found only in such holy places). Here, in the eternal Jerusalem, it was no longer possible to localize the divine Presence, for that Presence was everywhere. The **Lord God the Almighty and the Lamb are its sanctuary**, and their Presence floods the city.

That is also why the city **does not have need of the sun or of the moon to shine on it**. The **glory of God** and of **the Lamb** has **illumined it** and is its **lamp**. The Presence of the Father and His co-equal Son together form a single light that ceaselessly illumines those who dwell there, so that they never need walk in darkness any more (John 12:46). Thus all God's creation (imaged by all **the nations** and their **kings**) will **walk by** this **light**. The darkness of sin and death that clouded our existence will be banished forever. In this darkened age, men lavished their **glory and honor** on idols, only to find that the idols were powerless to save.

V. The New Beginning — Revelation 22:1–5

In that blessed age to come, creation will be healed of such folly, and **the kings of the earth** will **bring their glory** to God alone. The city will ceaselessly resound with this offering of praise, as all men **bring the glory and the honor of the nations** to lay at the feet of the King. The **gates will never be shut by day**, but will be always open to receive such homage (for **there will be no night there**). In the ancient world, city gates were shut at night to keep out the threat of invasion, but such precautions will not be needed there. Isaiah foresaw a day when Zion's gates "would be open continually and not be shut day or night, that men may bring into it the wealth of the Gentiles and their kings in procession" (Is. 60:11). That prophecy of glory for the people of God would now be fulfilled.

The redeemed will thus enter the city to bask in the radiance of the Father and the Son and to offer their glorious praise. But the redeemed alone have such access. For **no unclean thing** will ever enter into the city. Evil men defile cities in this age, darkening them with crime and oppression. But the eternal city is safe from evil. These evil men will never defile it with their presence, nor will **one who does abomination** such as idolatry or **lying. Only those whose names are written in the Lamb's book of life** have access to that bliss. Those acknowledged by Christ may enter into the joy of their Lord.

Once again, this word is addressed not so much to those who have never heard the Gospel, but to Christians who have heard it and might be tempted to apostatize in the coming persecution. These are challenged to hold to their faith, for only so will their names not be erased from the Lamb's book of life (3:5). If they would enter that shining city, they must persevere in their Faith.

---

୬ ୬ ୬ ୬ ୬

22 1 And he showed me a river of the water of life, bright as crystal, proceeding from the throne of God and of the Lamb,
2 in the middle of its street. On this *side* and that

> *side* of the river was the tree of life, making twelve fruits, rendering its fruit each month; and the leaves of the tree *were* for the healing of the nations.
>
> 3 There will no longer be any curse; and the throne of God and of the Lamb will be in it, and His slaves will worship Him;
>
> 4 they will see His face, and His Name *will be* upon their foreheads.
>
> 5 And night will be no longer; and they do not have need of the light of lamp or sun, because the Lord God will enlighten them; and they will reign to ages of ages.

Boundless life shall forever flow there, streaming from God's Presence. John was shown **a river of the water of life proceeding from the throne of God and of the Lamb**. (Once again the Father and His co-equal Son are portrayed as sharing the same authority and throne.) Earthly rivers can be muddy, but the river of the City was **bright as crystal**, since it contained the life of God. The river went down **the middle of its street**, accessible to all. On either side of it was **the tree of life**, bearing the fruit of immortality. This was the life men were denied in Paradise after the Fall (Gen. 3:22), but which is finally restored to those who conquer in Christ (2:7). The tree produced **twelve fruits, rendering its fruit each month**, and **the leaves of the tree** were for **healing**. That is, in the Kingdom, there is abundant variety and satisfaction and healing for every one of life's wounds.

The image of the life-giving river is found in Ezekiel 47:1. In the vision of Ezekiel, the river gave life to all the land of Israel, but here life is given to all **the nations**. (We note again that the ancient promise to Israel that they would be "His people" is widened in the Apocalypse to include all men.) There is a generous universality in the Apocalypse. All the nations might feel God's wrath, for all were involved in the worship of the beast (13:8; 17:2). But God's will is

V. The New Beginning — Revelation 22:1–5

to bless all the nations and for all nations to walk in the light of the Lord. Thus all nations are portrayed as finally being liberated from error (20:3) and as bringing their earthly glory and praise into the city of God (21:24). The healing offered by God is for all the world.

The glorious vision now reaches its climax. In the city of God, **there will no longer be any curse**. The curse of death and hardship, of suffering and sorrow, which has darkened the steps of man since he left the Garden (Gen. 3:17–19), will darken them no more. **The throne of God and of the Lamb** (that single source of authority and blessing) **will be in** the city, and God's **slaves** and servants will approach it with joy to **worship Him**. At last the pure in heart **will see His face** (Matt. 5:8); they will look to Him and be radiant (Ps. 34:5). In this age, no one could behold His face without dying (Ex. 33:20). In that blessed age, His servants will look the King full in the face and live forever. Moreover, **His Name *will be* upon their foreheads**. Even as the beast had stamped its devotees as its own property (13:16), so God will know His own children as they reflect His holiness.

In that day, the uncreated light of **the Lord God will enlighten them** and will flood the city, so that **night will be no longer**, and they will **not have need of the light of lamp or** of the **sun**. They will bask in that gladsome light forever and **will reign** with God **to ages of ages**. In the Law, God had promised that He would lift up the light of His countenance upon His people and give them peace (Num. 6:24–27). In that day, the light on His face will indeed shine upon His people, and there will come a day that will know no evening, the eternal Pascha.

It is with this triumphant vision that the Apocalypse reaches its conclusion. There were terrifying visions of judgment and the predictions of fearful persecution and death. But this is given as the final word, a word of peace, a vision of joy. This is the sight God would leave in the hearts of His Church—the sight of the heavenly Zion glorious and triumphant, eternally secure in the invincible joy of heaven. This hope would sustain the Church in the dark days of this age that were to follow.

§V.3. Conclusion

> 🙶 🙶 🙶 🙶 🙶
>
> 6 And he said to me, "These words *are* faithful and true; and the Lord, the God of the spirits of the prophets, sent His angel to show to His slaves the things which must happen soon."
> 7 ("And behold, I am coming soon! Blessed *is* he who keeps the words of the prophecy of this book.")
> 8 And I *myself*, John, *am* the one who heard and saw these things. And when I heard and saw them, I fell down to worship before the feet of the angel who showed me these things.
> 9 And he says to me, "See *that you do* not *do that*! I am a fellow-slave of yours and of your brothers the prophets and of those who keep the words of this book. Worship God."

We begin now with the final commendation of the Revelation to St. John. Once again, the **words** of the prophecy are certified as **faithful and true** (compare such assurances in 19:9; 21:5), and therefore certain to be fulfilled. **The Lord, the God of the spirits of the prophets** (both in the Old Covenant and the New), **sent His angel** with this vision **to show to His slaves the things which must happen soon** (compare 1:1).

It is possible that verse 7 is part of the quotation begun in verse 6 and belongs to the same speaker. If that is so, then the speaker of both verses is Jesus Christ. It would appear, however, that the speaker of 21:9–22:5 is "one of the seven angels who had the seven bowls full of the seven last plagues" (21:9), the one who showed John the heavenly city (21:9–10, 15; 22:1; compare 22:8). That being so, verse 7 represents an interjection by Christ into the angelic narrative. As with a similar insertion in 16:15, this interrupts the narrative flow, much as the Second Coming will interrupt the flow of history and bring it to an end.

V. The New Beginning Revelation 22:6–9

The Lord promises that He is **coming soon**. This imminence is not such as can be measured by calendars; it is the imminence of the divine timetable. All that God had to accomplish for the salvation of men has been done; nothing now remains but the final things. As St. John elsewhere writes, "it is the last hour" (1 John 2:18). The ends of all the ages have come, and the Church since Pentecost has been living in the last days (Acts 2:17; 1 Cor. 10:11). Thus **he who keeps the words of the prophecy of this book** and resists the beast will be **blessed** and inherit all these things after the Lord comes (Rev. 21:7).

John emphatically testifies that he was the one **who heard and saw these things** (the pronoun **I** is emphatic), and he can vouch for their accuracy. And after he **heard and saw them**, he once again **fell down to worship before the feet of the angel who showed** him the holy city. Once again, he was rebuked for this act, and the angel told him that he was but the **fellow-slave** of John and the other **prophets** and of all those Christians **who keep the words of this book**. John must **worship God** only.

An identical rebuke was given in 19:10 (where see comments). In 19:9–10, the identity of the speaker is not clearly stated. (We have suggested that it was Christ's angel, who mediated His Presence and thus resembled Him.) Here in 22:8 it is clearly stated that the speaker was the angel who showed John these things. That is, the angelic nature of the speaker is stressed, and John relates this second mistake and rebuke to make doubly sure the churches of Asia Minor do not stray into the worship of angels.

One may ask in passing, how is it that John made the same mistake twice? If we are correct in surmising that his first mistake in 19:10 was caused by the angel's outward resemblance to Christ, how could he make the same error again? The answer may be found in Christ's inserted word in 22:7. We are given only a verbal account of this experience and are not told what John actually saw when the angel spoke with him in verse 6, nor what he saw when Christ spoke in verse 7. We gratuitously assume the same consistency of person that we experience in our daily waking life. But this apocalyptic vision was more akin to our dreams than to our waking experience, and in our dreams one speaker can freely be transformed into another. I would therefore suggest that the angelic speaker of verse 6 appeared to John as if he were Christ at the time he carried His words of verse 7, and this was the source of St. John's mistake.

> ॐ ॐ ॐ ॐ ॐ
> 10 And he says to me, "Do not seal up the words of the prophecy of this book, for the time is near.
> 11 "He who is unrighteous, let him be unrighteous still; and he who is filthy, let him be filthy still; and he who is righteous, let him be righteous still; and he who is holy, let him be holy still."

When Daniel was given his visions, he was told to "seal up the book until the time of the end" (Dan. 12:4), for the visions pertained to a time far distant to Daniel's. St. John, however, is told, **"Do not seal up the words of the prophecy of this book,"** since **the time** when they would begin to be fulfilled **is near**. The persecution from the state had already begun (of which John's presence in Patmos was evidence), and the spread of the cult of emperor worship was soon to face all Christians with the decisions of their lives. All must now decide—there was no time to slowly ponder one's allegiances and weigh the issues, no time to let one's thinking on the matter mature. One must take sides now and be either hot or cold (compare 3:15). This is the meaning of the challenge, **"He who is unrighteous, let him be unrighteous still . . . he who is righteous, let him be righteous still."** It is not that God calls the unrighteous man to *persevere in his wickedness*; it is that God calls all men to *decide now*.

It would seem that the speaker of verses 10–11 is the angel who rebuked John in verse 9, for this would make these instructions about sealing the book parallel to the instructions about sealing the book in Daniel. It was an angel who spoke to Daniel about sealing the book in Daniel 12:4, and it would be fitting if it were an angel who spoke to John about this issue also.

V. The New Beginning — Revelation 22:12–16

> ꙮ ꙮ ꙮ ꙮ ꙮ
>
> 12 "Behold, I am coming soon, and My reward *is* with Me, to render to each man as his work is.
> 13 "I *Myself am* the Alpha and the Omega, the first and the last, the beginning and the end.
> 14 "Blessed *are* those who wash their robes, so that they may have their authority to *eat of* the tree of life, and may enter by the gates into the city.
> 15 "Outside *are* the dogs and the sorcerers and the fornicators and the murderers and the idolaters, and everyone who loves and makes a lie.
> 16 "I *Myself*, Jesus, have sent My angel to witness to you *people* these things for the churches. I am the root and the descendant of David, the bright morning star."

In verses 12–16, Jesus speaks once again. The decision about one's moral and spiritual stance is urgent because Jesus is **coming soon**, and His **reward *is* with** Him, **to render to each man as his work is**. Whatever decision and choice men make, Christ will render the appropriate reward. He is the One (the pronoun **I** is emphatic) who is **the Alpha and the Omega**, and as such, He has authority to judge. He is not only **the first**, the **beginning** and source of all who live, He is also **the last**, the One who will preside over the fate of men when history has ended.

We note that God the Father declared *Himself* to be "the *Alpha* and the *Omega*," "the beginning and the end" in 21:6, as He did in 1:8. Can there be two *Alphas*, two beginnings? How can both the Father and Christ be *Alpha* and *Omega*? Here is further proof of the co-equality and consubstantiality of the Father and the Son. Both God the Father and Christ the Son are *Alpha* and *Omega*, for Christ is one with His Father (John 10:30).

Christ pronounces the final blessing of the Apocalypse upon **those who wash their robes** in His precious Blood, making them white (7:14). By their trust in the Cross of Christ and by their steadfast confession of Him even to death, these **have their authority to *eat of* the tree of life** and partake of immortal life. These **may enter by the gates** and come boldly **into the city** of God, where only the blessed and righteous are allowed to dwell.

For they are righteous. They are not like those excluded from the city and banished to the **outside**, far from the light of God. Such are **the dogs** (that is, the sexually impure; compare its use describing homosexual cult prostitutes in Deut. 23:18), **the sorcerers and the fornicators and the murderers and the idolaters, and everyone who loves and makes a lie**, delighting in lies such as the idolatrous lie of beast worship. Those who refused to come out of the city of Babylon and repent of her sins (18:4) are now refused access to the city of New Jerusalem. Such impenitent pagans have chosen which city they belong to, and they must abide forever in their choice.

The Lord **Jesus** reaffirms the authenticity of the revelation. It is He who speaks (again the **I** is emphatic); He has **sent** His **angel to witness to you *people*** (the **you** is plural) **these things for the churches**. What John had written was by His authority and will—let no one disregard the message.

The Lord then describes Himself as **the root and the descendant of David** and as **the bright morning star**. As the true Messiah of Israel, He is **the root** and source of David, the One who called him to his destiny as king in Jerusalem. He is also **the descendant** of David, the One who became incarnate through David's historical line. That is, He is both transcendent, ruling history as God, and a participant in history as Man.

He is also **the bright morning star**. As said above (in the comments on 2:28), the morning star is the first "star" seen in the morning, usually known as the planet Venus. Christ here describes Himself as the bright morning star because the sight of this star in the sky is the sign that the night is over and that the morning is at hand. His Church would have to endure the long dark night of persecution and suffering. But the night would not last forever. The

V. The New Beginning   Revelation 22:17–19

morning would come, and Christ reigns from the throne of God as the promise of that future dawning.

> ༄ ༄ ༄ ༄ ༄
>
> 17 And the Spirit and the bride say, "Come." And let the one who hears say, "Come." And let the one who thirsts come; let the one who wants take the water of life freely.

Once again **the Spirit** speaks (compare His last utterance in 14:13). What is significant is that **the bride** of Christ, the Church, speaks as well, and these two share a common message. More accurately, the Spirit speaks *as the voice of the Church*, through her prophets such as John, inviting the world to **come** to Christ. Christ will come, rising in glory as the morning star, to banish all darkness from the world. He does not wish that any should perish, but that all should come to repentance and life, and He wills that **the one who thirsts** for life **come** and **take the water of life freely**, without cost (compare Is. 55:1).

John invites **the one who hears** this call to echo it to the world as well. Let all the Christians say, **"Come,"** and open the doors of the Church to the penitent seeker. The water of life was promised to the Christians, to those who conquered (21:6–7). The world may come and join the Christians, and slake its thirst at the eternal fountain. One might imagine that persecution would harden the hearts of the Christians against their persecutors and cause them to delight in their overthrow. But it is not so. They too invite their enemies to come and join them in the Kingdom of God.

> ༄ ༄ ༄ ༄ ༄
>
> 18 I witness to everyone who hears the words of the prophecy of this book: If anyone adds to them, God will add to him the plagues which are written in this book;

> 19 and if anyone takes away from the words of the book of this prophecy, God will take away his part from the tree of life and from the holy city, which are written in this book.

Before the final words, there is a warning not to distort or tamper with the divine message. Many ancient texts concluded with similar warnings, since in the days before the printing press, subsequent copies could be easily changed and adapted according to the views and whims of the copyist. Since this is a divine message, distorting its message will bring not just human complaints, but divine wrath. **If anyone** would **add** to these words, inserting his own teachings and counsels and claiming they were God's teachings, **God** Himself would **add to him the plagues which are written in this book**. Such a person would be a false prophet, and God would judge him as such.

Similarly, **if anyone** would dare to **take away from the words of the book of this prophecy**, omitting sections because he objected to them, **God** would **take away his part from the tree of life and from the holy city**. Apostates would be judged as apostates. In both these judgments, God would deal with the offenders appropriately: if they unlawfully added to God's message, God would add judgment to them. If they unlawfully took away from God's message, God would take away something from them.

> ꙮ ꙮ ꙮ ꙮ ꙮ
> 20 He who witnesses to these things says, "Yes, I am coming soon." Amen! Come, Lord Jesus!

Christ speaks His final word. He has **witnessed** to all that John has done in fulfilling his charge (1:19), and He adds a word of both warning and promise: **"Yes, I am coming soon."** With this word, the Apocalypse comes to an end. The blessed hope and earnest expectation of the churches was that Christ would come with the clouds, and that they would see Him (1:7). This was the great theme and climax of the Apocalypse. Speaking with the voice of the Church,

V. The New Beginning — Revelation 22:21

St. John cannot but add to His Lord's final word his own heart's cry: **Amen! Come, Lord Jesus!** This was the hope by which the Church lived, and through which it would survive throughout this long age. This is the perseverance of the saints.

§V.4. Epistolary Blessing

> ॐ ॐ ॐ ॐ ॐ
> 21 The grace of the Lord Jesus *be* with all. Amen.

The Apocalypse was written as an epistle, a circular letter to the churches of Asia. As an apostle, St. John concludes his epistle with the usual apostolic blessing.

A Practical Conclusion

Having read the Apocalypse, we must ask ourselves the question, "Now what?" The Book of Revelation was not given to the Church as a mental exercise or as a merely edifying early Christian version of *Star Wars*. It was given to bless us (compare the proffered blessing of 1:3). In other words, it was given to change us.

How do we receive this blessing so that we "have the authority to eat of the tree of life" (22:14)? There is only one way in the Christian Faith to receive the blessing of God. And that is to be holy, to live as the true disciples of Jesus Christ.

This is described in many different ways. The Lord Himself describes it as being *in* the world but "not *of* the world" (John 17:16). St. Paul describes it as "not being conformed to this age" but rather being "transfigured by the renewing of your mind" (Rom. 12:2). St. James describes it as refusing to be "a friend of the world" and thus "an enemy of God" (James 4:4). St. Peter urges us "as aliens and strangers, to abstain from fleshly lusts . . . keeping our behavior excellent among the Gentiles" (1 Pet. 2:11–12). St. Jude, in his short epistle, says, "Keep yourselves in the love of God, waiting anxiously for the mercy of our Lord Jesus Christ to eternal life" (Jude 21). And St. John himself, in one of his own epistles, tells us, "Do not love the world, nor the things in the world" (1 John 2:15).

All the writers of the New Testament, in fact, tell us the same thing and describe the same attitude that must be ours if we would receive God's blessing. This attitude and call to discipleship is sounded also in the Apocalypse. In answer to the practical question, "Now what?" it says three things:

Firstly, it says to *be prophetically critical of the world*. The world, with all its values, joys, sorrows, and turmoil, has a subtle and deadly way of capturing the heart and making us believe that if the whole world thinks something, it must be so. What's the big problem with burning a bit of incense before the image of your emperor and simply saying, "Caesar is Lord"? Everybody does it! It's no big deal. *Everyone* says it's okay: who are you to say the whole world is wrong?

Against such persuasion, the Apocalypse reveals that the whole world *can* be wrong. It was wrong when it crucified the Lord of glory. It is wrong now, when it says it holds the ultimate values. If we would be faithful and blessed, we have to learn to be discerning and not accept whatever the world offers us. Some of what it offers is good. Some of it is lethal and, if accepted, will lead us to being "tormented with fire and sulfur to ages of ages" (14:10–11).

Secondly, the Apocalypse says *we must be ready to die for our Lord*. Here we must be very careful and precise. We are not told to be or to feel courageous. (This is fortunate, since feelings are next to impossible to simulate or produce on one's own.) We need not work ourselves into a state where we think that if the world threatened to kill us for our Faith, we would remain steadfast. What is required is not *a psychological state*; it is a *decision*. The Lord will give the required courage when we need it. (And probably not before.) We must decide in advance, in the present quietness and peace, before the police or the armies of Antichrist come and knock on our door, that we will never deny the Lord. We will die for Him if we have to. We offer this decision to Him as an act of self-oblation. It is for Him to give us the strength to carry it through at the proper time.

Thirdly and finally, the Book of Revelation says *we should always look forward to the Second Coming*. That is why it is placed prominently at the beginning of the book in 1:7 ("Behold, He is coming with the clouds") and at its ending in 22:12 ("Behold, I am coming soon"). This is what the Apocalypse would have us focus on—the joy of "the blessed hope and appearance of the glory of our great God and Savior Jesus Christ" (Titus 2:13). We are to have the cry of *Maranatha* always in our hearts. It is this that saves us from being lukewarm and complacent. As Fr. Sergius says (in the essay quoted in the Introduction), "A non-apocalyptic, non-eschatological Christianity is a dangerous counterfeit of the real thing and a secularization of it." Amen. Come, Lord Jesus.

About the Author

Archpriest Lawrence Farley currently pastors St. Herman of Alaska Orthodox Church (OCA) in Langley, B.C., Canada. He received his B.A. from Trinity College, Toronto, and his M.Div. from Wycliffe College, Toronto. A former Anglican priest, he converted to Orthodoxy in 1985 and studied for two years at St. Tikhon's Orthodox Seminary in Pennsylvania. In addition to the books in the Orthodox Bible Study Companion series, he has also published *The Christian Old Testament: Looking at the Hebrew Scriptures through Christian Eyes; A Song in the Furnace: The Message of the Book of Daniel; Unquenchable Fire: The Traditional Christian Teaching about Hell; A Daily Calendar of Saints: A Synaxarion for Today's North American Church; Let Us Attend: A Journey Through the Orthodox Divine Liturgy; One Flesh: Salvation through Marriage in the Orthodox Church; The Empty Throne: Reflections on the History and Future of the Orthodox Episcopacy;* and *Following Egeria: A Visit to the Holy Land through Time and Space.*

ANCIENT FAITH RADIO

Visit www.ancientfaithradio.com to listen to Fr. Lawrence Farley's regular podcast, "No Other Foundation: Reflections on Orthodox Theology and Biblical Studies."

A Complete List of the Books in the Orthodox Bible Study Companion Series

The Gospel of Matthew
Torah for the Church
• Paperback, 400 pages, ISBN 978-0-9822770-7-2

The Gospel of Mark
The Suffering Servant
• Paperback, 280 pages, ISBN 978-1-888212-54-9

The Gospel of Luke
Good News for the Poor
• Paperback, 432 pages, ISBN 978-1-936270-12-5

The Gospel of John
Beholding the Glory
• Paperback, 376 pages, ISBN 978-1-888212-55-6

The Acts of the Apostles
Spreading the Word
• Paperback, 352 pages, ISBN 978-1-936270-62-0

The Epistle to the Romans
A Gospel for All
• Paperback, 208 pages, ISBN 978-1-888212-51-8

First and Second Corinthians
Straight from the Heart
• Paperback, 319 pages, ISBN 978-1-888212-53-2

Words of Fire
The Early Epistles of St. Paul to the Thessalonians and the Galatians
• Paperback, 172 pages, ISBN 978-1-936270-02-6

The Prison Epistles
Philippians – Ephesians – Colossians – Philemon
• Paperback, 224 pages, ISBN 978-1-888212-52-5

Shepherding the Flock
The Pastoral Epistles of St. Paul the Apostle to Timothy and Titus
• Paperback, 144 pages, ISBN 978-1-888212-56-3

The Epistle to the Hebrews
High Priest in Heaven
• Paperback, 184 pages, ISBN 978-1-936270-74-3

Universal Truth
The Catholic Epistles of James, Peter, Jude, and John
• Paperback, 232 pages, ISBN 978-1-888212-60-0

The Apocalypse of St. John
A Revelation of Love and Power
• Paperback, 240 pages, ISBN 978-1-936270-40-8

Other Books by the Author

The Christian Old Testament
Looking at the Hebrew Scriptures through Christian Eyes
Many Christians see the Old Testament as "the other Testament": a source of exciting stories to tell the kids, but not very relevant to the Christian life. *The Christian Old Testament* reveals the Hebrew Scriptures as the essential context of Christianity, as well as a many-layered revelation of Christ Himself. Follow along as Fr. Lawrence Farley explores the Christian significance of every book of the Old Testament.
• Paperback, 200 pages, ISBN 978-1-936270-53-8

A Song in the Furnace
The Message of the Book of Daniel
The Book of Daniel should be read with the eyes of a child. It's a book of wonders and extremes—mad kings, baffling dreams with gifted interpreters, breathtaking deliverances, astounding prophecies—with even what may be the world's first detective stories added in for good measure. To argue over the book's historicity, as scholars have done for centuries, is to miss the point. In *A Song in the Furnace*, Fr. Lawrence Farley reveals all the wonders of this unique book to the receptive eye.
• Paperback, 248 pages, ISBN 978-1-944967-31-4

A Daily Calendar of Saints
A Synaxarion for Today's North American Church
Popular biblical commentator and church historian Fr. Lawrence Farley turns his hand to hagiography in this collection of lives of saints, one or more for each day of the calendar year. His accessible prose and contemporary approach make these ancient lives easy for modern Christians to relate to and understand.
• Paperback, 304 pages, ISBN 978-1-944967-41-3

Unquenchable Fire
The Traditional Christian Teaching about Hell
The doctrine of hell as a place of eternal punishment has never been easy for Christians to accept. The temptation to retreat from and reject the Church's traditional teaching about hell is particularly strong in our current culture, which has demonstrably lost its sense of sin. Fr. Lawrence Farley examines the Orthodox Church's teaching on this difficult subject through the lens of Scripture and patristic writings, making the case that the existence of hell does not negate that of a loving and forgiving God.
• Paperback, 240 pages, ISBN 978-1-944967-18-5

Let Us Attend
A Journey Through the Orthodox Divine Liturgy
Fr. Lawrence Farley provides a guide to understanding the Divine Liturgy, and a vibrant reminder of the centrality of the Eucharist in living the Christian life, guiding believers in a devotional and historical walk through the Orthodox Liturgy. Examining the Liturgy section by section, he provides both historical explanations of how the Liturgy evolved and devotional insights aimed at helping us pray the Liturgy in the way the Fathers intended.
• Paperback, 104 pages, ISBN 978-1-888212-87-7

One Flesh
Salvation through Marriage in the Orthodox Church
Is the Church too negative about sex? Beginning with this provocative question, Fr. Lawrence Farley explores the history of the Church's attitude toward sex and marriage, from the Old Testament through the Church Fathers. He persuasively makes the case both for traditional morality and for a positive acceptance of marriage as a viable path to theosis.
• Paperback, 160 pages, ISBN 978-1-936270-66-8

The Empty Throne
Reflections on the History and Future of the Orthodox Episcopacy
In contemporary North America, the bishop's throne in the local parish stands empty for most of the year. The bishop is an honored occasional guest rather than a true pastor of the local flock. But it was not always so, nor need it be so forever. Fr. Lawrence Farley explores how the Orthodox episcopacy developed over the centuries and suggests what can be done in modern times to bring the bishop back into closer contact with his flock.
• Paperback, 152 pages, ISBN 978-1-936270-61-3

Following Egeria
A Visit to the Holy Land through Time and Space
In the fourth century, a nun named Egeria traveled through the Holy Land and wrote an account of her experiences. In the twenty-first century, Fr. Lawrence

Farley followed partially in her footsteps and wrote his own account of how he experienced the holy sites as they are today. Whether you're planning your own pilgrimage or want to read about places you may never go, his account will inform and inspire you.
• Paperback, 160 pages, ISBN 978-1-936270-21-7

Three Akathists:
Akathist to Jesus, Light to Those in Darkness
• Staple-bound, 32 pages, ISBN 978-1-944967-33-8

Akathist to the Most Holy Theotokos, Daughter of Zion
• Staple-bound, 32 pages, ISBN 978-1-944967-34-4

Akathist to Matushka Olga Michael
• Staple-bound, 32 pages, ISBN 978-1-944967-38-3

Other Books of Interest

The Orthodox Study Bible: Old and New Testaments
Featuring a Septuagint text of the Old Testament developed by outstanding Orthodox scholars, this Bible also includes the complete Orthodox canon of the Old Testament, including the Deuterocanon; insightful commentary drawn from the Christian writers of the first ten centuries; helpful notes relating Scripture to seasons of Christian feasting and fasting; a lectionary to guide your Bible reading through the Church year; supplemental Bible study articles on a variety of subjects; a subject index to the study notes to help facilitate Bible study; and more.
• Available in various editions. Visit store.ancientfaith.com for more details.

The Whole Counsel of God
An Introduction to Your Bible
by Stephen De Young
In *The Whole Counsel of God*, popular writer and podcaster Fr. Stephen De Young gives an overview of what the Bible is and what is its place in the life of an Orthodox Christian, correcting many Protestant misconceptions along the way. Issues covered include inspiration, inerrancy, the formation of the biblical canon, the various texts and their provenance, the place of Scripture within Orthodox Tradition, and how an Orthodox Christian should read, study, and interpret the Bible.
• Paperback, 128 pages, ISBN: 978-1-955890-19-9

The Names of Jesus
Discovering the Person of Jesus Christ through Scripture
by Fr. Thomas Hoko
In this book based on his popular podcast series of the same name, the late Fr. Thomas Hopko shares meditations on over 50 different names and titles used for Jesus in the Bible. Learn what each name uniquely has to tell us about the character of the Son of God, His role in our salvation, and the relationship we can choose to cultivate with Him.
• Paperback, 400 pages, ISBN 978-1-936-70-41-5

The Rest of the Bible
A Guide to the Old Testament of the Early Church
by Theron Mathis
A beautiful widow risks her life to defend her people while men cower in fear. A young man takes a journey with an archangel and faces down a demon in order to marry a woman seven times widowed. A reprobate king repents and miraculously turns back toward God. A Jewish exile plays a game of riddles in a Persian king's court. Wisdom is detailed and exalted. Christ is revealed.

These and many other stories make up the collection of writings explored

in this book—authentic books of the Bible you've probably never read. Dubbed "Apocrypha" and cut from the Bible by the Reformers, these books of the Greek Old Testament were a vital part of the Church's life in the early centuries, and are still read and treasured by Orthodox Christians today. *The Rest of the Bible* provides a brief and intriguing introduction to each of these valuable texts, which St. Athanasius termed "the Readables."
• Paperback, 128 pages, ISBN 978-1-936270-15-6

Christ in the Psalms
by Patrick Henry Reardon
A highly inspirational book of meditations on the Psalms by one of the most insightful and challenging Orthodox writers of our day. Avoiding both syrupy sentimentality and arid scholasticism, *Christ in the Psalms* takes the reader on a thought-provoking and enlightening pilgrimage through this beloved "Prayer Book" of the Church. Which psalms were quoted most frequently in the New Testament, and how were they interpreted? How has the Church historically understood and utilized the various psalms in her liturgical life? How can we perceive the image of Christ shining through the psalms? Lively and highly devotional, thought-provoking yet warm and practical, *Christ in the Psalms* sheds a world of insight upon each psalm, and offers practical advice for how to make the Psalter a part of our daily lives.
• Paperback, 328 pages, ISBN 978-1-888212-21-7

Christ in His Saints
by Patrick Henry Reardon
In this sequel to *Christ in the Psalms,* Patrick Henry Reardon once again applies his keen intellect to a topic he loves most dearly. Here he examines the lives of almost one hundred and fifty saints and heroes from the Scriptures—everyone from Abigail to Zephaniah, Adam to St. John the Theologian. This well-researched work is a veritable cornucopia of Bible personalities: Old Testament saints, New Testament saints, "Repentant saints," "Zealous saints," "Saints under pressure" . . . they're all here, and their stories are both fascinating and uplifting. But *Christ in His Saints* is far more than just a biblical who's who. These men and women represent that ancient family into which, by baptism, all believers have been incorporated. Together they compose that great "cloud of witnesses" cheering us on and inspiring us through word and deed.
• Paperback, 320 pages, ISBN 978-1-888212-68-6

For complete ordering information, visit our website: store.ancientfaith.com.

We hope you have enjoyed and benefited from this book. Your financial support makes it possible to continue our nonprofit ministry both in print and online. Because the proceeds from our book sales only partially cover the costs of operating **Ancient Faith Publishing** and **Ancient Faith Radio**, we greatly appreciate the generosity of our readers and listeners. Donations are tax deductible and can be made at **www.ancientfaith.com**.

To view our other publications,
please visit our website: **store.ancientfaith.com**

ANCIENT FAITH RADIO

Bringing you Orthodox Christian music, readings, prayers, teaching, and podcasts 24 hours a day since 2004 at **www.ancientfaith.com**

www.ingramcontent.com/pod-product-compliance
Lightning Source LLC
LaVergne TN
LVHW090435100425
808241LV00002B/371